THE GEORGE CROSS

The
GEORGE CROSS

by
Lieutenant-Colonel
Ian Bisset

*

LONDON
MACGIBBON & KEE
1961

FIRST PUBLISHED 1961 BY MACGIBBON & KEE
© IAN BISSET 1961
PRINTED IN GREAT BRITAIN BY
THE CHELTENHAM PRESS LIMITED
CHELTENHAM

To men and women
who have given their lives
to save others.

CONTENTS

++

APPENDIXES

I *Part I:* Lists of names of men and women awarded the George Cross in replacement of the Medal of the Order of the British Empire for Gallantry.

Part II: List of names of men and women awarded the George Cross since the institution of the award.

II Royal Warrant defining the conditions of the George Cross.

CONTENTS

INTRODUCTION

WRITING this book has been an absorbing task that has occupied much of my spare time over the past two years. To have done full justice to the subject I could have spent far longer in research but it was planned to publish it to mark the twenty-first anniversary of the institution of the George Cross.

A rewarding aspect of the work has been my contact with many examples of personal sacrifice. I have come to realize that the world is not always so godless a place as it would appear from the evidence of the columns of the average newspaper. I suppose delinquency has a greater news value than selflessness.

As no comprehensive record of the deeds that have resulted in the award of the George Cross has previously been published, nor even a complete list of the names of the men and women who have won it (until 1960, Whitaker's Almanack published lists of surviving holders of the G.C. but I have found some inaccuracies in these), one of my aims has been to repair this omission. I have, therefore, made a point of giving some details of every award made since the institution of the Cross and, in an appendix, I have shown the names and descriptions of every recipient. Against the names I have given references to the chapters in which the deeds are mentioned.

I shall be surprised if there are not some errors and omissions in the list as, apart from anything else, I have found inconsistencies in official records. I have, however, taken some pains to cross check different sources of information and I have done my best to make it both complete and accurate.

As I explain in Chapter I, the George Cross is unusual as it has been given in recognition of many acts that were performed long before its institution; to surviving holders of the Medal of the Order of the British Empire for Gallantry, and to men and women who received that medal posthumously since the beginning of World War II. It has not been practicable to give details of the majority of these earlier awards though I have mentioned a number that were made in the early months of the war.

I have tried to put the deeds into perspective with the assistance of background information about both events and the people concerned in them. I hope, as a result, that this has helped to give depth to the significance of the story of the George Cross and that this book has been made more readable than a straightforward catalogue of acts of gallantry might have been.

For a variety of reasons my accounts of these acts of gallantry vary in length. I have devoted only a few lines to some stories because they have been identical with others in the same chapter. Sometimes I have had to describe an act briefly because I have been short of information, or because it was a momentary thing; performed in an instant and on the spur of the moment. On the other hand, some awards have been made in recognition of gallant behaviour that has been continuous over many months, or even years, and far longer descriptions have been necessary. In no case, however, has the space devoted to any award been meant to represent any assessment of the degree of gallantry. I believe that such comparisons would often be impossible as well as odious. How, for example, could anyone draw comparison between the bravery of a man who, to save his comrades, throws his body onto a bursting grenade, and a woman who allows her toe nails to be drawn out one by one, rather than reveal the names of her accomplices?

The George Cross was a product of World War II and, in the main, it has been given for war-time deeds. Thus, inevitably, this book is primarily another 'war-book' and it has seemed right, when writing of such things as the Blitz and the resistance movement, to tell briefly of the circumstances that led up to them. Members of my own generation have vivid memories of these events, but they may be little more than names to many who have now reached maturity.

Originally, I had not foreseen any great difficulty in unearthing the general details of all George Cross awards, but I had forgotten the effectiveness of war-time security precautions and I quickly made the disturbing discovery that over half the London Gazettes which announced awards of the George Cross did not publish the citations. Luckily, although the George Cross has been called the 'civilian's V.C.,' it has, in fact, been won far more often by service men and women than by civilians, and I was able to get the details of a great many of the awards from the three service ministries.

In the case of some of the civilian awards, and others made to certain Commonwealth servicemen, it was a different story and up until the last moment I despaired of ever being able to collect all the material I needed. I had particular difficulty over the award to Captain Simmon Latutin of the Somerset Light Infantry. Neither the War Office nor the Colonial Office had a record of this officer's citation. (He had won the George Cross whilst seconded to the Somaliland Gendarmerie.) It was fortunate that he had a most unusual name, for I wrote to the only person of that name in the London telephone directory who turned out to be his widow. She was most helpful.

In the matter of decorations, the Royal Navy well merits the title of 'Silent Service,' for details of war-time awards to sailors were very rarely published. Fortunately the Chief of Naval Information at the Admiralty was extremely co-operative. Having said that, it is only right to add that the War Office and the Air Ministry, so far as they were able, gave me all the information that I asked for.

The war-time suppression of details of many acts of gallantry was an unfortunate thing in more senses than one. All forms of censorship are infuriating from the point of view of the historian but, when they are concerned with acts of gallantry, they have the effect of undermining the value of the whole idea of giving decorations. Their significance must be diminished if nobody knows what they have been given for.

The need for security in war-time is obvious but, having read all the suppressed citations, I can truthfully say that hardly any of them had very obvious security implications, and the few that had could very easily have been re-worded to remove them. It is difficult to get away from the impression that war-time censorship was too often in the hands of small-minded officials who regarded negative rulings as safe ones.

I will never cease to be amazed at the remarkable influence of the words, 'I am writing a book.' They act like a charm upon individuals and government departments alike and produce nothing but helpfulness in every quarter. I have already mentioned the assistance I have had from the three service ministries and I must also express my gratitude for information supplied by the Ministry of Transport, the High Commissioners for India, Pakistan, Canada, New Zealand and Australia, the Secretary of the Central Chancery of Orders of Knighthood, the Commissioner of the Metropolitan Police and several Chief Constables of county forces, Civil Defence authorities, and British Railways. Public Libraries are invariably both helpful and patient and my thanks go to the City Librarians in both Nottingham and Manchester. I do not grudge the former the money he has had from me in fines for keeping some of his books too long.

I have had invaluable help from the Headquarters of several Corps and Regiments and would like to make particular mention of the Institution of Royal Engineers. A remarkably large number of Sapper officers and men have won the George Cross, and I have had to ask that body for information many times, but their secretary, Brigadier John Lacey, invariably came to my aid.

It is of interest, by the way, that twice, when I wrote to the Headquarters of two famous infantry regiments, I found that I had given them the first intimation of the fact that members of these regiments had won the George Cross. Neither of the two soldiers concerned was serving with his own regiment when he earned the award.

Amongst the many individuals who have assisted me I must make special mention of the late Baron d'Amigo Inguanez, whose aid was invaluable when I was writing of the siege of Malta. He helped to unravel the truth behind several remarkably conflicting pieces of information given in some of the best known books on the subject and he corrected my drafts and made many useful suggestions. His last letter to me was written in a distressingly shaky hand from his sick-bed, during his last illness. Soon afterwards I heard of the death of this delightful person who was one of the most warm-hearted men I have ever met. I will always remember him for his puckish sense of humour.

Major M. R. Pennell, whom, to this day, I have never met, also gave me invaluable help. Mark Pennell is an expert on medals and decorations and I was put in touch with him by a mutual friend. The history of British awards for gallantry is obscure and complicated and I have found the few books that touch upon this matter to be difficult to follow. Mark Pennell clarified the obscurities and made it possible for me to write my first chapter and he also corrected my drafts of it.

I would like to express particular gratitude to Brigadier P. K. Benner, who took great trouble over supplying me with information and documents concerning the posthumous award of the George Cross to his son, Second Lieutenant Michael Paul Benner. At a later date he re-wrote and greatly improved parts of my account of this award. He also helped me to trace the details of an award to a Pakistani soldier when the Pakistan military authorities had lost trace of him.

In addition to the few people whom I have named, there were others, too numerous to list, who supplied me with valuable information and I deeply appreciate their help.

I must also give acknowledgement to the authors and publishers of the list of books shown in the Bibliography. From all of these I have extracted factual information and I should make particular reference to Major A. B. Hartley's book, *Unexploded Bomb*. Anyone reading my chapter dealing with awards made to the men who had to deal with these unpleasant things might think that I am something of an expert in this subject. The truth is that most of my information came from Major Hartley's interesting book.

In writing my account of the award to Sergeant William Fairfax of the Metropolitan Police, I gained some of my information from the account of the trial of Craig and Bentley in *The Times*. Back numbers of this newspaper are available in every worthwhile public library and they provide a source of accurate information which is, I suspect, used more often than it is acknowledged.

I.S.B.

Mobberley,
Cheshire.

While in the frailty of our human clay
Christ, our Redeemer, went the self same way.

ARKWRIGHT

CHAPTER I

‡‡‡

A NEW DISTINCTION

THE origin of the custom of awarding and wearing decorations is obscure, but as the custom of making monetary awards for distinguished and gallant service is probably older, the similarity between a medal, one of the oldest forms of decoration, and a coin, suggests that the two customs may be connected. Possibly the earliest medals were, in fact, specially minted coins.

The Romans decorated a man who saved the life of a comrade with a crown of oak leaves and it is interesting that, today, a bronze oak leaf on the ribbon of a campaign medal, is the symbol of a Mention in Despatches.

There are references in some early writings of 'Honorary Badges' being presented and worn in the reigns of Queen Elizabeth I and King James I and VI but little is known about them. It is on record, however, that Charles I presented a gold medal to a certain Sir Robert Welch for gallantry at the battle of Edgehill.

A number of gold medals were given to senior officers during the reigns of William and Mary and Queen Anne but, at that time, it still seems to have been normal to reward the bravery of ratings and soldiers with money.

The earliest equivalent of a campaign medal was given to the Parliamentary troops who took part in the battle of Dunbar, in 1650, and no more were issued until a silver medal was struck for certain loyal petty officers and ratings after the Nore mutiny, at the end of the eighteenth century. They must have been more commonly used on the Continent, however, for when Napoleon surrendered to the British in 1815, he was received by a 'Captain's Detachment' of Royal Marines and he expressed surprise that none of them had had any active service. When he was assured that they were all veterans he asked why they were not wearing their medals.

Although, during the first half of the nineteenth century, the issue both of decorations for gallantry and campaign medals had become a fairly common practice it seems to have been a haphazard business; very much dependent upon the whim of the monarch, parliament, individual Admirals, Colonels of Regiments and, more than once, private citizens. No standard decoration for gallantry was instituted until, in 1856, Queen Victoria was persuaded that something should be done to reward conspicuous acts of heroism in the Crimean War. The original idea came from William Howard Russell, the celebrated *Times* war correspondent.

The result of his inspiration was, of course, the Victoria Cross and, to this day, it remains the nation's highest award for bravery. It is, as well, the senior British award and is worn on the right of all other decorations. The Cross was designed by the Prince Consort and it was at his suggestion that it was made from the bronze of captured enemy guns. This idea had a particular appeal for the Treasury and the acrimonious arguments about cost which followed the submission of designs for certain later decorations did not take place.

It is of some interest, by the way, that the original supply of Crimean bronze is not yet exhausted and considerable stocks are still held, in ingot form, in the Command Ordnance Depot at Didcot.

It was the Queen herself who thought of the simple but effective motto that was incorporated into the design of the Victoria Cross, *For Valour*. She also involved herself in framing the conditions of the award which specified that it could only be won by members of the fighting services who performed acts of conspicuous bravery in the presence of the enemy. In 1858, however, they were amended to include civilians serving under military command and four have actually received the award; all in the Indian Mutiny.

Originally there were two ribbons for the Cross, blue for members of the Royal Navy and red for the Army, but after 1918 the Cross hung from a red ribbon for all services.

Several different Royal Warrants, making changes in the conditions, have been issued since Queen Victoria's death and, for a period of four years, the clause that insisted that the act of bravery should have been performed in the presence of the enemy was suspended. One Royal Warrant made all ranks of the Indian Army, Colonial Forces and native levies eligible for it and another, issued in the reign of King Edward VII, made it possible to give the award posthumously. In 1918, when the Royal Air Force was formed, the decision was made that, in future, the Cross would hang only from a red ribbon.

Five years after the institution of the Victoria Cross the Prince Consort died and, five years after that, his name was given to a new award, the Albert Medal. Originally it was intended to be given only for acts of heroism in saving life at sea. Two years later its application was extended to the saving of life on land as well. The original ribbon was blue with two white stripes, but it was decided that, when the medal was awarded for an incident on land, it would hang from a red ribbon with white stripes. Normally the medal was made of bronze but provision was made for the award of gold Albert Medals in circumstances of particularly outstanding bravery. The ribbon of the gold medal has four white stripes.

The conditions that governed the award made all British citizens eligible for it but, just as the Victoria Cross was intended primarily for servicemen, the Albert Medal was meant for civilians. It was never the Queen's intention, however, that it, or any other medal, should be as highly cherished as the Victoria Cross and she stubbornly resisted a later suggestion that a new decoration should have the form of a cross, for fear of any possible confusion. Nevertheless the Albert Medal has, in practice, been awarded far more sparingly than the Victoria Cross. Up to the outbreak of the Second World War only 107 were given, compared with 522 Victoria Crosses.

Between the Crimean War and the Second World War a number of new decorations for gallantry were instituted but the majority of them were intended for members of the armed forces. The Distinguished Conduct Medal of the Army, and the Conspicuous Gallantry Medal of the Royal Navy, were instituted soon after the Victoria Cross and were designed only for non-commissioned ranks. A few years later came the

Distinguished Service Order which was only intended for commissioned officers of the fighting services and, in 1901, the Conspicuous Service Cross that became the Distinguished Service Cross in 1914. World War I produced a whole crop of new decorations such as the Distinguished Service Medal, the Military Cross and the Military Medal. Then, with the formation of the Royal Air Force, came the Distinguished Flying Cross, the Distinguished Flying Medal, the Air Force Cross and the Air Force Medal. The ribbons of these latter awards were original in that they had horizontal stripes, but they were later changed to diagonal ones.

Several special awards for the Indian Army and other Imperial and Colonial Forces were also instituted between the Crimean and the Second World Wars.

An award for gallantry that was specifically designed for civilians was instituted a few years before World War I. It was the Edward Medal, and the original Royal Warrant, published in 1907, said that it was intended to be given only in recognition of acts of bravery by quarry-men and miners. Two years later the conditions were changed and it was made applicable to heroism in industry generally.

One further award for gallantry was instituted during the reign of Edward VII; the King's Police Medal. This was not well named for it could be won by members of Fire Brigades as well as by the police.

With the exception of Indian and colonial decorations, the above summarizes the various awards for gallantry that were instituted by Royal Warrant before 1919. (Details of all the British gallantry awards are given in Appendix III.) However, a number of different bodies started to issue medals and several of these are highly prized. Important amongst them is the Board of Trade Medal for Saving Life at Sea and this is issued under the authority of the Merchant Shipping Acts of 1854 and 1894. Awards are notified in the London Gazette and the medal is normally presented by the monarch.

Less official but equally worthy are the gold, silver and bronze medals of the Royal Humane Society—which may be worn in uniform on the right breast by members of the services

—and the Royal National Lifeboat Institution, the gold and silver medals of the Shipwrecked Fishermen's and Mariners' Society, the medal of the Liverpool Shipwreck and Humane Society, the Lloyd's Medal for Saving Life at Sea, the Life Saving Medal of the Order of St. John of Jerusalem, the Bravery Medal of the Glasgow Corporation, the London County Council Fire Brigade Medal, the Margaret Wheatley Cross and the silver and bronze medals of the R.S.P.C.A. The Boy Scout and Girl Guide Associations, as well, have their own gallantry awards. Finally there is the *Daily Herald* Order of Industrial Heroism. Medals of this order are presented by Labour Members of Parliament or trades union officials. One is tempted to the view that the *Daily Herald* award smacks of political and journalistic enterprise. However, a study of the details of the heroic acts that have earned it makes it difficult to sustain the criticism.

Ignoring unofficial ones there were, by the end of World War I, fifteen different British decorations for gallantry and it is reasonable to argue that there were, in fact, too many. A case could possibly be made for confining some decorations to the fighting services and others to civilians. It is more difficult to see why it was necessary for each of the three fighting services to have parallel series of virtually identical ones, or different decorations for different ranks. In any event one would have thought that by 1918 there were sufficient awards to ensure appropriate recognition of any distinguished act of bravery by any British subject. Events during the war had shown, however, that this was not the case.

The difficulty arose from the fact that all the gallantry decorations of the fighting services applied to acts of bravery either in the presence of the enemy, under fire or, in the case of the A.F.C. and the A.F.M., in the air. The Victoria Cross, as well, could only be won in the presence of the enemy. The civilian decorations, on the other hand, were confined to heroism in saving life (the Albert Medal), heroism in industry (the Edward Medal), and acts of heroism by members of the Police Forces and Fire Brigades (the King's Police Medal). But, between 1914 and 1918, there were many acts of bravery, performed by both civilians and servicemen, that were not covered by any of these special conditions. During the Zeppelin raids, for example, hundreds of brave men risked their lives fighting fires, handling unexploded bombs and clearing masonry. In France, far behind the lines, there were many fires and explosions in ammunition trains and depots that were only brought under control through feats of individual heroism. Regrettably, more than once the Army was called on to aid the civil power at moments of unrest and many soldiers showed great personal courage, not in the face of any enemy, but in handling their own countrymen.

As a result of this, in 1922, King George V instituted the Medal of the Order of the British Empire, for Gallantry. Its shorter title was the Empire Gallantry Medal and recipients were allowed to use the letters 'E.G.M.' after their names. The conditions of the award were far less fettered than those that governed any of the earlier ones. It could, in fact, be won by any person of any rank or station who performed an act of gallantry that merited recognition by the Crown, anywhere in the world.

The medal was made of silver with, on the obverse, a representation of Britannia, the motto of the Order of the British Empire, *For God and Empire*, and the words *For Gallantry*. On the reverse was the Royal and Imperial Cypher and the words, *Instituted by King George V*. It hung from the purple ribbon of the Order. This was later changed to the now familiar rose pink with pearl grey edges, and a narrow grey stripe in the centre in the case of the Military Division.

The Empire Gallantry Medal filled an important gap in the list of official British decorations for gallantry and it is a pity that its existence was given very little publicity. When, in 1940, it was replaced by the George Cross it had been awarded less than a hundred times and surprisingly few people had ever heard of it.

The need for a further change in the means of giving recognition to acts of outstanding bravery became evident when the first waves of the Luftwaffe attacked the south of England in the summer of 1940. Britain had been bombed before but the

Zeppelin raids of the First World War had been mild compared with this onslaught, and the risks and privations that were faced by the civilian population of the British Isles had been trifling compared with the horror of life in the trenches of Flanders. But now, for the first time, large sections of the civilian population were not only in the front line of the battle but, very often, they were under heavier fire than the majority of the members of the fighting services.

Throughout history fighting men had known a measure of hardship and danger that few civilians had ever had to face and nobody had grudged them higher recognition of their gallantry. For almost a hundred years the Victoria Cross had stood on a plane of its own—as Queen Victoria had always intended that it should—and the fact that, in practice, it could virtually only be won by a serviceman was accepted as reasonable and natural. But, with the wider spread of the conflagration of war, this situation seemed no longer to be justified and there was little reason why the bravery of servicemen should be more highly honoured than that of civilians.

One of the first people to recognize this changed situation was King George VI and, as it happened that the study of medals, decorations and orders was one of his favourite hobbies (the late King's collection at Windsor Castle was reputed to be one of the most complete in the world), he set himself the problem of dealing with it. He probably appreciated the fact that there were already too many gallantry awards and resisted the simple solution of adding to their number. He must have considered the obvious alternative of making another change in the conditions of the Victoria Cross and it is likely that he abandoned this idea out of deference to his great-grand-mother's wish that it should be given only for valour in battle. In the end he decided to replace an existing award with one that had the status of the Victoria Cross. The award that he selected was the Empire Gallantry Medal and the new name that he chose was the George Cross. (It was once suggested to the author by the late Lord Hardinge of Penshurst, Secretary to King George VI, that, although the whole credit for the inspiration that resulted in the creation of the George Cross was given to the King, the idea emerged from a long discussion between the King and Winston Churchill. He wrote to Sir Winston to ask if he was not, in part, responsible for the idea and received a sharply worded reply which stated that Sir John Wheeler Bennett's account of the institution of the George Cross, in his biography of the late King, was correct. Sir John gives the credit wholly to King George.)

The King took particular pleasure in planning every detail of the new decoration and he made several rough sketches of the Cross himself. The final design was drawn by the late F. W. Barry MVO who worked, until his death, in the Royal Library at Windsor. It was decided to make it of silver and the Royal Warrant that laid down its conditions described it as:

. . . *a plain cross with four equal limbs, the cross having in the centre a circular medallion bearing a design showing Saint George and the Dragon, that the inscription, 'For Gallantry,' shall appear round this medallion, and in the angle of each limb of the cross, the Royal Cypher 'G VI' forming a circle concentric with the medallion.*

The Cross was to be worn, the Royal Warrant said, immediately after the Victoria Cross, suspended from a dark blue ribbon. (Despite the fact that the Royal Warrant describes the ribbon as dark blue it is, in fact, 'Garter Blue.') When the ribbon was worn alone it was to have a miniature replica of the Cross fixed in its centre and a further replica for each subsequent award to the same person. The same arrangement has existed in the case of the Victoria Cross since the abolition of blue and white ribbons in 1918.

All the King's subjects in the British Commonwealth and Empire were to be eligible for the award but the Warrant said that it was intended primarily for civilians and should only be given to members of the fighting services for actions for which military honours were not normally granted. In fact, just over three-quarters of the men and women awarded the George Cross since the institution have been members of the services.

It was to be awarded only for 'acts of the greatest heroism or the most conspicuous courage in circumstances of extreme danger.' As with the Victoria Cross, provision was made for its posthumous award.

The King announced the creation of the George Cross in a broadcast to the nation on the evening of 23rd September 1940. He said:

'Many and glorious are the deeds of gallantry done during these perilous but famous days. In order that they should be worthily and promptly recognized, I have decided to create at once a new mark of honour for men and women in all walks of civilian life. I propose to give my name to this new distinction which will consist of the George Cross. It will rank next to the Victoria Cross.'

The original Royal Warrant laying down the conditions of the award was published next day, but it was superseded by a new Warrant dated 21st January 1941. This made provision for surviving holders of the Empire Gallantry Medal, and men and women who had won the award posthumously since the outbreak of the war, to have the medal replaced by the George Cross. The complete Royal Warrant is reproduced in Appendix II.

The new award was meant to be prized only below the Victoria Cross and it is significant that it captured the interest and imagination of the nation in a way that no new honour has done since the institution of the Victoria Cross. It is now twenty-one years since its creation and during those twenty-one years it has been won by 132 men and women. It has been won, as well, by the Island of Malta in recognition of the bravery and fortitude of the people of the Island when they withstood two and a half years of bombardment and siege. The story of those years of siege is one of the epics of the late war. That story is told, briefly, between the covers of this book. The rest of the book is devoted to telling of some of the other feats of incredible heroism that have merited the award of the George Cross.

CHAPTER II

THE BLITZ

In 1933 Adolf Hitler came to power in Germany and the Third Reich was born. The Versailles Treaty became a meaningless scrap of paper as, in defiance of it, the German fighting forces were rebuilt, the Rhineland reoccupied, and German industry and economy were harnessed to the production of tanks, submarines and dive-bombers.

At first Britain's political leaders convinced themselves, and the majority of the general public as well, that the whole thing was nothing more than a gigantic bluff; that the Führer was playing a game of poker and the best way of calling his bluff was to sit tight until he over-called his hand. It was authoritatively reported that his tanks were clad with plywood and he had insufficient petrol to put a mechanized army into the field.

But Hitler, confounding the theorists, marched into Austria and, not long after that, started to threaten Czechoslovakia. This had the effect of jerking the British Prime Minister, Neville Chamberlain, from his platitudes and, with an umbrella in his hand and a worried frown on his brow, he scuttled off to Münich to meet the German Leader. There, Chamberlain made a shameful agreement that Britain would not act if Hitler would content himself with the Sudetenland, and the two men put their signatures to a piece of paper that avowed that war between Britain and Germany was unthinkable.

Chamberlain returned to London, convinced by the Führer's assurance that the annexation of the Sudetenland would satisfy his last territorial demand in Europe, and was acclaimed as the saviour of peace. But not by everyone, for there were men such as Churchill and Duff Cooper who were less gullible than the Prime Minister, though their warnings were dismissed as the sabre rattlings of war-mongers.

Within months of Münich Hitler annexed the whole of

Czechoslovakia and then started to threaten Poland. At last Chamberlain realized that his intentions were dishonourable. The youth of Britain was conscripted, hasty plans for the evacuation of women and children were made, and everyone was issued with a gas-mask in a little cardboard box.

Soon afterwards Germany swept into Poland, and Britain and France declared war. Their two armies were mobilized and occupied a defensive position which stretched from the Swiss frontier to the English Channel.

Along most of their frontier with Germany the French had built, at huge expense, the Maginot Line; a carefully planned corridor of tank traps, pill-boxes and underground emplacements. But there were gaps in it. In the Ardennes, reckoned to be impassable to armoured formations, the defences were sketchy and they stopped altogether at the Franco-Belgium frontier. It was along part of that frontier that the little British Army of five regular divisions was deployed. Later it was re-inforced with a few hastily mobilized divisions of the Territorial Army.

For eight months nothing happened and then, on 10th May 1940, the German Army struck. Holland was over-run in a few days, mobile troops poured into Belgium, and the group of Panzer and motorized divisions, under General Kleist, tore through the allegedly impenetrable Ardennes, as though they were in open desert, and crossed the French frontier on a fifty-mile front at Sedan.

On 27th May Belgium capitulated and the British Expeditionary Force, together with the First and Seventh French Armies, found themselves with Kleist's Panzers to the south and west, the sea at their backs, and an open flank to the east. By some miracle, well over a quarter of a million soldiers were evacuated from Dunkirk to England, and with them went some thirty thousand Frenchmen. The Panzers regrouped and turned towards Paris.

Although Hitler's hordes quickly over-ran the greater part of the mainland of Europe, they halted on the English Channel and there followed a second uneasy pause. Nobody, including Hitler himself, was at all certain what the next move would be.

Britain began hurriedly to prepare for invasion and there were reports of barges and landing-craft being assembled in the ports of Belgium and northern France. But there was reason for believing that some of the German arrangements for an assault across the Channel were as improvised as the British arrangements for defence. The truth was that events had moved more quickly than either side had expected and both attacker and defender were caught unprepared.

The course of the war would have been vastly different if Hitler had had airborne and seaborne forces poised ready to cross the Channel whilst the British Expeditionary Force was fighting to extricate itself from Dunkirk. But he had not and, not for the first time in history, Britain was saved by sixteen miles of salt water.

However, by 1940 salt water had become less of a bulwark of defence than in the past. It was no barrier to aircraft and, in the Luftwaffe, Hitler possessed the most powerful air force in the world. And there can be no doubt that he realized that he held a trump card though he was uncertain how to play it.

In 1921 an Italian General named Douhet wrote a book entitled *Command of the Air*. In it, he put forward the theory that a country with a powerful bomber force could, by blasting the principal cities of an enemy, reduce it to surrender within a very few weeks, if not even days, without the use of land armies. But, though Douhet had his adherents, his theory was not universally accepted in military circles, and there were powerful members of the German General Staff who held the more generally accepted view that infantry was necessary to overthrow an enemy, whilst the main task of an air force must be to destroy the enemy air power and prevent it from hindering the movement of soldiers on the ground.

A study of the air strategy that Hitler adopted during the ten months that followed Dunkirk does not make it clear whether he accepted the theory of Douhet or that of his own General Staff. In the main it would seem that, as in other things, he was more than a little mixed up.

The first bombs that fell on the British mainland were dropped on the 10th May, the day that Germany launched her attack against Belgium and Holland. They came down close to Canterbury. Then, for the next three weeks, the Luftwaffe was preoccupied with the battle in Europe, and Britain was left alone.

Early in June small-scale attacks started again and the target areas were widely scattered; the Midlands, East Anglia, Cambridge and Portland. In July, the size of the attacking formations began to increase and a force of seventy aircraft bombed Swansea, killing thirty people. Sharp attacks were also made on Norwich, Cardiff, Bristol, Aldershot, Portsmouth and R.A.F. stations in Berkshire and Caernarvon.

In August it began to look as though there was some logic in the pattern of the German tactics, for the main weight of attack was against Britain's fighter airfields. But scattered raids on other targets continued and, whilst some of them, such as industrial centres and naval bases, had military significance, others had none. One place in the latter category was the little Yorkshire seaside town of Bridlington, which was hit several times, and it was there that the first George Cross of the war was won by a civilian—a thirty-five years old A.R.P. worker named Thomas Hopper Alderson, Works Supervisor of the Bridlington Corporation and Detachment Leader in charge of Rescue Parties.

In his twenties, Thomas Alderson had qualified as a ship's Chief Engineer and had spent several years at sea. In 1932, however, he had married and decided to settle on dry land; first as an employee of the West Hartlepool Borough Engineer's department and later in his appointment at Bridlington.

His job made him an obvious choice for the task he was given in the A.R.P. and, as soon as that organization was set up, he started to recruit and train volunteers for his Rescue Parties. Many of these men came from the Borough Engineer's department.

In the first of the raids on Bridlington, a pair of semi-detached houses were demolished and Alderson and his men were quickly on the scene. He learned that there was a woman trapped below the wreckage and, at once, he tunnelled under it and succeeded in bringing her out.

Five days later two five-storey buildings were demolished and eleven people were trapped in the cellars beneath them. Again Alderson drove a tunnel into the wreckage to rescue them and, this time, he had to work for three-and-a-half hours before he reached them. His tunnel was fourteen feet long.

Alderson had been badly bruised when he worked his way down into the cellars, and he was hampered by gas and water that flowed from fractured pipes, but he took no notice of any of these things as he scrambled on to the trapped people and, one by one, released them and helped them into the tunnel he had dug. There, others waited to pull them to safety.

Thomas Alderson had not fully recovered from his bruising when, a few days later, Bridlington suffered yet another attack and five more people were trapped in a cellar below a four-storey house. Again, he was one of the first to reach the scene and once more he started to burrow towards the foundations of the building.

Close to the spot he selected for the start of his tunnel a wall of the building, three storeys high, was still standing but its fabric was in a perilous condition and it swayed ominously in a high wind. It looked as though it might topple at any moment and bury Alderson and the men who were working alongside him. But neither he nor any of the other men took any notice of it and they went on, quietly and methodically, with their work of rescue.

It took three hours to complete the tunnel and then Alderson spent a further five hours under the building, struggling with masonry and timber in his efforts to free the people who were trapped. He had to saw away large sections of a staircase that had pinned down one woman but in the end he freed her and dragged her to the mouth of the tunnel. She was still alive when she reached the fresh air above but, this time, Thomas Alderson's efforts proved to have been in vain, for she died soon afterwards.

This woman was the last of the trapped people to be brought out. The Rescue Teams had worked throughout the night and the sun was high in the sky when they finished their task. Their leader went quietly home for breakfast and a quick wash and shave. Then he returned to supervise the work of clearing up the shattered buildings of Bridlington.

On 30th September 1940, the London Gazette published the news that Thomas Alderson had been awarded the George Cross. But this was not the last time that he was to be decorated for saving life. A few months later he was given an R.S.P.C.A. Medal for heroism in saving the lives of two horses trapped in a bombed stable.

Whilst Bridlington seemed to be a senseless target, others did not and, for a time, the Luftwaffe concentrated its efforts on the advanced fighter airfields of the Royal Air Force and on coastal shipping. The intensity of these raids mounted and, in the south of England, the summer skies were rarely without a dog-fight somewhere on the horizon. Then, attacks were switched onto the Royal Air Force Sector Stations in the London area and they were bombed persistently for several days.

Whilst these attacks, obviously aimed at destroying the defensive power of the Royal Air Force, were in progress, continual reports of concentrations of troops and boats at the Channel ports were reaching London and it was believed that invasion was imminent. On 6th September Goering arrived in the north of France and assumed personal command of the Luftwaffe's operations. On the following day 250 bombers crossed the coast and made the first heavy raid on London, killing over a thousand people.

This attack on London was thought to be the prelude to the seaborne assault and the code-word *Cromwell*—stand by to repel invasion—was issued and resulted in church bells being rung in more than one village. (This ringing of church bells was intended as the signal that a landing was in progress.) Hurried troop movements took place and defence posts were fully manned. When dawn arrived, tired eyes scanned the calm waters of the Channel and the North Sea but no attackers came into sight.

The bombardment of London went on and so did the dog-fights and more and more German bombers fell victim to our Spitfires and Hurricanes. On 11th September, in broad daylight, a bomb struck a wing of Buckingham Palace where the King and Queen were still living and they had a narrow escape. Four days later 200 bombers attacked the capital and sixty of them were shot down. Actually official reports at the time credited the R.A.F. with 185 enemy aircraft, but it was discovered after the war that this figure was much exaggerated. Hitler cancelled Operation Sealion, his seaborne attack, and stopped daylight bombing. It was a turning point in the war and, for the first time in history, an air force had won a major victory; though not in the manner that General Douhet had forecast.

The situation, in a nutshell, was that, although the Royal Air Force could not claim to have achieved supremacy in the skies over Germany, the Luftwaffe had patently failed to win it and, without it, Hitler had been persuaded that Operation Sealion was not feasible. Nor did his advisers feel that large scale daylight raiding could continue, for Germany was losing bomber aircraft more quickly than they could be replaced. Hitler still believed, however, that the people of Britain could be brought to their knees by aerial bombardment and so the Blitz went on by night.

Unfortunately we had no effective defence against night bombing. Our anti-aircraft artillery served almost exclusively as a booster of public morale and a satisfactory night fighter was not developed until the following year. Thus, night after night, the Luftwaffe dropped its load of high explosives and incendiaries over London and the greater part of the population went into their shelters, whilst the members of the Fire and A.R.P. Services did what they could to clear up the mess and prevent the spread of the flames.

There were many acts of great heroism at this time and typical of them was the bravery of the late Albert Ernest Dolphin, a porter at the South Eastern Hospital at New Cross. In one of these autumn raids one of the hospital blocks was hit by a high explosive bomb which landed in the kitchen, killing four nurses there, and injuring nurses and patients in the adjacent ward.

One of these nurses was thrown through a gaping hole in the floor into a passageway below and several people, including

Albert Dolphin, went to her rescue. They found her alive but pinned down by a great block of masonry. Whilst helpers were struggling to remove this from the injured woman there was a loud noise close by. It was the cracking of stonework and, looking up, the workers there saw a great rent forming in the wall beside them and it was beginning to sway drunkenly. It was obviously about to crash down on them.

With the single exception of Albert Dolphin, everyone did the natural thing and ran for their lives. He, however, remained with the imprisoned nurse and when, seconds later, the wall began to fall he threw himself on top of her.

It took some time to remove the fallen masonry, but when anxious workers eventually succeeded in digging down to where Dolphin and the nurse were, they found that he had been killed but the woman was still alive. Though she was very severely injured, she eventually recovered. Albert Ernest Dolphin's posthumous award of the George Cross was announced in the London Gazette of 17th January 1941.

His was not the only posthumous award of the Cross to be announced in that issue of the London Gazette. Another went to an Air Raid Warden, Leonard John Miles, for great bravery in a raid on Ilford. He was standing close to a shelter when he was warned that an explosion was imminent, although it is not clear what was going to explode or how this was known. The men who had warned him then rushed into the shelter but Miles, instead of following them, ran to warn the occupants of some nearby houses. He was mortally wounded but, whilst he lay waiting for an ambulance that had been called, he refused all aid and directed the operations of A.R.P. workers who were fighting a fire that had been caused by a fractured gas main.

By the middle of October the Germans seemed to have realized that the Luftwaffe had had a second failure; their efforts to bring their enemy to their knees by bombardment of their capital had been as unsuccessful as their attempt to destroy the R.A.F. Their tactics were therefore changed again and a systematic attempt to disorganize and destroy key factories and production centres up and down the country was begun.

2

One of the first places to suffer in this phase of the blitz was Birmingham, which was heavily attacked on 15th October. And it was on that night that a George Cross was won for the first time by a member of the Home Guard—Section Commander George Walter Inwood of No. 10 Battalion. The award was posthumous.

The area around Bishop Street had suffered badly and the police sent an urgent call to Inwood's Section Post to ask if he could help with rescue work in that part of the city. He responded by rushing to the scene with some half-dozen volunteers.

Below a demolished house a number of people were imprisoned in a cellar. There was grave risk of the roof, and the great heap of rubble above it, crashing down on top of them, but, worse, a gas main had been broken and the atmosphere in the cellar was becoming more and more lethal as every minute went by.

The men of the Home Guard set to work with such tools as they had and drove a narrow shaft down to the cellar. Then Inwood was lowered by a rope into it. It was full of gas and none of the occupants was conscious, but two men were still breathing and the Section Commander decided to rescue them first. He caught hold of one of the men and, after a desperate struggle, managed to get him out into the fresh air above. He then returned for the other man and, although he was beginning to suffer from the effects of the gas himself, he also got him to safety.

George Inwood was not content with having saved two lives and, despite the protestations of his subordinates, he entered the gas filled cavern for a third time. But by now he had inhaled too much of the deadly gas and he had scarcely dropped down onto the floor below when he collapsed.

The Assistant Section Leader, Leonard Tidball, climbed in after him and dragged his leader out into the open air. But it was too late and, although a doctor and a nurse did everything they could to revive him, Section Commander George Inwood never regained consciousness.

Exactly a month after this raid the Luftwaffe went in strength to another great Midland city, Coventry, and there, on 14th

November 1940, they delivered one of the most devastating raids of the whole blitz. From dusk until dawn wave after wave of German bombers dropped high explosive and incendiary bombs over the densely populated city and there was hardly a street or alley that did not suffer damage. Important gas and water mains were ruptured, the telephone system put out of action and, in some areas, whole rows of houses were razed to the ground. The pride of the city, its lovely cathedral, was demolished, although throughout that terrible night the clock in the tower kept chiming the hour until the city's electricity supply failed. When the raid ended the German propaganda service announced: 'Coventry, the centre of the British aircraft industry, has been obliterated.'

Coventry had not been obliterated but grievous damage had been done. 450 of her citizens had been killed and most of them were buried in communal graves. 100 acres of the centre of the city had been razed to the ground but, despite it all, dazed men and women went back to their jobs in damaged factories and, though there were gaps in their ranks, their spirit was unbroken.

The indomitable courage of the men and women of Coventry was typified in one man—one of the many who had displayed great gallantry on the night of the raid—who was singled out to receive the George Cross for his bravery. That man was Special Constable Brandon Moss.

Moss, thirty years old at the time, was a fitter in the Armstrong-Siddeley works and had been a 'Special' since before the beginning of the war. On the night of the raid he was on duty and was patrolling in Clay Lane when the bombs began to fall. He had just met three men that he knew and they ran and took refuge in an alley between two houses. Moss chose instead to lie, face down, on the road. He chose wisely for within seconds most of the houses around him were mounds of rubble.

He picked himself up and shook the dust from his clothes. The two houses on each side of the alley where his friends had gone were completely flat, but another one was less badly damaged and he knew that there were three people inside it.

He decided that his first task was to try to save them if they were still alive.

The Special Constable was on his own and he had no tools or other equipment. Bombs and incendiaries were still dropping all around him but, with his bare hands he began to tunnel into the ruins of the house and eventually his efforts were rewarded. Under the debris, he found the three occupants, suffering from no more than bruises and cuts.

This task over, Brandon Moss turned his attention to the place where his three friends were buried. He believed that the chance of saving any of them was remote. Nevertheless, he decided to try and, after several hours of hard digging, he eventually came on their bodies. As he had feared, all three were dead. Next, Moss turned his attention to another nearby house and, after further arduous work, he came on two more people, one of whom was alive.

Brandon Moss worked alone and without respite from 11 in the evening until 6.30 on the following morning, and in those hours he saved four lives. Throughout the whole of that time bombs were falling close by, many of them simply throwing up showers of rubble from buildings that had already been flattened. He never once thought of his own safety and his only interest was to do everything in his power to save the lives of others.

Exactly one month after the night of the Coventry raid the award of the George Cross to Special Constable Brandon Moss was announced in the London Gazette. This was the only wartime award to any member of the Police Force.

The attack on the provinces went on and few places suffered more severely than Birmingham. It was bombed fifty-one times and suffered eight major night attacks. In all, over 1,800 tons of high explosives were dropped on the city and this tonnage was only exceeded in London and the Liverpool-Birkenhead area. It suffered its heaviest raid only five days after the attack on Coventry, when 400 tons of high explosives and 30,000 incendiaries were dropped. Three weeks later, on 11th December, the Luftwaffe returned in force and it was on that night that Station Officer William Radenhurst Mosedale of the

National Fire Service won his George Cross for saving no less than twelve lives during operations that lasted for over twelve hours. Throughout this period Birmingham was under the most intense bombardment and, according to the London Gazette of 28th March 1941, Station Officer Mosedale displayed outstanding gallantry and resource and risked his own life repeatedly.

He had been born in Birmingham in 1894, and at the age of sixteen—he gave it as eighteen—he had joined the 5th Royal Irish Lancers. He reached the rank of corporal within three years, but then his parents died and he had to leave the Army to support his widowed grandmother and his younger brothers and sisters. He became a railway porter and, soon afterwards, a member of the Birmingham City Fire Brigade. He remained in that force for thirty years having been promoted to the rank of Station Officer in 1940.

It was at about 3 a.m. in the morning of 12th December that William Mosedale was ordered to go to a house where three people were trapped and to take breathing apparatus with him. He set off in a fire tender at top speed but he finished up with the machine crashed in the bottom of a bomb crater. He struggled out of the wreckage and made his way, in another vehicle, to the scene of the incident.

There, Mosedale extricated two people from the ruins of a house without a great deal of difficulty, but he found that the third victim, a man, was unconscious under a pile of debris. He administered oxygen and revived the man before he set to work clearing away the rubble. After a hard struggle he dragged him to safety.

Mosedale then returned to his station but he had not been there for very long when the 'phone rang again and he was given the news that the Fire Station in Grantham Road, Sparkbrook, had been hit and fourteen men were buried there. He raced to the scene and found little more than a pile of rubble with faint cries coming from below it.

He took charge of the situation and started to dig a tunnel but it collapsed under the weight of the debris above. He sent somebody off to find timber for props and, wedging them into position as the tunnel went deeper, he eventually reached the Fire Station Control Room but found his way barred by a great lump of stone and a girder. It was impossible to move them and he was forced to drive another shaft from a different angle.

Eventually Mosedale reached the trapped men and, by the light of a hand torch, he administered oxygen to those who were still alive and then superintended their removal to safety.

It was daylight when the Station Officer emerged from the ruins of the Fire Station and learned that there were seven men trapped in the cellar of another house next door. A few A.R.P. workers were struggling desperately to clear away a great mound of bricks which blocked the entrance to the cellar but so far their efforts had met with little success.

Mosedale at once took charge and was the first person to crawl into the cellar beside the trapped men. Three of them were already dead but he was able to pass the other four to the A.R.P. workers outside.

This operation over, Station Officer Mosedale heard that there were still several firemen unaccounted for in the ruins of the Fire Station and he at once started work on yet another tunnel.

Again Mosedale was the first man into the wreckage and, this time, he found four more firemen still alive, as well as several dead. First, he superintended the release and removal of the living and then he had the men who had been killed taken out. When they had all been removed, he was the last man to leave the tunnel. He had only just climbed clear of it when there was a surging movement in the great mound of rubble above, and the whole length of it collapsed.

The London Gazette that announced the award of the George Cross to Station Officer Mosedale was published on his forty-seventh birthday.

Although, throughout the winter of 1940-41, the Luftwaffe's main effort was directed against Britain's industrial centres, London was by no means left alone and the German High Command was guilty of the error of pursuing several objectives simultaneously. It seemed that, despite the fact that faith was now pinned upon the policy of destroying British war industries, the theory that victory could come through bombing the Londoner into submission had not yet been finally abandoned; and it never was.

The outcome of this situation was that the capital was rarely given more than a few days respite and it was during one of these winter raids on London that a second member of the National Fire Service won the George Cross—Auxiliary Fireman Harry Errington. He was in the basement of a building with two other firemen when the place received a direct hit and he was blown right across the room by the force of the blast. He was hurt and badly shaken when he picked himself up and, as he slowly recovered his senses, he realized that his two comrades were trapped under fallen debris and the building had caught fire.

The flames crept into the room and the heat was intense. Smoke filled the place and burning pieces of timber were crashing down. Harry Errington had no tools and so, with his bare hands, he began to tear away the rubble that imprisoned the other two men. After a while he was driven back by the heat but he grabbed hold of a blanket and, wrapping it around him, he returned to his task.

After a while the fabric of the building started to creak and the ceiling above began to rock. Clearly the whole place was on the point of collapse but Errington ignored this and worked on until he had extricated both of the two firemen.

Neither of them could walk and so he grabbed hold of one of them and struggled up a narrow stone stairway with the man on his back. Then he returned and brought out the second man.

Errington and his two comrades all recovered but they were more fortunate than many of the firemen who perished in the fires that raged across London. Sixteen of them died in a single night, the 29th December, the night of the 'Great Fire Raid' when 136 bombers dropped 613 canisters of incendiaries and a hundred tons of high explosives on the City.

This was not the heaviest raid on London but it happened at a time when the level of the Thames was exceptionally low and the shortage of water was made worse when several of the principal water-mains were shattered by high explosive bombs. As a result, London's Fire Service had to stand by, almost helpless, whilst 1,500 fires raged; 1,400 of them within the City.

It was on that night that the historic Guildhall was gutted and eight Wren churches were lost.

Following this devastating raid, London had a raid free period when the Luftwaffe went back to the provinces and blasted one or other of our great cities on almost every night until the 19th January. Then, over a period of some six weeks, there were only five raids; one on London and two on Cardiff and Swansea.

On March 8th the pressure was turned on again and over the next two months there were few nights on which the Luftwaffe did not attack some target in Britain. A city that was singled out for particular attention was the great port of Liverpool which had already been heavily raided at the end of November when three George Crosses were won by men who had to handle unexploded mines and burning ammunition; Sub-Lieutenant G. G. Turner, Lieutenant H. R. Newgass and Mr Norman Tunna. In one of these later raids a further Cross was won by a Corporal of the Royal Pioneer Corps, James Patrick Scully.

Corporal Scully was a member of 256 Company, R.P.C., which had been moved into Liverpool a few weeks earlier to reinforce the overloaded A.R.P. organization, and had been employed mainly in rescue and demolition duties. On the night of the incident that won him his award he was a member of a party that went, under the command of an officer, Lieutenant C. C. Chittendon, to look for survivors in the remains of a row of houses that had been demolished.

After some time Scully located a man and a woman below a great heap of debris. He and Chittendon managed to burrow down to them and, with pieces of wood, they began to shore up the masonry that buried them. Eventually they managed to wedge a long plank under it and, by raising it on props, removed some of the weight.

Despite the efforts of the two soldiers, it was impossible to release the trapped civilians, who were badly hurt. More men were summoned and they worked furiously to try and clear some of the wreckage.

In the meantime Scully stayed beside the injured people, trying to prevent any more debris from falling. After a while the plank that had been fixed over them began to sway and the props supporting it started to creak. Realizing the danger, Scully put his back under the plank to ease the load on the props and he held it until the weight began to increase and the props slipped away.

By the time that this happened Chittendon had climbed back into the hole and, somehow, the two men managed each to support an end of the plank and so to prevent the man and the woman from complete burial. Most of the weight was on the end that Scully was supporting and gradually he was forced down until he lay flat on the ground with the plank across his shoulders and his face almost covered with dust and rubble. Every now and then the Lieutenant leaned across and cleared away enough to let the Corporal breathe whilst he, though practically exhausted, kept up a stream of cheerful Irish witticism with the object of cheering up the woman. The man was by now unconscious.

It was seven hours after the two soldiers first found the buried people that rescue parties managed to reach them; still, with their bodies, the two men were supporting the plank that was holding up several tons of rubble.

An account of this act of gallantry was contained in the London Gazette of 8th July 1941, which announced the award of the George Cross to Corporal Scully and the George Medal to Lieutenant Chittendon. Both men, the Gazette explained, could have escaped at any time but they chose to remain for seven hours, in the gravest personal danger, in a situation that seemed hopeless.

Soon after Corporal Scully won his George Cross the period that has been called the Blitz came to an end. There were several more raids on various places and a particularly heavy one on London on 19th April, when 712 German bombers dropped 1,026 tons of high explosives and 4,252 canisters of incendiaries. 750 people were killed, 80 of them in a shelter at

Poplar. This raid—the heaviest German air-raid of the war—was generally regarded as a reprisal for the bombing of Berlin. Then, in the early part of May, there was another very heavy raid on Birmingham and, on the 10th May, 550 Luftwaffe bombers delivered the last devastating raid of the war, during the course of which they killed 1,436 Londoners. It was on this night that the Chamber of the House of Commons was destroyed and Westminster Abbey damaged.

The Blitz came to an end because the bulk of the Luftwaffe was moved from bases in France, Belgium and Holland to new ones in the east, posed for the offensive that Hitler had decided to launch against Russia. It began on 22nd June 1941.

Despite preoccupation with this new venture, the Luftwaffe did not leave Britain completely neglected, and even whilst the process of regrouping was in progress, Manchester, Hull and Merseyside all suffered sharp raids. Three months later Manchester was again attacked by a force of fifty aircraft.

During the autumn of 1941, and the winter that followed, there were no raids of any significance. Then, in the spring of 1942, came the notorious 'Baedeker' raids when some of England's lovely cathedral cities, such as Bath, Canterbury and Exeter, were subjected to attacks of unpleasant severity. As these places were of little military importance, it has generally been supposed that these raids were reprisals for R.A.F. attacks on Germany.

The 'Baedeker' raids came to an end in the summer of 1942 and for the next eighteen months very few German aircraft crossed the British coastline. The few that came rarely arrived in formations of more than two or three machines, normally dropping a few bombs on some port or harbour and then making off again at low altitude, often only a few feet above the sea. Attacks of this kind were commonly called 'tip-and-run raids' and the general impression was that the pilots were more concerned with their own escape than the accuracy of their bombing.

By the beginning of 1944 the man in the street had come to believe that the nightmare of German air offensive was a thing of the past and the government was criticized for retaining able-bodied men and women in Anti-Aircraft Command and the A.R.P. services, when they were desperately needed in the ranks of the great army that was assembling for the liberation of Europe, and in the munitions factories. But the Government had been wise, for Hitler had not yet been shaken in his belief that the war could be influenced by the bombardment of London and, in February, he launched a fresh series of air attacks, probably in the hope of disrupting the effort that was going into the assembly of the Allied invasion force.

The effectiveness of R.A.F. raids on German munitions centres and the need to keep the Luftwaffe deployed on other fronts made it impossible for them to attack on the same scale as in the winter of 1940-41. Despite this, the 1944 raids were relatively severe and, in a period of about five weeks, a greater tonnage of bombs was dropped on London than had fallen on the whole of Britain throughout the previous year. This period of the war has been christened the 'Little Blitz.'

One of the heaviest of these raids was on the night of 23rd February and it was the borough of Chelsea that suffered most. On that night a Chelsea A.R.P. worker won a George Cross. He was a chimney-sweep named Anthony Smith.

Mr Smith was no youngster when he performed the act of gallantry that won him this high distinction; he was, in fact, in his fiftieth year and had already seen service in the First World War and had lost three fingers when serving with the Royal Marines at the Gallipoli landing. With the approach of another war, however, he decided that he would not be left out of it and he was one of the earliest volunteers for the Chelsea A.R.P. Service. He was attached to a Heavy Rescue Squad.

When the Blitz began, in 1940, though Chelsea did not suffer so badly as the City, there was plenty of work for Anthony Smith and his comrades. His squad, for example, were involved in a serious incident in Pont Street and another very unhappy one when a shelter was hit in Beaufort Street. Other isolated incidents followed and then, for nearly two years, the men of the Heavy Rescue Squad were rarely, if ever, needed and it began to look almost as though their contribution to the war effort had ended.

Then came the 'Little Blitz' and the heavy raid on Chelsea. One heavy bomb landed in Edith Grove, off Chelsea's Kings Road, at 10.30 p.m. and Anthony Smith's squad were rushed to the scene. When they arrived, they found a large mound of rubble where, a few minutes earlier, there had been a neat row of six four-storied houses. Gas and water mains had been cut, flames enveloped the ruins and water flooded the street.

Someone told Smith that there was a man alive in a basement room in the front of the building and he at once began to dig into the debris to reach him. He forced a way through into the basement surprisingly quickly, but to get the man out proved to be a more difficult job for, by now, what had once been the front of the building was a wall of flame and what remained of the upper floor was crashing down onto the roadway.

Somehow, the chimney-sweep forced his way through dense smoke and flames to the back of the building and succeeded in passing the man through to helpers there.

Anthony Smith was an inveterate smoker and he disposed of a quick cigarette whilst he recovered from his exertions. Then he hurried off into the remains of the next door house to help a comrade who was trying to extricate a woman trapped in the basement there. The place was being flooded with water and within a few minutes of entering the room it was up to his chest. All around him the walls of the basement were rumbling and cracking and great splits opened in them as the two men worked.

Fortunately the woman was trapped with her head above the level of the water and, after struggling for some time, Anthony Smith and his companion managed to get her free and to carry her to safety.

Another George Cross was awarded to a member of the London A.R.P. Rescue Service at this time. His name was Leslie Owen Fox and he was called to an incident in the adjacent borough of Fulham, where some houses had been destroyed. Incendiaries had set fire to the wreckage and there were cries for help coming from underneath.

Leslie Fox immediately began to drive a tunnel towards the spot where the cries were coming from. His most serious problem arose from the fact that the timber of the fallen buildings was burning so fiercely that the heat was almost intolerable. One of his comrades knelt behind him as he worked and sprayed him with water, and the debris that he passed back as he burrowed downwards was almost too hot to handle.

After working for two hours, Fox had travelled fifteen feet and had succeeded in locating two trapped people. Then, when he had climbed out of his tunnel to discuss plans for rescuing them, it collapsed. Undeterred he started again, and this time he cleared a way to the two prisoners and a medical officer was able to climb in and drag them to safety. Throughout most of the time that this brave man was working high explosives and incendiary bombs were falling.

On the night of 12th June 1944, the German air assault on Britain entered a new phase when three pilotless aircraft with high explosives in the nose fell in Sussex, Kent and Bethnal Green, the last killing six people. These new weapons were officially called V1s, but they were more popularly known as 'buzz-bombs.' For a time about a hundred a day fell in Britain and in one fourteen-day period they killed 1,600 persons. Most of them dropped in the south of England but a few went further afield and, over the Christmas holiday period, a number were launched against Manchester.

By the beginning of September 1944, the menace of the V1 had largely been eliminated. Most of the launching sites had been either destroyed by the R.A.F. or overrun by advancing Allied armies, and on 7th September the Joint Parliamentary Secretary to the Ministry of Supply, Mr Duncan Sandys, informed a press conference that 'the Battle of London was virtually over.'

At twenty minutes to seven on the following evening two violent explosions at Chiswick and Epping happened within seconds of each other. There were no aircraft overhead and nobody had heard the now familiar buzz of the V1s. They were caused by the first of the V2s, Hitler's newest secret weapon, long range rockets.

Over the next six months an average of six V2s fell daily over the south of England and they did a good deal of damage.

Worse, arriving in complete silence and often without warning, they had an unfortunate effect on public morale. Happily this had been boosted by allied victories on land but it was very noticeable that, whilst many jokes were made about the buzz-bombs, the V2s gave rise to none.

It was one of these weapons that fell on the Dockland Roman Catholic Church in Parkers Row, Bermondsey, at 11 p.m. on the night of 2nd March 1945. And it was as a result of this incident that the last George Cross of the war was awarded to an A.R.P. worker. He was Albert Edward Heming, another early volunteer to the service who had become something of a specialist in first-aid duties.

It was a call from roof-spotters that summoned the Belling Road Light Rescue Section to Parkers Row and when they reached the spot they found the area devastated. Heming, who was the Section Leader, made some enquiries and was told that there were four priests, a nun and a housekeeper below the ruin, but there seemed little prospect of any of them being alive. But, as Heming walked round the area, suddenly, from far below his feet, he heard a weak voice shouting: 'I'm down here. I'm down here.' The voice came from the direction of the crypt of the church.

At once, Heming began to drive a narrow shaft towards the voice, but he had not gone far before it was realized that the weight of the ruins above the shaft was likely to close it again. In addition to this danger, there were bad escapes of gas making the air in the shaft highly poisonous.

By now, the Regional Commissioner, Sir Edward Evans, had arrived on the scene and decided that the conditions were far too dangerous to go on with an attempt at rescue and he gave orders that all A.R.P. workers were to be withdrawn from the scene. In response to this instruction, Heming ordered all his Section, except one man, to leave. This man he posted at the mouth of his tunnel to keep contact with him, and then he slid head first into it again and returned to his task.

For two hours Albert Heming dug his way into the ruins of the church, guided by the faint voice below. He worked upside down, in constant danger of being buried alive and with his inadequate air supply poisoned by coal gas. But, in the end, his bravery was rewarded and he was able to see a priest's head and to speak to him. He had tunnelled to a depth of thirty feet.

Then he broke through into the cavity in which the other man had been imprisoned and found that he was badly wounded in the head and had a broken arm. His legs were trapped under a heavy baulk of timber.

First, Heming did what he could for the priest's wounds and then he turned his attention to the problem of trying to free him. A great weight of masonry rested on the baulk of timber and it was impossible to move it. However, Heming did manage to cut away some of the wood and free one of the priest's legs but he failed in all his efforts to free the other one.

By now, the priest, Father Arbuthnot, was on the verge of unconsciousness and he announced that he was ready to die and would like another priest to administer the Last Sacrament. This was arranged and administered by a priest who had managed to force his way into the crypt, close by.

But Albert Heming was not yet convinced that Father Arbuthnot had to die and he explained to him that he thought they might be able to free his leg if both men pulled as hard as they could. Arbuthnot agreed and they both paused for a moment to gather breath; Heming then put his arms under the priest's shoulders and both men heaved with all their might. For a moment it seemed as though the effort was in vain, and then the leg came clear.

Heming was a small slight man and the tunnel he had dug below the church was a very narrow one but, by good fortune, Father Arbuthnot was little bigger than his rescuer and Heming managed, with a good deal of difficulty, to drag him out of the ruins.

Father Arbuthnot was taken to Guy's Hospital and, for a while, it looked as if Albert Heming's efforts to save him had been in vain, for the doctors despaired of being able to save him. But, in the end, he rallied and made a fine recovery. In 1959, Father Arbuthnot appeared as the subject of the B.B.C. Television programme, *This is Your Life*, and Albert Heming was one of the men who came forward to speak of the self-sacrificing work of the little dockland priest.

Five days after the V2 fell on Bermondsey, one landed on Smithfield Market and killed 110 persons. Then, as the Allied armies advanced more deeply into Germany and more and more launching sites were overrun, the attack diminished. On 27th March 1945, the 115th V2 fell on Britain, at Orpington in Kent. It was the last German missile to land on British territory.

+++

CHAPTER III

U.X.B.

ONE of the less pleasant by-products of the Blitz was the unexploded bomb, or 'U.X.B.' as it was familiarly called. The primitive bombs of the First World War were fitted with a simple impact fuse that was designed to detonate when it struck its target and, if it failed to go off after having been dropped from several thousand feet, providing it was handled with reasonable care, it was equally unlikely to explode on being removed to a place suitable for its destruction. But these bombs suffered from certain drawbacks. Exploding, as they did, on impact, they did not inflict as much damage as bombs that plunged to the basements of buildings before detonating. When dropped from a low-flying aircraft they endangered the machines that released them.

Between the wars a German firm invented and patented an electrical fuse in which the impact of the bomb closed a circuit that fired the charge. With this type of fuse there was a short delay between impact and detonation and the delay varied with the height from which the bomb was dropped.

Elements of the Luftwaffe operated on the side of General Franco in the Spanish Civil War and they dropped bombs that were fitted with the new electrical fuse. In addition, of course, this was the first time in history that bombing of industrial areas had taken place on an appreciable scale. Thus, it was not until this war that the problems of dealing with unexploded bombs first came to be realized.

The new electrical fuses were found to be more temperamental than the old impact ones. Sometimes they would go off several minutes, hours, or even days, after they had been dropped and some of them displayed an aversion to being shaken or jolted. As a result it needed brave, or foolhardy, men to remove the bombs to safe places and often large areas of cities had to be evacuated, roads closed and vital war plants shut down until they were dealt with. In many respects the unexploded bomb was becoming a greater menace than the one that exploded.

Reports of the disorganizing and disrupting effects of unexploded bombs came back to London but they were filed in the archives of the Home Office. A year or two later the inevitability of war began to be recognized and Civil Defence planning—it was then known as Air Raid Precautions—started in earnest, but the problem of the unexploded bomb had been forgotten. When Germany attacked Poland in the summer of 1939, and the Luftwaffe, with its dive bombers, provided the spearhead of the attack, fresh reports of the menace were received. Then, at last, the Home Office began to give some attention to the problem.

The reports that had come from Spain can hardly have been studied very carefully, however, for the first Home Office instruction on the handling of unexploded bombs recommended that they should be collected into dumps by Air Raid Wardens and exploded by the armed forces. This optimistic and impractical instruction was quickly followed by an announcement that the Home Office was setting up a special civilian organization that would be trained in the handling and disarming of live bombs.

But the Home Office failed to find the men to staff it, and, in November 1939 the job was handed over to the War Office and the War Office gave it to the Royal Engineers. Thus the first Bomb Disposal Sections were born; parties of three men commanded by Corporals, utterly ignorant of the intricacies of the weapons they were meant to handle and equipped only with pickaxes, spades and sandbags. Their only instructions were, when they found an unexploded bomb, to cover it with sandbags and detonate it.

That is the story of the makeshift beginnings of an organization which, within a year, contained thousands of skilled men whose work was backed by the brains of some of the country's best scientific and civil engineering establishments. The work of the Bomb Disposal units demanded the most cold-blooded courage, and it was never lacking. Twelve uniformed members of the organization had their bravery recognized by the award of the George Cross and scores more received George Medals and other awards. The only outward symbol of the bravery of the remainder was the gold bomb on a crimson flash that the Bomb Disposal sappers wore on the sleeve of their uniforms. It was an emblem that had the respect of the nation.

As well as being dangerous, the work of the Bomb Disposal units was arduous and often frustrating. They received tens of thousands of requests for help and all had to be answered. The first thing that had to be done, on receiving a call, was to make sure that their services were really needed. Often some unusual object had caused unnecessary alarm. Sometimes, after hours of fatiguing digging, it was discovered that the alleged un-exploded bomb was, in fact, a small bomb that had bored deeply into soft ground and gone off there.

One of the early surprises of the war was the tremendous depth to which some bombs penetrated; sometimes as much as sixty feet. This involved the Bomb Disposal units in hours, and often days, of back-breaking labour and it also introduced serious engineering problems in connection with the casing and timbering of the shafts that had been dug.

Having unearthed a bomb the Sappers then had to decide whether or not it was safe to detonate it on the spot and, if it was not, how it could best be made harmless. Sometimes this was impossible and, if there was a risk of it doing serious damage where it lay, the thing had to be removed in its dangerous state.

Typical of this was an incident at Lougher railway station, in Wales, where a bomb fell on 24th August 1940. The officer in charge of the nearest Bomb Disposal Section was 2nd Lieutenant Ellis Edward Talbot and he went with his men to the spot. There they found that the bomb had penetrated deeply into the ground and the party had to dig for twelve and a half hours before they reached it. Then Talbot put a rope around it and the thing was hoisted carefully to ground level.

The young officer sent his men to a safe distance and examined the bomb himself. He had had no proper training for the dangerous work that he was doing—few had in those early days—but he had seen some of the first types of fuses that the Germans had used. This one, however, was of a kind that he had not seen before and he was uncertain either of how to withdraw it or how safe such an operation would be. He decided, therefore, not to meddle with it.

The bomb was one of a light variety that was often used in the early part of the war and so, shouting to his men to keep behind their cover, he hoisted it onto his shoulder and carried it to a field two hundred yards away. There he covered it with sandbags and detonated it.

For this act of bravery 2nd Lieutenant Talbot was given the Empire Gallantry Medal and this was then replaced by the George Cross. A year later he was killed in action.

Talbot's reluctance to tamper with a fuse that was strange to him was understandable, for only a few days earlier the first news of the use of delayed action fuses had reached him. Eleven days before a Bomb Disposal officer had taken a fuse from one of the three thousand unexploded bombs that were, by now, scattered over Britain from the Shetland Isles to the South Coast. As he examined it, he suddenly noticed that there was a faint ticking coming from its interior. He sent it to Woolwich Arsenal.

There an Experimental Officer tried to unscrew the base from its casing but it was obstinate and he failed. He then put it on a lathe and carefully cut through the casing with a cutting tool. Inside he found a clockwork mechanism that was obviously intended to delay the explosion of the bomb. He was, in fact, able to calculate that this particular fuse had been set to go off forty hours after dropping.

A couple of days later another of these fuses was discovered. This had been set to go off at seven hours but had jammed. Others came to light and examination of them produced some interesting information. It became clear, for example, that none of the fuses then being used by the Germans was capable of being set to delay for more than seventy hours. It was also discovered that the clockwork was particularly prone to jamming a short while before the fuses were timed to explode.

Once they stopped, however, they were very liable to re-start again when jolted or shaken.

All this added to the difficulties and dangers of the work of the Bomb Disposal Sections and orders were given that all un-exploded bombs were to be treated as though they were of the delayed action type and, unless their immediate removal was vital, they were not to be approached until eighty hours after they had fallen.

When bombs had to be handled it became important to know, if they had delayed action fuses, whether or not the clockwork mechanism was still running. To start with, doctors' stethoscopes were issued but the clockwork was embedded deep inside the weapons, behind a thick wall of explosives, and it was by no means always easy to hear it with an ordinary stethoscope. Eventually, therefore, highly sensitive electric microphones were produced to take their place.

Very shortly after the arrival of the first delayed action fuse it was discovered that the Germans were fitting them with anti-handling devices. These were mechanisms that were de-signed to explode when any attempt was made to withdraw the fuse. The first of these was found by an officer who was subsequently given the George Cross in recognition of a number of daring feats.

His name was Lieutenant (later Lieutenant-Colonel) Bertram Stuart Trevelyan Archer. He was called, with his Section, to the great tank farm in the Anglo-Iranian Oil Company's re-finery at Llandarcy, near Swansea, where a stick of four bombs had fallen amongst the oil tanks, none of them going off. One had bored a slanting shaft into the ground and settled itself right below the concrete foundations of one of the huge tanks; a second had buried itself a hundred and fifty yards away between two other tanks, and the other two were in safer spots. Close by, several tanks of oil were on fire.

The greatest danger came from the bomb under the tank and Archer decided that that was the one that must be tackled first. He therefore set his men to work to reach it. The heat from the blazing oil was intense but they dug in relays. After working for an hour or so, there was a violent explosion. It was the closest of the other three bombs but, happily, it did no damage. A few minutes later one of the more distant ones went off.

The sweating soldiers must have wondered whether the one below the tank would be the next to explode but they went on digging and, after almost five hours of back-breaking effort, they reached it and removed sufficient earth from around it for their Section Commander to climb down the shaft and make an examination.

By the light of an electric torch he was able to see that the bomb casing had a wide split down one side and through this he could see the fuse casing; a hollow steel tube stretched across the centre of the bomb like a ladder rung. It had become detached from the main casing at one end.

Using a cold chisel and a hammer, Archer removed the base plate of the bomb and then working partly through the split in the casing and partly through the place where the base-plate had been, he scooped out the explosive filling. That done, he wrenched out the partly dislodged fuse.

A little while later he examined this and removed the fuse mechanism. When he did this there was a sharp crack as a small cap detonated. He looked at the mechanism again and noticed that in addition to the usual electrical fuse there was a small clockwork motor and another gadget that he could not recognize. Sensibly, he made a parcel of all the bits and pieces and sent them to the War Office by dispatch rider. There they were examined by experts who, for the first time, discovered that the Germans were employing clockwork delayed action fuses with an anti-handling device.

Winston Churchill became interested in the subject of fuses and he minuted the Department of Scientific Research demanding that high priority should be given to the development of equipment for dealing with live bombs. His exhortations were not without effect and a spate of gadgets were produced. The earliest of these was a simple device that was designed to short-circuit the fuse and drain off its electrical charge. It worked well but, before it could be put into production, changes in the design of the German fuses rendered it useless.

A later and more effective device for draining the charge from an electrical fuse was a mechanism that injected a strong solution of salt into the fuse case.

Various means of stopping the clockwork of delayed action fuses were tried out and the most successful was an instrument called the 'Q' Coil. This was simply a large coil that was slipped over a bomb like the collar of a cart horse. A current was then passed through the coil and this set up a strong magnetic field that magnetized and stopped the clock just as a wrist watch can be made useless if it is not made of anti-magnetic materials and it is brought too close to an electro-magnet.

Another piece of equipment that proved most useful was called the 'steam steriliser.' This cut a hole in the bomb casing and then discharged steam into it, causing the T.N.T. filling to turn into a glutinous liquid and drain from the bomb.

One of the more fantastic ideas was the conception of firing a bullet through a fuse casing to disarm it. This was the brainchild of a remarkable member of the Department of Scientific Research: Charles Henry George Howard, twentieth Earl of Suffolk and thirteenth Earl of Berkshire.

Lord Suffolk succeeded to his titles at the age of eleven when his father, serving as a Major in the Royal Artillery, was killed in action in the First World War. He went to school at Radley where his main interests were sailing, riding, plumbing, welding, woodwork and metalwork. When he left school he sailed, for a time, before the mast in one of the last of the clippers. Next, he took a commission in the Scots Guards.

Unfortunately, in 1927, he suffered a severe attack of rheumatic fever and had to leave the Army. He went to Australia and for a while ran a sheep farm in Queensland. In 1930 he decided that he had seen enough of the rough and tumble of the world and that the time had arrived for him to settle down and run his family estate at Charlton Park, in Wiltshire. But it did not take him long to realize that he was not cut out for the life of a landed aristocrat and he packed his bags again and went to Edinburgh where, in 1934, he graduated as a Bachelor of Science. He was then twenty-eight. He achieved one other success whilst he was at the University of Edinburgh. He met, wooed and married the then popular musical comedy star, Mimi Crawford. Lord Suffolk was a contemporary of mine at Edinburgh University and I met him several times. He had delightful manners and great personal charm combined with high intelligence. I then knew nothing of his earlier history, except that he had had rheumatic fever and still suffered much pain. I would certainly not have picked him out as a potential hero, but this is not the first time I have been wrong in this.

Having acquired a degree and a wife he was happy to return to Charlton Park and, for the next five years he divided his time between running his estate and conducting scientific experiments. Then the war came and he applied to rejoin his regiment but, hardly surprisingly, he was rejected and, instead, he found himself a job as an Experimental Officer in the Department of Scientific Research.

Lord Suffolk spoke perfect French and he was sent to France as the personal representative of the Director General of Scientific Research. When France fell he made his way across country from Paris to Bordeaux and, from there, back to England. With him he brought a group of French scientists, a large quantity of industrial diamonds and a supply of heavy water. Other valuable equipment he hid on the French coast and it was later recovered by the Royal Navy.

By now, the Department of Scientific Research had become responsible for research into methods of handling and de-fusing unexploded bombs and, on his return to England, Lord Suffolk volunteered for this work. For eleven months he toured the British Isles visiting the sites of bomb incidents. Whenever news reached him of a bomb with a new type of fuse he made a bee-line for the spot. Always he was accompanied by his chauffeur, Fred Harts, and his secretary, Miss Morden, and the trio were well known to the members of many of the Bomb Disposal Sections who christened them 'the Holy Trinity.' It became a common sight to see the Earl crouching contentedly in the bottom of a pit alongside a live bomb, smoking a cigarette in a long black holder and working away with a welding set, a spanner or a hack-saw. Fred Harts would hover around the top of the hole, handing down tools and instruments at the request of his master, whilst Miss Morden would squat on some piece of fallen masonry taking down in shorthand the notes that the Earl made as he worked.

Lord Suffolk had an inventive brain and, in addition to his scheme for firing a bullet through a fuse, he developed the idea of destroying bombs by burning, instead of exploding them, and of removing the charge by sawing the casing in half. His particular interests were fuses and anti-handling devices and he conducted hundreds of experiments with them both. Nobody could have been more fully aware of the dangers that he faced than the titled scientist himself.

On Tuesday 12th May 1941, Lord Suffolk took a live 500 pound bomb to a desolate part of Richmond Park that had been set aside for the destruction of bombs. Nobody knows what he intended to do with it. All that is known is that it exploded and the 'Holy Trinity' were killed. A non-commissioned officer and four Sappers of an experimental Bomb Disposal unit of the Royal Engineers perished with them.

The Earl of Suffolk and Berkshire was posthumously awarded the George Cross and the Port Laureate wrote of him:

> He loved the bright ship with the lifting wing:
> He felt the anguish of the hunted thing;
> He dared the dangers which beset the guides
> Who lead men to the knowledge nature hides.
> Probing and playing with the lightning thus
> He and his faithful Friends met death for us.
> The beauty of a splendid man abides.

One other Experimental Officer of the Department of Scientific Research was awarded the George Cross for his work in connection with unexploded bombs. He was Arthur Douglas Merriman. On many occasions Arthur Merriman volunteered to remove new and unknown fuses from German bombs and, often, they were fitted with anti-handling devices. He recovered the fuses from the very first German bombs that were dropped on Britain and failed to explode. They fell on the Shetland Isles. In the late summer of 1940 he went to Southampton and took out the fuses of ten bombs in the bomb-bay of a crashed German aircraft. All were delayed action fuses with anti-handling devices.

In September 1940, Merriman, in company with Dr H. J. Gought, the Director General of Scientific Research, went to the site of an unexploded bomb that had fallen in Regent Street. A delayed action mechanism was ticking and the two scientists tried, for some time, to stop it but all their efforts failed. It was then decided to remove the main charge of the bomb and Arthur Merriman stayed and helped with this task whilst someone else listened to the regular beat of the clock, ready to shout a warning if it stopped, in the vain hope that the workers would be able to reach some sort of cover before the bomb exploded. But the ticking did not stop and Merriman and his helpers were able to remove the greater part of the charge. Soon after they had finished their work the bomb went off but with little force and the only damage that it caused was a few broken windows.

Unlike his colleague, Arthur Merriman survived the war despite his dangerous occupation. He was more fortunate than many of the Bomb Disposal Sappers for, by the end of 1940, no less than 123 of them had been killed.

Amongst those that died was another officer who was decorated with the George Cross, Captain Michael Floud Blaney. On 13th December he was in charge of a party that was trying to hoist a bomb from its entry hole in Romford Road, Manor Park, by means of a derrick and pulleys. His plan had been to fit a 'Q' Coil around the bomb and to keep it there whilst it was being dragged out. Unfortunately this cumbersome piece of equipment interfered with the lifting tackle and, in the end, he had to remove it again and withdraw the bomb without it. He was anxious that the bomb should not jolt against the sides of the hole but, as it neared the end of its journey, he noticed that it was swinging dangerously. He went forward to steady the bomb as it was dragged clear of the hole. A moment later, whilst Captain Blaney was still holding on to it, it exploded. Another officer, a Staff-Sergeant, five soldiers and a senior police officer were also killed. A second Staff-Sergeant who had been listening to the electric stethoscope from behind cover lived to tell what had happened.

Another Bomb Disposal officer who was killed at this time and was posthumously awarded the George Cross was 2nd Lieutenant Alexander Fraser Campbell. He was called to deal with an unexploded bomb that had fallen in Chapel Street, Coventry. When he examined it he found that it was so distorted that it was quite impossible to withdraw the fuse. He decided, therefore, that the only thing to do was to remove the bomb for destruction as it was. He and his men handled it with the same care that they would have shown to a badly wounded man and loaded it into a truck. They then drove it to a stretch of empty country that was being used as a bomb cemetery and, still using every care, began to unload it again.

It is tragic that, having loaded the bomb and driven it several miles, it chose to explode as it was being unloaded again. Six soldiers died with Campbell.

More fortunate was 2nd Lieutenant Launcelot Andrews. He was in charge of a Bomb Disposal Section that was attempting to disarm an unexploded bomb on a hot August day in 1940. He managed to withdraw the fuse a short distance out of the bomb casing when it suddenly snapped back again, apparently under the influence of a strong spring. After that nothing would budge the thing.

The bomb was needed for examination by the Department of Scientific Research and he had been given strict orders to disarm it and deliver it to Woolwich. He made several more attempts and then he sent his men to a safe distance and tied one end of a long length of cord to the exposed part of the fuse. He went with the other end of the cord behind cover some thirty or forty yards off. He gave a sharp tug and the bomb went off with an explosion that shook the neighbourhood and sent a shower of debris in all directions.

Several of Andrews' men were cut and bruised by flying stones and masonry. He himself was thrown several yards but he suffered from nothing worse than shock and superficial injuries. He was awarded an Empire Gallantry Medal, later replaced by a George Cross.

Other early members of the Bomb Disposal Organization who won the same award and are now on the list of George Cross holders were 2nd Lieutenant Edward Womersley Reynolds and Lance-Sergeant William John Button. Reynolds, although he had had no proper training in the task, removed one of the first clockwork fuses from a 250 kilo bomb that was lying in the middle of a council estate and had driven several hundred people from their homes. Three weeks later he performed a practically identical act.

Sergeant Button was the non-commissioned officer in charge of a party that dug desperately to reach a delayed action bomb before it went off and destroyed a row of houses. They lost the race against time and the whole party was blown up. Button and a couple of other men survived the explosion. Five sappers were killed.

A George Cross award to a Bomb Disposal officer that received more publicity than any other was that made to Lieutenant Robert Davies. This was not because what he did— brave though it was—was any braver than many other acts that won the George Cross. It was because he was responsible for saving a great national shrine, if not from destruction, at least from very severe damage.

On the night of Thursday 12th September 1940, the City of London was heavily bombed. When the light came somebody noticed a large and deep hole in the pavement close to the west front of St. Paul's Cathedral. A shaft sloped away from the road towards the cathedral wall and, inside it, a fire was burning from a ruptured gas main. The cause was obvious and an urgent call was sent to the Bomb Disposal Organization.

A party of Sappers under the command of Lieutenant Davies quickly arrived on the scene and, without any waste of time, they began to dig. The toiling men had to contend not only with the burning gas main but another unruptured one, close by, and several electricity cables. One man said later that he was more frightened of being gassed and electrocuted than of being blown up.

After several hours of digging a large bomb was found some

twenty feet below ground level. It lay on its side firmly wedged in heavy black clay.

Sapper George Cameron Wylie was given the difficult task of scraping away the clay from the sides and top of the bomb and then fitting a harness to it. This was no easy job at the foot of a twenty-foot shaft where the air was foul and the light poor. Every minute he spent on it could have been his last.

Eventually the bomb was withdrawn and loaded onto a cradle in the back of an army truck. As soon as it was safely in the vehicle, Davies dismissed his men and climbed into the cab alone. The streets along his route were cleared by the police and he took the bomb to Hackney Marshes where it was destroyed.

Sapper Wylie, as well as Lieutenant Davies, was awarded the George Cross for the part he had played in saving the great Wren masterpiece that had taken forty years to build.

Shortly after this two further awards of the George Cross were announced. The first went to Captain Herbert John Leslie Barefoot, of No. 4 Bomb Disposal Company R.E., who played a part in a large number of incidents and had been continuously engaged in dangerous investigations into fuses and other mechanisms of new designs of bombs. The other award was won by Sergeant Michael Gibson, of No. 9 Company, who took charge of a particularly difficult and hazardous operation in an important factory.

One other civilian was decorated with the George Cross for bomb disposal work in 1940. That was Mr Roy Thomas Harris, Staff Officer of the Croydon A.R.P. Engineer Service, and a member of the Borough Engineer's Department. In 1940, Croydon received its fair share of bombs and the normal proportion of them failed to explode on impact. The nearest Bomb Disposal unit was at Kingston and Mr Harris was nominated to act as Liaison Officer between the local A.R.P. Service and the Sappers at Kingston.

To begin with, he did little more than locate and pin-point the bombs and then lead the Sappers to them. But, as the Bomb Disposal unit became more heavily engaged, it was often necessary for them to send small parties of junior ranks to deal with incidents at Croydon and Mr Harris would often assume un-official charge of the operations. More than once he disarmed highly sensitive bombs himself.

Having taken on the role of a Bomb Disposal officer it was hardly surprising that, some time later, Mr Harris joined the Army and was commissioned in the Royal Engineers, eventually reaching the rank of Lieutenant-Colonel.

In 1941 the work of the Bomb Disposal Sections was bedevilled by the arrival of magnetic and acoustic mines that were sometimes accidentally dropped on land. One of the earliest of these was found in the back garden of a terrace house. It had, apparently, been there for some time and the occupant of the place, under the impression that it was a harmless aeroplane part, had rigged up an elaborate erection of steps over it so that he could get to and from his coal cellar.

Next year, the Germans began to drop phosphorus bombs and these were particularly unpleasant things. Often they would lie harmlessly in the soil until they were exposed by the activities of the bomb disposers. The moment that they came into contact with the air, however, they would burst into flames and several soldiers suffered very severe burns from them.

An equally unpleasant innovation of 1942 was the butterfly bomb. This was a little canister that weighed less than five pounds and floated down to earth on veins, after the manner of a sycamore seed. They were dropped by the thousand and were fitted with varying types of fuses. Some detonated on landing, some had a time fuse and some went off on being moved. They were unpleasant to handle and difficult to find.

The use of these new weapons did not mean that high explosive bombs were not still being dropped in large numbers, nor that more complicated and dangerous fuses were not being developed by the enemy. There was, unhappily, little doubt that the German intelligence of our bomb disposal methods was far too good, for it was noticeable that every new British bomb handling technique was quickly countered by a new fuse.

One day in January 1943, a bomb fell on Lord's Cricket Ground and penetrated the Bakerloo tube line that runs underneath. It eventually came to rest between the underground rails.

Whilst the bomb lay there the tube traffic was halted and its immediate clearance was ordered. The task was allotted to a Bomb Disposal Company commanded by Major W. G. Parker. (He served in Bomb Disposal units throughout the whole of the war and had a particularly distinguished career. He disarmed many dangerous bombs and, though his bravery was never rewarded by any decoration, it received unique recognition from the proprietors of Odeon Cinemas Ltd, who presented him with a medallion that entitled him to free entry to any of their cinemas for life. This was given to him when, as a subaltern, in 1940, he had removed an unexploded bomb from an Odeon Cinema in Birmingham.) Parker supervised the clearance of the bomb himself and he decided to make the fuse safe by the then well established method of pumping brine into it. This done, he had the bomb hauled up through its own entry hole to the cricket ground. From there it was taken, by lorry, to Hampstead Heath.

At Hampstead, another officer extracted the fuse, a particularly difficult job that, in the end, he had to accomplish with a hammer and chisel. When he had achieved this he found that its reluctance to come out had been due to a new internal locking device but, more than that, the fuse was of an entirely new design. Parker was sent for and, after a quick look at the fuse he rushed it to the Department of Scientific Research.

Experts made a careful examination of the thing and discovered that it was fitted with a highly sensitive mercury switch that completed a firing circuit on the slightest movement of the bomb. Worse than that; whilst the electrical charge in all other earlier fuses could be drained away by pumping brine into them, in this device the charge came from a dry battery in another part of the bomb and the effect of pumping in brine was to close the circuit and fire the bomb. By a stroke of amazing good fortune, in this particular bomb, one of the battery leads had been broken when it fell.

The news of the discovery of this very dangerous fuse was rushed to all Bomb Disposal units, together with details of its markings. (At no time did the Germans ever employ bogus markings on fuses and, as soon as a new type of fuse had been identified, it could always be recognized again. Presumably this was done for the benefit of German armourers who often had to disarm the bomb-loads of machines that had returned without having dropped them.) The news had barely gone out when a heavy bomb fell on a warehouse in Battersea.

The bomb had torn its way through roof girders, packing cases and machines, and finally came to rest below the bed-plate of a large lathe. It was badly distorted and it looked as though it would be impossible to withdraw the fuse casings. There were two of them. Further examination, however, revealed that they bore the same markings as the bomb that had fallen at Lord's.

A large flour mill next door had had to be closed down and much valuable machinery in the warehouse was in danger. The matter was discussed between representatives of the Ministry of Supply and the Regional Commissioner and it was decided that, despite the risk, the bomb would have to be removed as quickly as possible.

Major Cyril Arthur Joseph Martin volunteered to handle the bomb and, after examining it, he decided that the best method would be to try to remove the explosive filling. After a long struggle he managed to unscrew the base plate but discovered, to his horror, that the bomb was filled with a solid block of cast T.N.T. He thought of using a steam-sterilizer which would liquefy the filling and could be worked by remote control, but decided that the high temperature or any movement from the force of the steam jet might move the mercury in the switch sufficiently to fire the fuse. He decided, therefore, that the safest approach to the problem would be to apply a steam jet by hand, using it for short periods only, for long enough to soften and scrape away small quantities of T.N.T. at a time.

Helped by one other officer, Major Martin worked away at this arduous job for nearly twenty-four hours, lying in a cramped position in a hole that was filled with steam and water and pressed against one of the largest bombs that the Luftwaffe had dropped on London. Piece by piece, he succeeded in scraping away the T.N.T. until it was safe to move away the hollow casing that now only contained the two fuses. These were a valuable acquisition in themselves for, of course, only one other mercury switch fuse had so far been recovered.

Watchers who saw Major Martin at work said that, throughout the long hours of his task, he remained cool and calm and seemed to have a complete disregard for the risk that he was running. This would probably not have surprised anyone who knew him well, however, for Cyril Martin had been continuously engaged on bomb disposal work in the London area for over three years and had always shown the same cold-blooded courage when handling countless other bombs during the heavy raids of 1940-41. It is on record that at least ten of these were fitted with new and unknown types of fuses.

This brave officer's exploits were recognized by the award of the George Cross and, later in the war, he won the Military Cross as well. But he did not get the former decoration until he had had at least two other encounters with the terrifying new fuse.

Before these events, British scientists had, once again, succeeded in keeping pace with advances in German fuse design. It will be recalled that the mercury switch mechanism depended upon a dry battery lodged inside the bomb and it so happens that a dry battery, when its temperature is reduced to well below freezing point, ceases to be effective. The technique that was introduced to combat the new fuse was to build a ring shaped plasticine cup round the bomb and then pour a powerful freezing agent into it. Liquid oxygen was used for this purpose.

No sooner had the mercury switch fuse been mastered than a bomb fitted with one was located in the Old Kent Road and a Bomb Disposal officer was given the job of dealing with it. He succeeded in freezing it but then broke off the head of the fuse casing when he was trying to extract it. Major Martin then took charge himself and the problem that he had to face was the danger of the bomb defreezing whilst he was still wrestling with the fuse. He decided to break away the fuse piece by piece with a chisel until he had exposed the mercury switch. To overcome the danger of the temperature rising and the battery becoming active again, he dribbled liquid oxygen into the fuse casing as he worked.

3

In the end, he succeeded in disarming the bomb and, whilst he was doing this, he relayed a running commentary on his work over a microphone to somebody who was at a safe distance.

A few days later he disarmed another mercury switch bomb by the freezing method and, again, he broadcast a running commentary. He wrapped a greatcoat around the bomb to insulate it and then spent over two hours, crouched beside it, pouring liquid oxygen into the plasticine cup until he was satisfied that the temperature was sufficiently low for the battery to have been made inert.

It took him exactly twenty minutes to remove the fuse after he had taken off the plasticine cup. This was a critical time for the experts had calculated that, once the freezing process had been stopped, precisely twenty minutes would be available for work on the fuse before the freezing process had to start all over again.

Major Martin's well earned George Cross was the last one to be given to the Army for bomb disposal work but this did not mean that, after this, the work of the Bomb Disposal Sections was diminished. Admittedly after 1943 there were relatively few bombing raids on Britain but there were still many thousands of unexploded bombs from earlier raids waiting to be dealt with. No new fuses or anti-handling devices were appearing, however, and suitable techniques for dealing with all the old ones were by now in use.

In addition, X-ray photography of bomb fuses had become common practice and this added immeasurably to the safety of bomb disposal workers. Another development was the bomb locator, an instrument very similar in principle and appearance to a mine detector. With these, unexploded bombs were being more quickly located and excavated.

In the London area, a fair number of German bombs that had been dropped in the Zeppelin raids of World War I came to light. In addition, large numbers of our unexploded anti-aircraft shells and rockets had to be dealt with.

When Hitler decided to use his secret weapon the Bomb Disposal Sections were presented with yet another variation in their work, but at no time did either the V1 or the V2 present them with any serious problem. By the time that the first V1s fell our intelligence was so good that working drawings of them were already in the War Office and the Department of Scientific Research and plans for dealing with them were complete.

The V2 was fitted with a radio fuse, set to explode them ten feet above ground, and it was not difficult to disarm. Anyway, only four out of the thousand or so that fell in England failed to go off.

With the end of the bombing and then the end of the war, it was possible to disband a large part of the Bomb Disposal Organization, but several units had still to be kept in being, and even today, sixteen years after the end of hostilities, one still remains and, every now and then, we read in the press of its activities.

++

CHAPTER IV

FRENCH RESISTANCE

WHILST brave feats were being performed in Britain, courage was also abroad on the continent of Europe, particularly in occupied France where gallant men and women were facing danger just as great as from German bombs. They were the men and women of the Resistance. But to appreciate their story we should look, for a moment, at the fall of France.

It was not easy to understand French willingness to go hand in hand with the British pacifism that failed to resist the re-armament of Germany. The British knew nothing of life under German domination, but on no less than five occasions since 1800 the fire of Prussian guns had been heard from the suburbs of Paris and life under the Teutonic heel was a living memory for millions of Frenchmen.

In the mid-thirties France had by far the strongest army in Europe but Hitler gambled on the belief that she was politically rotten and his gamble succeeded. The inner weakness of France was a complex thing, due in part to a spirit of disillusionment that began in the army with the Dreyfus affair and spread throughout the nation with the Stavinski scandal. More than a decade of political restlessness had bred disunity and dis-content whilst the common Frenchman's natural love of peace was overhung with fear, and Communism was abroad. A new industrial plutocracy, which lacked conscience and loyalty, had been born and it had powerful influence. Important elements, fearful of Communism, leaned towards Fascism.

The complete collapse of France, when Germany eventually marched against her, was another strange thing; partially caused by her lack of inner strength but, just as much, by the shortcomings of her high command. There was a time when the French General Staff had been regarded as the centre of military science. But, in 1940, its senior officers were old and inflexible, resting on past laurels instead of moving with the time. In the age of the tank and the bomber they still thought in terms of linear defence. They strung their finest divisions, and all their tanks, along the length of the Maginot Line and deployed no reserve to deal with any penetration.

Thus it was that when Kleist's Panzers smashed through the second-rate French formations that had been allotted the task of defending the supposedly impenetrable forests of the Ardennes, little but the problem of their own lengthening lines of communication stood between the Germans and Paris. The French Government was in utter despair. However, on the very day that Germany attacked, Chamberlain's government had fallen and been replaced by a coalition with Churchill at its head, and four times between 16th May and 11th June, that remarkable man flew to France to encourage Reynaud to continue the fight and to offer him such meagre help as he was able. He was persuaded to fight on but, three days after Churchill's final visit, the German army marched into Paris and the Maginot Line was breached in front of Saarbrucken.

The government moved to Tours and Reynaud sent for the British Ambassador and told him that France was lost and he had decided to establish a centre of French authority in North Africa. But he was opposed in this by the elderly Marshal Petain who had placed himself at the head of the defeatist element of the cabinet, and decision was deferred. Churchill determined, once again, to visit France in a desperate last bid to bolster up the last remnants of crumbling morale.

This time the British Prime Minister decided to travel by cruiser but, as he climbed into the Southampton train at Waterloo station, news was brought to him that stopped his mission. Reynaud's government had been overthrown and the President had sent for Petain.

The Marshal formed a government of defeat and asked Hitler for an armistice. This was given and, under its terms, the whole of the northern and western regions of France became German occupied territory, whilst Petain's government, established at Vichy, was given autonomy over the rest of the country.

So far as the war against Germany was concerned, France,

as a nation, was finished and out of the battle. Amongst her
new leaders there were even some, such as the neo-Fascist
Pierre Laval, who were prepared to side with Hitler. But the
French are a race of individualists and the country was by no
means solidly behind Petain. In many a French heart, hatred
of the traditional enemy burned deeply and many a Frenchman
decided that, if he could not continue the battle as a part of
a nation, at least he could do so as an individual.

The lead was given by de Gaulle and, on the day that
Reynaud's government fell, he slipped quietly away to England
by air. He was followed by thousands of other brave Frenchmen, but there were many more who were either unable to
escape or preferred to remain behind and await their opportunity. Thus the French resistance movement was born.

At least one Englishman refused to believe that the true spirit
of France was dead. It was, of course, Winston Churchill, and,
despite his ultimate failure to rally the French government, he
remained convinced that the country was not yet out of the
fight. Towards the end of December 1940, he went to the
microphone and, in schoolboy French, addressed himself to the
people of France:

'Frenchmen!

'For more than thirty years, in peace and war, I have
marched with you and I am marching with you still along the
same road. Tonight, I speak to you at your fireside wherever
you may be, or whatever your fortunes may be. I repeat the
prayer around the *louis d'or, God protect France!* Here, in England,
under the fire of the Boche, we do not forget the ties that unite
us to France. . . .'

He went on to say that the British were unflinching in the
face of the Luftwaffe's assault and the Royal Air Force was
holding its own. The task of Britain was to clear Europe of the
Nazi pestilence and France would share in the ultimate victory.
He told Frenchmen everywhere that they might see their way
to useful action but he refused to go into details with hostile
ears listening. He ended:

'Good night, then: sleep to gather strength for the morning;
for the morning will certainly come. Brightly will it shine upon

the brave and true; kindly upon all who suffer for the cause; glorious upon the tombs of heroes. *Vive la France!* Long live also the forward march of the common people in all the lands towards the true and fuller inheritance, and towards the broader and fuller age.'

Churchill's call to be ready for action was something more than a dark and meaningless threat to the Nazis. He was already resolved to set up an organization that would foster and give material support to resistance movements throughout occupied Europe.

The organization was called the Special Operations Executive, or S.O.E. for short. It was established in London, where a section was formed for each territory in which it was to operate. There were difficulties over the formation of a French Section, however, and they stemmed from a relationship with General de Gaulle that was not always happy. He had, and still has, a stout heart but, as is well known today, a difficult personality. He was ever ready to take offence at the least slight, whether real or imagined. In addition, he regarded himself as the supreme and sole leader of Free France and he was not ready to recognize any authority except his own in matters that concerned France.

The British Chiefs of Staff, however, felt that it was necessary for all aspects of the war effort to be co-ordinated by them. In particular, they wanted to be in a position to order any specific acts of sabotage that might fit into the general pattern of the war strategy. In addition, it was known that there was some leakage of information from the Free French Headquarters and they were not ready, for this reason, to take de Gaulle into their full confidence on every occasion.

As a result of this situation the resistance movement in France had two parts. The larger consisted of groups of workers who had some measure of allegiance to de Gaulle and were in communication with the Free French Headquarters. The remaining groups worked under the direction of the British Government.

Throughout the war de Gaulle resented the British controlled groups and refused to co-operate with them. The British Government, on the other hand, accepted the fact that de Gaulle's groups were doing useful, if sometimes misdirected, work and agreed to supply them with arms and equipment.

The outcome of all this was that two separate sections were set up in S.O.E. to deal with the French resistance movement. The first of these, the one that was generally known as the French Section, was under the command of Major Maurice J. Buckmaster and had the task of recruiting and training agents to operate with the British controlled groups, organizing their activities and supplying them with arms, explosives and equipment. The other section, called the R.F. Section, had a number of different chiefs during its existence and was responsible for liaison with the Free French Headquarters and arranging the supply of arms and equipment to the groups that they controlled.

Maurice Buckmaster ran the French Section from soon after its formation until the end of the war and he was promoted to the rank of Colonel in the same appointment, as its importance grew. One of his most difficult jobs was the recruitment of suitable people for training as agents. Not only had their French to be good enough to let them pose as Frenchmen but they had to have the type of temperament that was suited to the work. He might have drawn recruits from the many French officers who were finding their way to England but it had been agreed with de Gaulle that Buckmaster would have no call on French nationals. Instead, therefore, he had to seek amongst dual-nationals and non-Frenchmen who had, as he himself, lived for long periods in France. Later a number of French Canadians offered their services and were accepted.

Training, for the would-be agents, started with a three-week course in the grounds of a remote country house in the south of England. Here the new recruits were taught to use explosives and to shoot. All instruction was given in French and no other language was spoken either on or off duty. During this period all the students were carefully watched to make sure that their behaviour and personality was suitable for the work that lay ahead. The man whose tongue was loosened under the influence of alcohol, for example, was quickly eliminated.

Those who survived the first part of the training were sent for another three-week period to the West of Scotland. There they went through a toughening-up process and learned to climb and stalk, to poach game and cook it over an open fire. They learned the ignoble sport of fishing with a stick of gelignite, and to lay an ambush. They trudged for miles over mountain and glen and many of them had good reason to remember this part of their training when, at a later date, they had to make their escape from France across the Pyrenees. They also learned to jump by parachute.

In Scotland they were also taught to send wireless messages by means of the morse code. Those who showed particular aptitude for this then went to a wireless school in the Midlands for more advanced training.

Those who had not been eliminated as temperamentally unsuitable, nor found the rigours of the training in Scotland too much for them, went to the New Forest for the final stage of their instruction. There they learned all the finer points of their new trade; the subtle tricks of the skilled agent. They were taught how to slip through a security screen or pass messages unseen in a crowded place, the art of the locksmith and not a few skills of the underworld.

Whilst brave men and women were being trained at home, in France the resistance movement was growing daily and, as it grew, the need for British agents increased. But few suitable candidates had been found and more than a few of the available ones fell by the wayside for one reason or another. Thus the newly trained agents seldom had long to wait before they were given the chance of practising their arts in the field.

Ninety per cent of them jumped into France from Royal Air Force bombers, for landing aircraft on the Continent was a hazardous business. Sometimes, however, the hazards had to be faced when it was necessary to take agents and others out of France. On such occasions Lysander aircraft were normally used and some agents landed by this means. On rare occasions, when suitable landing grounds could be found, bombers touched down on such missions. A few agents entered France by rowing or swimming from submarines or from small fishing craft that had sailed from Gibraltar.

By one means or another, almost five hundred trained men

and women found their way into France and, of that number, one hundred and thirty-three never returned. Theirs was a dangerous occupation; as dangerous as any other in the war and it is not surprising that a high proportion of them were decorated both by the King and, after the liberation, by the President of France. Three of them, all women, were given the George Cross but it is sad that all but one of these awards were posthumous for, in common with many of the other agents who never returned, two of these women were put to death in Hitler's concentration camps.

For almost two years the French Section of S.O.E. resisted the idea of employing women on this work. Then, towards the end of 1942, this policy was changed and one of the first women to volunteer and be accepted was Assistant Section Officer Nora Inayat-Khan of the Women's Auxiliary Air Force. She was the first woman agent to be sent to France and, fifteen months later, she was murdered in the infamous camp at Dachau. For her bravery, she was posthumously awarded the George Cross, but it was not until five years after her death that her sisters went to Buckingham Palace to receive the decoration from King George VI. It had taken a long time to piece together the fragments of her story.

It is difficult to imagine a less likely candidate for the work that Nora Inayat-Khan volunteered to do. She was a confirmed believer in fairies and wrote children's books that were published in France, England and the United States. Often, before the war, she read her own stories over the radio in children's programmes, from both London and Paris, in a soft voice that had a rich musical quality. She played the piano and the harp and she wrote music for both of these instruments.

She loved children, horses and dogs, and she was an accomplished horsewoman. She was a skilled linguist, talking six languages, and had a deep interest in oriental philosophy. This, no doubt, she inherited from her father who had been Professor of Philosophy and Psychology at the University of Paris and was a descendant of the ruling family of Mysore. Her mother was American; a first cousin of the founder of Christian Science, Mary Baker Eddy.

Professor Inayat-Khan had held a post in Moscow before he went to Paris and it was there that Nora had been born and spent the first part of her childhood. She was in England when the war broke out and she at once joined the Women's Auxiliary Air Force and it was with that service that she received her early training as a wireless operator. She spoke perfect French and knew France well, particularly Paris.

Her training finished, Nora was selected for duty as a wireless operator with a resistance group in Paris. Her dispatch there was planned and the time and place of her arrival was confirmed to a British agent in France by means of a bogus message at the end of a news bulletin in the B.B.C.'s French programme. By now, this was the established method of confirming all drops and landings of agents and supplies and, to those who held the code, which was frequently changed, a message such as, 'Ninette sends her love and birthday greetings to Georges,' could well mean, 'R.A.F. bomber will drop three hundred rifles at Dropping Zone "X" at midnight tonight.'

The message confirming the arrangements for Nora's dispatch to France went out on the evening of 16th June 1943, and as a result of it a British officer collected together a small group of French resistance workers and they made their way to an open field in a country district somewhere in the centre of France. There they waited anxiously for the sound of an aircraft and, after one or two false alarms, a Lysander flew low over their heads.

All the members of the reception party had electric torches and they separated and switched them on to indicate the limits of the temporary landing ground. Then one of the Frenchmen signalled the code letter of the operation, in morse. This was a necessary precaution to guard against the possibility of the Gestapo having laid a trap.

The little plane made a bumpy landing on the uneven ground and came to rest at one end of the field. The members of the reception committee gathered round it and helped Nora Inayat-Khan to the ground. A few quick words were exchanged with the pilot, and then a French officer who was escaping to join de Gaulle's forces climbed up into the Lysander and took the seat the girl had just left. Then, almost within seconds of its arrival, the plane was taxied over the rough grass and climbed up again into the darkness of the night. Nora was taken off to a farmhouse some miles away by her new friends and given food and a bed to sleep on.

She had been supplied with a new name, a forged identity card and ration books, and a false story to tell if she had to account for her presence in France. She was, for all practical purposes, no longer Nora Inayat-Khan. Not even the people that she was now working with knew her true name. To them she was 'Madeleine.'

Somehow she made her way to Paris and to an address that she had been given. There she met a man who had been described to her and they exchanged passwords. He gave her another address to go to, where she was welcomed by the members of one of the groups that was operating inside the capital of France, almost within a stone's throw of the Headquarters of the Gestapo, on Avenue Foch.

The job of wireless operator was a particularly dangerous one, for the Gestapo made much use of directional equipment for locating illicit transmitters and it was rarely possible for anyone found beside one to talk their way out of the situation. But, despite the dangers, Madeleine was soon at work and in contact with London.

By the summer of 1943 the resistance movement in France had grown from small beginnings into a vast underground network with many thousands of members. Large quantities of high explosives, rifles and anti-tank mines were being parachuted to the men of the Maquis—a Corsican word meaning 'bush' and applied to people who, for various reasons, have to 'take to the bush'—and they were using them with effect. The British officers who were attached to resistance groups had been carefully trained in the use of explosives and they passed on their knowledge to the Frenchmen. Two large German petrol dumps at St Ouen and L'Aumonier had gone sky high and the turn-tables in the railway yards at Le Mans were no longer usable. Another target that had been successfully attacked was the lock gates at St Quentin and, as a result, the Germans had to cease sending submarine parts through the canal route to the Mediterranean for assembly there. One particularly energetic worker, a dentist by profession, specialized in de-railing German trains. He had dealt successfully with no less than sixty-three.

It was becoming clear to the German High Command that many of these acts of sabotage were parts of a master plan and that their main aim was to interrupt the movement of reserves and supplies to their defensive positions on the coast. They also realized that invasion of the Continent by British and American forces was by now inevitable. Clearly, if the activities of the French resistance workers went unchecked they would have a profound influence upon the capacity of the German Army to resist invasion.

The Gestapo was ordered to smash the resistance movement. In particular they were told to round up as many as possible of the British agents that were known to be operating in France and directing the sabotage operations.

The Germans knew only one way of dealing with such a situation and that was by means of a rule of terror. Through a process of mass arrests and mass shootings the weaker elements in the movement could be terrified into betraying their comrades. The method was effective and, during July 1943, a large number of underground workers in the Paris area were rounded up and sent to Germany. With them went several British agents and, by the end of the month, Madeleine was the only wireless operator left in the city.

Madeleine herself had only escaped arrest by the skin of her teeth and the Germans not only knew of her existence but they knew her name and had a very full description of her in their files at Avenue Foch. The Gestapo were determined to find her.

When news of conditions in Paris reached the Headquarters of S.O.E., in London, Madeleine was told that her situation was too dangerous and she was ordered to make her way out of the capital as quickly as possible: plans to fly her from France would then be made. But she was a woman of independent spirit and she signalled back to say that she was not prepared to leave the Paris resistance workers without communications and she had plans for rebuilding one of the groups that had been smashed. For the present, therefore, she proposed to remain at her post.

Colonel Buckmaster was powerless to enforce his orders and so Madeleine remained and communication between London and Paris went on. Her coded messages were picked up by the Germans and they became more and more determined to catch her and break this last remaining link with England. A large number of Gestapo men were given the sole task of hunting this slight, quiet-spoken girl who believed in fairies and loved children and animals.

For a week or so, moving almost daily from house to house with her small transmitter, she eluded all their efforts. Then a French traitor gave away her hiding place and a score of Gestapo men surrounded the house that she was in. They caught her with her wireless set, a pad of messages, and her book of codes.

Madeleine was taken to Avenue Foch and there she was made an offer. The Germans wanted to be in a position to send false messages to London and promised the girl that, if she would co-operate in this plan, she would be well treated. She refused contemptuously and the senior officer who saw her, realizing that the plan had failed, threatened her with death, or worse, if she would not give the names of resistance workers and British agents who remained free in Paris. She remained silent.

The Gestapo decided that a spell of solitary confinement would soon break Madeleine's spirit and she was shut up in a cell on the fifth storey of their Headquarters. From time to time she was brought before Gestapo officers and threatened with every known penalty. She may well have been tortured but this is not known for certain, for all the meagre information that is available about this period of Madeleine's life has come from German sources and all that has been said is that she refused to speak.

She made two separate attempts at escape from her prison and, as a result, she was told that unless she would give an undertaking not to try again she would be sent to a concentration camp in Germany. She made no answer to this demand

and, five weeks after the day of her arrest, she was put, under close escort, on to an eastbound train.

For a time she was imprisoned at Karlsruhe and then she was sent on to Pforsheim. There, she was kept in a cell that was apart from the main camp and, in it, she was interrogated almost daily by Gestapo officers. By now she was becoming weak and ill but she still refused to speak.

Madeleine was held a prisoner in Germany for ten months and, throughout that time, the Gestapo never gave up hope of getting information from her. However, by the early part of September 1944, it became clear that she was ready to die in silence. And, in any event, the Allied armies were already in France and the information that she was able to give had become of relatively little importance. It was decided that Madeleine was of no further value to the Third Reich.

She was moved to the notorious concentration camp at Dachau on the 12th September 1944. On arrival there she was taken straight to the crematorium and shot. Her body was then burned. Nora Inayat-Khan was in her thirtieth year when she died.

A second posthumous award of the George Cross to a woman agent with the French resistance movement was made to Violette Szabo of the First Aid Nursing Yeomanry, the Corps into which all women volunteers for this work were recruited if they were not already a member of another Corps or service.

Violette Szabo was the British born widow of a French officer who had died fighting with the Eighth Army. Her parents had retired to live in France when she was still a young girl, and she knew the country and spoke the language as a native. She volunteered to work with the French Section early in 1944 and was quickly accepted and sent off to begin her training.

By then the resistance movement had grown into an organization that controlled several large areas of the interior of France, particularly in the mountains and forests to the northeast of Lyon, where one disciplined force of over 5,000 men, commanded by a French Colonel, held regular parades and exercises. Another place where the Maquis was equally strong, although still more or less underground, was Marseilles, where the labyrinths of the old town provided excellent hiding places and escape routes. The final area of strength and, from the German point of view, the most dangerous, was the industrial region of the North East. There the movement was based on Lille but it was strongly represented in all the larger cities of that part of France and the main targets of the resistance workers were the centres of communication.

By now the second front was imminent and the Germans were becoming extremely sensitive about the havoc to their communications that was resulting from the activities of the Maquis. A focal point that gave them particular concern was the city of Rouen which straddled the main road and rail routes over the Seine. The High Command ordered an all-out attack on the resistance movement there and extra Gestapo were moved to the spot.

Their activities bore fruit and, by the beginning of April 1944, French resistance in Rouen had been effectively smashed and all the British agents in the city had either been captured or had to make their escape to other parts of France. The city was cordoned off by the Gestapo and communication with London had been cut.

This turn of events did not suit the Allied Chiefs of Staff for the effective disruption of communications through Rouen played an important part in their invasion plans and several important jobs had to be done by the resistance forces there. S.O.E. was ordered to restore the situation.

The first essential was to discover the precise position, for all that was known in London was that communication had been lost, a number of agents and French workers had been arrested, and the city was alive with Gestapo. It would be no easy task to slip an agent past the German security cordon and, if anyone was to stand a reasonable chance of success, it was essential that they should be able to pose as French under the closest interrogation. Risks had been successfully taken in sending British officers with doubtful French accents to work in parts of the interior where the Maquis was in control. Such a person could not be expected to get through to Rouen, however.

The mission was a dangerous one and Colonel Buckmaster

would have preferred to have given it to a man. But no suitable man was available. In fact, the only suitable agent that he had was Violette Szabo, who had recently finished her training.

The young and very beautiful woman was parachuted into France and successfully slipped through the German cordon that surrounded the city. She spent several weeks there and succeeded, not only in making contact with the remnants of the broken resistance groups, but also in helping them to re-form. Twice she was arrested by the Gestapo and each time she managed to escape again. Then, having done all that she felt she could do, she slipped out of the city again and returned to England by Lysander.

A week or two later she was dropped into France a second time. She was sent to join a group in the Haute Vienne, in central France, and she landed on the day after D Day.

Three days later, when she was driving along a narrow lane with a French resistance worker, the pair of them ran into a German road block. The non-commissioned officer in charge ordered Violette and her companion to get out of their car and walk towards him. The pair dismounted from the car but dived behind some cover and opened fire on the Germans with sten guns.

A pitched battle developed and it lasted for the best part of half an hour and only ended when Violette and her companion had exhausted their ammunition. Then they were captured, but not before Violette had killed one of the Germans.

The girl was sent to Germany by rail and, during her journey, she learned that at the far end of the train there was a cattle truck with several British officers in it. Some of them were badly wounded.

Soon after she heard this the train was attacked by the R.A.F. and the German sentries locked the doors and ran from it for shelter. Violette, although she was handcuffed, made her way along the whole length of the corridor with a tin of water and managed to force her way into the truck where the officers were imprisoned. She gave her water to the badly wounded and encouraged the rest of the prisoners so cheerfully that, as one of them reported afterwards, everyone's morale was greatly raised.

Inside Germany, Violette was held for a time in the concentration camp at Ravensbruck and, there, the Gestapo tried to make her give details of British agents who were still at large in France. She was kept in solitary confinement and subjected to every sort of torture but she refused to speak. She was then sent, for a time, to work in a forced labour camp in East Prussia. In January of the following year she was returned to Ravensbruck and, after two days, was sent to the gas chamber.

Reports of the circumstances of Violette Szabo's captivity and death did not come to light until nearly two years after her murder but, when they did, it became clear that she faced everything, even her last walk to the gas chamber, with unbelievable bravery and cheerfulness. More than that, her constant concern seemed to have been to encourage others to show the same courage that she did herself. This brave woman was in her early twenties when she died and she left a four-year-old daughter.

The third agent of the French Section to be decorated with the George Cross was also a mother. When she agreed to undertake this dangerous work she left three young girls in the care of the Sisters of Mercy at St. Helen's Convent, in Essex. She was Odette Sansom, the subject of Jerrard Tickell's well known book and the film, *Odette*.

Odette was of French birth and her maiden name was Brailly. Her father, Gaston Brailly, was a bank clerk but died as a Sergeant of the 52nd Infantry Regiment, at the battle of Verdun. Before he was killed, however, he was decorated with both the Croix de Guerre and the Medaille Militaire. If bravery is capable of being inherited, one has not far to look for the source of Odette's.

In 1931, when Odette was nineteen, she married an Englishman, Roy Sansom, who lived in France. Three years later the couple moved to England and, in the years that followed, the young Frenchwoman acquired an affection for England—particularly for the English countryside—but this in no way quenched her ties to the country of her birth.

Odette Sansom's name was brought to the attention of the French Section of S.O.E. as the result of a broadcast appeal for photographs of the Continent. It was, in fact, made on behalf of the Admiralty, but Odette, who tended at the best of times to be somewhat unscientific in her methods, wrote to the War Office explaining something of her background and offering to send some photographs of the Boulogne area.

Her letter resulted, not in a request for Odette to send her photographs, but in one that she should present herself in person at the War Office. She went, more out of curiosity than anything else and, at the end of a somewhat lighthearted and rambling conversation with an officer, it was suggested that her knowledge of France and the French might well fit her for some sort of war work. The suggestion was casually made and the type of work was not specified. Odette did not take it very seriously but said that she might consider doing some translations during the few hours that she could spare from her virtually full-time occupation of running a house and looking after three children.

A few days later she was invited to visit the War Office again. There she had another conversation with a different officer but discussion was confined to the war and her attitude to France and the Nazis. As soon as her interviewer had convinced himself of her love of France and hatred of its enemies he asked her if she would like to go there to help to make life unpleasant for the occupation forces. Odette replied, quite firmly, that the idea did not appeal to her in the very least. Shortly after that she left and returned to her war-time home on the borders of Somerset and Devon. When one of her daughters asked why she had been summoned to London she told her that the whole thing was a stupid mistake and her name had been mixed with that of somebody else.

A week later, on 5th July 1942, Odette telephoned to a number that had been given to her and was connected with Maurice Buckmaster. She told him that she had decided to accept the appointment that she had been offered.

The report that went to the French Section at the end of the first part of Odette's training very nearly ended any further idea of her going to France as an agent. She was enthusiastic, highly patriotic and had absorbed all the instruction, it said, but it went on to describe her as impulsive, lacking in clarity of mind and experience of the world, excitable and unwilling ever to admit to being in the wrong. Maurice Buckmaster shook his head sadly over it and then motored off into the country to interview the young woman of whom it had been written.

The head of the French Section tried, as kindly as he could, to explain to her that the work of a British agent called for a cold-blooded calculating outlook on life, whilst her temperament seemed to be the complete reverse. An agent who was at all impulsive or excitable could easily let down her comrades in an emergency. This roused Odette, who said that she would never let down anyone and she seemed so distressed at the prospect of not going to France that Buckmaster relented and agreed that she should go on with her course.

Odette had one other setback during her training. She had a nasty fall when she was jumping from an aeroplane mock-up in her parachute instruction. At first it was feared that she had broken a bone in her foot but an X-ray showed that she had nothing worse than a badly sprained ankle. With it, she had a very nasty black eye.

She was eventually earmarked for duty with a resistance group in Auxerre, in the German occupied zone and, her training over, she was given a false identity and a false background that would, if necessary, account for her presence there. The name on her forged Carte d'Identite was Odette Metayer. If her history was enquired into, she was briefed to say that she was the widow of an elderly shipping agent who had died of bronchitis in the winter of 1936. Since his death she had been living with old family friends, sometimes in Le Touquet and sometimes in Amiens. Her marriage to old M. Metayer had been childless.

Other parts of her manufactured past coincided with the truth. Her father, for example, though he had a different name, had died fighting with the 52nd Infantry Regiment and she had been educated, until her eighteenth birthday, by the nuns of the Ecole St Therese. In common with all British agents her true identity was to remain a secret on the files of S.O.E. and she was given a code name by which she would be known to her fellow workers. It was Lise.

Arrangements were made to send Odette to Gibraltar in a Whitley bomber and details of the B.B.C. message that would confirm her departure were sent to an agent in France. She set off from Paddington in a west-bound train, taking with her her false identity papers, fifty thousand francs and some little pills. One of them was lethal and some, if dropped into somebody's drink, were guaranteed to divert his mind from everything except his own condition and give him an uncomfortable and pre-occupied couple of hours. The remainder were what are commonly known as pep pills.

She left the train at Bristol and went to a nearby airfield. There she was helped into a waiting Whitley and, a few moments later, she was in the air. Seconds after that the bomber crashed on the end of the runway and, by the following morning, Odette was back in London again.

This was merely the beginning of a chapter of accidents that invaded all efforts to get Odette to France. A few days later plans were made to send her by Lysander but, whilst it stood on the runway waiting to take off, news came that the reception committee that was preparing to meet her had been rounded up by the Gestapo.

The third plan that was made involved her going to Gibraltar by seaplane and then on to the south of France in a fishing boat. This time she got as far as Plymouth, where she waited for several hours until she was told that the weather was too bad to take off and was unlikely to improve for several days. Once more she went back to London and from there to Cornwall where she climbed into a Whitley bomber that was airborne only for a matter of seconds before it hit the ground again with a violent jolt and came to rest on the edge of a cliff.

S.O.E. gave up the unequal struggle and, in the end, Odette sailed for Gibraltar in a troopship. The trip was uneventful. At Gibraltar she transferred to a small fishing vessel commanded by a young Polish officer who, to begin with, refused to sail on so dangerous a mission with an attractive young woman. Eventually he was persuaded and the little boat—it had been a sardine fisher before the war—set off with a small crew, Odette, and six other agents who were to be landed with her. The journey took eleven days and, throughout one of them, heavy seas made everyone desperately sick. But eventually the coast of France was sighted and Odette and her companions were landed in a small dinghy.

The main British controlled resistance group in the South of France had its headquarters at Cannes and the senior British agent who operated with the group was Captain Peter Churchill, an experienced and brave agent who was on his third mission to France and was a distant relative of the Prime Minister. He had been given the responsibility of looking after Odette whilst she was in the South of France and for arranging her move to Auxerre. They met shortly after the girl's arrival and their rendezvous was, of all places, a Cannes beauty salon.

Odette was impatient to start on her journey but Peter Churchill explained that arrangements were not complete and he gave her a job to keep her occupied. Some of the other agents who had landed with her had to go to Marseilles but spoke poor French. Odette was told to escort them.

She was delayed in Marseilles and had to spend the night there. She was directed to a house where she was told that she would be safe, and it turned out to be a brothel. Nevertheless, she was well looked after and, when the place was raided in the small hours by a German Army patrol looking for deserters, they were diverted from her room by the Madame telling the soldiers that her niece lay sick inside with small-pox.

Arrangements for Odette's move to Auxerre went wrong and there were further delays but there was also plenty of work for her in the south. Eventually it became necessary for Peter Churchill to return to England for discussions with Maurice Buckmaster and, after an exchange of signals with London, it was agreed that Odette should remain in Cannes for a time, to look after matters there in his absence.

Plans were made for Peter Churchill to be picked up by Lysander from a field near Perigueux and Odette went to see him off. As the plane was preparing to land, however, some German troops appeared on the scene and Odette and her companions were forced to scatter over the countryside. She was chased by a guard dog and only escaped from it by scrambling through a stream.

At Perigueux, news reached the two agents that somebody in Cannes had been talking and Peter Churchill's flat had been raided. Most of the members of his group were either in hiding or had fled from the area.

Instead of returning to Cannes they made their way to Annecy, in the Haute Savoie, and were met there by the group's wireless operator Captain Rabinovich, who had also escaped from Cannes.

A patriotic farmer provided Rabinovich with a loft where he could operate his wireless set and contact was re-established with London. It was also made with several other resistance groups in various parts of France and, for a while, Peter Churchill and Odette co-ordinated their activities. They also made contact with Frenchmen who were anxious to form a resistance group in the Haute Savoie and they organized the dropping of arms to them. Eventually, a fresh plan for Peter Churchill's return to England was made and Odette was left in charge of the organization that the two of them had set up.

Whilst Odette was at Annecy she had a visit from a certain Lieutenant Colonel Bleicher, of the German Counter Espionage Department, who explained that he had been directed to her by a resistance leader who was now in prison. He told her that there was a deep rift between Hitler and his followers and the German High Command. He represented the latter and wanted to make contact with the British Government. The moment had arrived, he said, when the High Command was ready to cut itself adrift from the Nazis and negotiate with the Allies. Odette could be their intermediary.

Odette asked for time to consider the proposition and the man went away. Then she signalled London for instructions and was told to have nothing more to do with Bleicher, to disband the group and prepare to vanish from the area. She was also told to select a dropping zone, for Peter Churchill had finished his business in England and was ready to jump back into France.

On 15th April 1943, Peter Churchill parachuted into Europe for the last time. He landed high in the Haute Savoie on a ridge between two peaks. Waiting on the ground to meet him were Odette and Rabinovich.

Peter Churchill scolded Odette for not having left the area already and insisted that they must now all leave at once. She refused and said that there was still work to be done and, as she had arranged to meet Bleicher next on the 18th April, they were safe for three days. On the following morning, the pair of them were arrested.

Over the next month Odette was held in a number of prisons in Italy and France and then, during the first week in May, she was moved to Fresnes Prison on the outskirts of Paris, the largest jail in Europe. For reasons that are not entirely clear, she and Peter Churchill pretended to be man and wife and though the Gestapo Headquarters had discovered enough about her to know that this was untrue, she was accepted as being Mrs. Peter Churchill by the authorities at Fresnes. She also stuck to the masquerade throughout her subsequent captivity in Germany and, in the end, it saved her life.

Bleicher visited Odette in Fresnes and offered her her freedom if she would talk, but she refused. Three days later he tried again and again he failed. She was not prepared to say anything in exchange for her freedom, nor in response to offers of extra food or books. A fortnight later she was taken to Avenue Foch and interrogated by a Gestapo officer but he did all the talking and Odette said nothing. Persuasion and bribes were clearly unavailing with this obstinate young woman but the Gestapo had other methods and they decided to use them.

Next day she was sent for once more and taken before the same Gestapo officer. As he sat, with a faint smile on his face, Odette's back was burned with a red hot iron and she gave a cry of pain but uttered no words. Then she was made to take off her shoes and stockings and she was told that, unless she would say where Rabinovich was hiding, her toe nails would be pulled out one by one.

'I have nothing to say,' she answered.

A man came forward with a large pair of pincers and, taking

hold of her left foot, pulled out the nail of her small toe. Despite the agony of this Odette retained sufficient sensibility to register horror when he spoke and she realized that he was a Frenchman.

The Gestapo officer fired another question and was given the same reply. Then another toe nail was removed. Half an hour later the gruesome operation had ended. Dazed, numb, bleeding and scarcely able to walk Odette was hustled back into a van and returned to her solitary cell at Fresnes. The Gestapo had learned nothing from her.

A few days later, still numb with pain and only able to hobble, she was taken before a German Court Martial. The proceedings, which were very short, were conducted entirely in German. Eventually, the President addressed himself to her in the same language and, when she said that she did not understand German, he said, in bad French:

'Madame Churchill, you are sentenced to death for being a British spy and a Frenchwoman.'

Though Odette had been condemned to death, nothing was done to put the sentence into effect and she languished in Fresnes for a year. During that time she had several more visits from Bleicher who went on trying, without effect, to persuade her to talk. Then, on 12th May 1944, she was taken with six other British women agents to Karlsruhe. Strange to say, she was the only one of the seven who had been sentenced to death and she was the only one who did not, in the end, die at the hand of the Gestapo.

After two months in Karlsruhe, Odette was moved to the dreaded concentration camp at Ravensbruck. There, for the next three and a half months, she was kept in solitary confinement in a cell that was in total darkness. She was given little food and she gradually became weak and very ill. Then, surprisingly, she was moved to a light, though bitterly cold, cell and given a better diet. She began to regain her health.

By the end of April 1944, the Russian armies were approaching Ravensbruck. Plans for the evacuation of the camp were considered and rejected. Then Himmler decided that every prisoner there must be killed and his orders were carried out, almost to the letter. But, for some reasons, seven women were not sent to the gas chamber and one of them was Odette. In her case it seems very probable that she was saved because the Commandant of the camp, Fritz Suhren, believed that she really was Mrs Peter Churchill.

On the morning of 28th April—it was Odette's thirty-third birthday—Suhren came to her cell and ordered her to follow him. He led her to a prison van and put her in the back. She was driven to the concentration camp at Neustadt where she spent three days. From there she was taken to another camp and the next morning, 3rd May, Suhren made her get into the front of his own car and he drove up to the American lines and surrendered to a sentry. It is significant that he told the startled man that he had a relative of Winston Churchill with him.

The story of the French resistance movement is an epic one. It is a story of great courage and terrible sacrifice. Nora Inayat-Khan, Violette Szabo and Odette Sansom were not the only ones whose efforts ended in unbelievable suffering in Hitler's concentration camps. They were but three of many. Thirteen women agents were killed by the Gestapo as well as many more men, including Captain Rabinovich. Hundreds, if not thousands, of French resistance workers suffered the same fate. But their suffering was not in vain. Throughout the time of the German occupation of France the resistance movement did incalculable hurt to the German military machine whilst, at the time of the Allied landings, it brought the movement of German reserves and supplies almost to a standstill.

CHAPTER V

BEHIND ENEMY LINES

Two further George Crosses were awarded to members of
S.O.E. and one of them went to another worker with the
French resistance movement. He was not a member of Colonel
Buckmaster's organization but belonged to the R.F. Section:
the section that worked in London and provided a liaison
between the Gaullist resistance groups and the British service
ministries.

He was of Welsh extraction and his name was Forest
Frederick Edward Yeo-Thomas, a Wing Commander in the
R.A.F.V.R. War-time heroes often had unexpected peace-time
occupations and Tommy Yeo-Thomas certainly had for he was
a director of the famous Paris fashion house of Molyneux. He
was nearly forty years old when the war broke out and had
already served, though under age, in the 1914-18 war, and
with the Polish forces in their Russian campaign of 1919-20.
Once he had been captured by the Bolsheviks and, under
sentence of death, escaped.

Tommy Yeo-Thomas came of a family that had lived in
France for almost a hundred years and, as a result, could pass
himself off anywhere as a Frenchman. He travelled to England
when war broke out and tried to become an air-gunner but he
was turned down on account of his age. Instead, he was given
a job as a corporal interpreter with a Forward Air Ammunition
Park of the Advanced Air Striking Force, the R.A.F. contin-
gent that accompanied the British Expeditionary Force to
France.

When France fell Yeo-Thomas, now a Sergeant, escaped to
England from Bordeaux. For a while he was employed as an
interpreter with the Free French Air Force and then he was
commissioned and became an Intelligence Officer with a Polish
fighter squadron. It was not until 1942 that he found his way

into S.O.E. and, in February of that year, he joined the R.F. Section as a junior Staff Officer.

He was well fitted for the job of an agent but he had joined the wrong 'firm' for that, for de Gaulle had sufficient Frenchmen for this type of work and was not prepared to consider using other nationals. So Yeo-Thomas had to spend his days pushing a pen and wading through voluminous reports on conditions in France, trying to extract a very little wheat from a great deal of chaff. Much of his time he devoted to thinking up ways of getting to France and, though one of his schemes almost worked out the way he meant it to, in the end it was not until well into 1943 that he eventually achieved his ambition.

Although the great mass of the French resistance groups were called 'Gaullist,' their only real allegiance to the Free French Forces lay in a readiness to co-operate over the dispatch of supplies and few of them were prepared to take orders from the exiled French leader or, for that matter, from anyone else. The only exception to this rule was that the Communist groups, and there were many of them, took orders from their political masters and there were some who held that a greater control of the French resistance came from Moscow than from London.

De Gaulle was not the man to accept such a situation and he decided to send two of his Staff Officers to France in an effort to set up a unified command. A secondary task was to investigate the activities of the British controlled resistance groups, for several members of the Free French Headquarters held the view that Buckmaster's agents were deliberately trying to divert Frenchmen from allegiance to de Gaulle. In the belief that the truth of this could be brought home to them, the R.F. Section was asked to provide a British Staff Officer to accompany the mission and Yeo-Thomas was selected and sent off to the R.A.F. Parachute School at Wilmslow, in Cheshire, to learn to jump.

Low clouds prevented Yeo-Thomas' party from spotting the dropping zone on their first flight to France but, two days later, they tried again and all went well. Tommy Yeo-Thomas spent two months in France and, at the end of that time, he was picked up and returned to London where he made a full report on the activities of the resistance movement. What he had to say about the activities of Buckmaster's agents has not been recorded but, although Yeo-Thomas has since expressed disapproval of some of their activities, nothing he said resulted in any curbing of their activities.

Five months later he went back to France, and spent over a year with the resistance men. Again he was accompanied by one of de Gaulle's Staff Officers and, this time, their main task was to investigate the efficiency, effectiveness and mobility of the resistance forces. But Yeo-Thomas was not inclined to confine his activities to mere investigating and reporting and he landed himself in all sorts of scrapes and came close to arrest on many occasions. Probably his most outstanding achievement was the occasion when he managed to purloin some plans of V1 emplacements from a flat that was being watched by the Gestapo.

On his return to London, Tommy brought back one main impression: that not nearly enough aircraft were being made available for the supply of arms to France. In an effort to put this right he succeeded in arranging an interview with Winston Churchill and, though the Premier was not in a receptive mood when he arrived and the interview started badly, the airman believed deeply in his case and, in the end, he won the day and Churchill ordered the immediate diversion of bombers from other tasks.

In February 1944, Yeo-Thomas went back to France for a third time and, a month later, whilst he was waiting in the street to meet one of his contacts, five plain clothes members of the Gestapo surrounded him. He was taken to their headquarters and beaten up so severely that he decided that the only safe way of making certain that he did not talk was to use his lethal pill. But this was hidden in a signet ring on his left hand and his hands were handcuffed behind his back. Before he could get at it the ring was taken from him by one of his captors.

For several days he was subjected to a succession of beatings and duckings in a bath of cold water and each time this happened he was only taken out when he was on the verge of drowning. Between times he was given gruelling cross-examinations, when he told his inquisitors everything under the sun except the things that they wanted to know. After a week or so of this treatment Yeo-Thomas was moved into Fresnes Prison and, after only a few days there, he was sentenced to three weeks solitary confinement, in an unlighted underground cell, for hurling verbal insults at Adolf Hitler. During this period he was given food only on every third day.

Whilst he was serving his sentence, Yeo-Thomas had the news, whispered down an air vent from a cell above, that the liberation armies had landed in Normandy.

In August 1945, Tommy Yeo-Thomas was put on a train for Germany and, as he was being marched along the corridor he noticed that one crowded compartment was full of women. By a strange coincidence, two of those women were Violette Szabo and Nora Inayat-Khan. He was shut in a carriage with other British and Allied officers and it was to that carriage, later on, that Violette Szabo and another girl crawled with a can of water when the German guards had deserted the train in a bombing raid.

Later in the journey Yeo-Thomas persuaded most of the occupants in the carriage to join him in a mass burst for freedom when a suitable opportunity occurred but, in the end, the plan had to be abandoned because a small number of faint-hearted threatened to reveal it to the guards.

The journey finished at Buchenwald and there Yeo-Thomas experienced the full horror of that dreadful concentration camp. But Tommy Yeo-Thomas was tough and it was not the hardships of the place that worried him so much as the knowledge that it was only a matter of time before he, like so many others, might finish his days on the camp incinerator. The only solution seemed to lie in escape and he set to work on the organization of a break out. Thirty-seven of his companions agreed to follow his lead but, for a variety of reasons, his plans came to nothing, and he and his supporters had to content themselves with retaining their morale and dignity by such achievements as shaving every morning, albeit they had only one razor amongst them.

When the liberation armies swept on towards the camp all the prisoners who remained alive were loaded into trains that headed for Czechoslovakia. Many were already on the brink of death and, on the second night of Yeo-Thomas' journey, one hundred and seventy of his fellow passengers died. The train had to make an unscheduled halt and the survivors were made to dig a great hole in the ground and then carry their deceased comrades to it.

The occasion gave Tommy the opportunity that he had long awaited and he hastily organized an escape party. They clung together and then, just after they had lowered a number of corpses into their communal grave, he and nineteen followers made a sudden dash for some nearby woods. Immediately the air was full of bullets but somehow, despite their weakened condition, Yeo-Thomas and several of the others evaded capture.

The airman became separated from his companions and for several days he roamed the countryside alone suffering from a severe attack of dysentry. Then, within a few hundred yards of an American post, he was recaptured by front line German troops. A day or so later he escaped again, in company with some French Air Force prisoners who were also being held by the Germans and, this time, he succeeded in leading his party into the American lines.

Wing Commander Yeo-Thomas was forty-four years old when he entered Buchenwald and, when he escaped, people who saw him said that he looked like a man of seventy. But he had retained the fighting spirit that had taken him into three wars and, in spite of everything that he had suffered, he had remained a leader to the end.

There was another man who worked with the underground in France and then had to suffer the torment of a German concentration camp. There he displayed the same qualities of leadership as did Wing Commander Yeo-Thomas and, for his courage, he was also decorated with the George Cross.

The man's name was Dr Albert Marie Guerisse, but the strange thing is that, in announcing his award, the London Gazette made no mention of his real name but referred to him

by his pseudo name: Lieutenant-Commander Patrick Albert
O'Leary, D S O. The 'Lieutenant-Commander,' however, was by
no means pseudo, for that was the rank that Dr Guerisse
achieved in the Royal Navy and, before winning the George
Cross, he had already been decorated with the Distinguished
Service Order. Afterwards, he was to add the Legion d'Honneur
and the French Croix de Guerre, the Belgian Croix de Guerre,
the American Medal of Freedom and a Korean decoration to
these two British awards.

At the outbreak of the Second World War, Albert Guerisse
was a doctor in the Belgian Army but, when his King capitulated, he made his escape to England and was accepted by the
Royal Navy in the assumed name of O'Leary. He was employed
on the dangerous task of landing agents in the south of France.

One night in April 1941, he was making his way back from
the French coast to the 'Q' ship, H.M.S. *Fidelity*, in a small
motor boat, when he had the misfortune to run into a cutter
belonging to the French Naval Gendarmerie. He tried to convince the Frenchmen that he was fishing but they would not
believe that story. Then he pretended that he was a compatriot
from the north trying to escape to join de Gaulle, but he mis-
judged the mood of official France and he was taken ashore
and marched off under escort.

As he was going along a street, O'Leary, as we will now call
him, made a sudden dart up a side alley but, shortly afterwards,
he was recaptured and put into the Naval prison at Toulon
where he was surprised to find that several of his fellow prisoners were serving five-year sentences for Gaullist activities. Four
days later he was moved to Fort Lamalgue, also in Toulon, and
from there to St Hippolyte du Fort where he made friends
with one of his jailors and, with his help, organized the escape
of a British officer. Next day, in company with another British
officer, he made a dash for the prison wall and helped his
comrade over it but failed to get away himself.

O'Leary was put into solitary confinement and kept there
for ten days. As soon as his punishment was over he made
contact with a number of British soldiers who were also in the
prison and started to organize a mass escape. They managed

to saw through some window bars with a small piece of a hacksaw blade and the venture succeeded. O'Leary made his way to freedom with the soldiers.

In Hippolyte, he had heard of an officer of the 51st Highland Division, named Ian Garrow, who had evaded capture when his Division was surrounded at St Valery and set up, in Marseilles, the beginnings of an organization for helping in the escape from France of British servicemen who were at large in the country. He made his way to Marseilles and succeeded in contacting Garrow, who told him that he was badly in need of someone who spoke good French to help him in his work and begged O'Leary to stay and join the organization. O'Leary, however, felt that his first duty was to try and get back to England but said he would stay in France if the Admiralty would agree to the plan.

Garrow had no wireless and communication with London was a slow process involving the passage of a written message to Gibraltar and a coded reply at the end of a B.B.C. French news broadcast, but O'Leary agreed to stay on whilst London was contacted in this way and, in the meantime, he escorted a young Sergeant Pilot of the R.A.F. to the Spanish frontier and handed him over to a mountain guide.

On his return to Marseilles, he was greeted with the news that Ian Garrow had been arrested by the Gestapo. There had still been no reply to the message to the Admiralty but he decided, there and then, that until he was given any contradictory orders he must assume charge of the organization.

An important member of it, operating in the north of France, was a certain Paul Cole, a non-commissioned officer who had been left in France when the British Expeditionary Force had gone from Dunkirk. Probably he had deliberately chosen to stay there, for he had a criminal record and was wanted by the British police. He had done some valuable work in organizing the movement of pilots from the Paris area to the south and this was no easy trip, for it involved crossing the demarkation line between the occupied and unoccupied zones.

Garrow had had complete confidence in Paul Cole but, for reasons that he did not find easy to explain, O'Leary quickly

4

began to have doubts about him and soon unearthed the fact that he was pocketing large sums of money that he was receiving as payments for a French agent. The man was, in fact, giving his services for nothing and Cole was spending the money on the upkeep of several mistresses and other forms of riotous living.

He confronted Cole in the presence of several other members of the organization and, in the end, the man confessed and cried for mercy. Some of O'Leary's companions were in favour of killing him, for they felt that a man who was not to be trusted was a danger to the organization so long as he lived, but O'Leary argued that he had only been proved dishonest in financial matters and there was, as yet, no evidence of treachery. They locked Cole in a bathroom while they continued to debate the matter but their arguments soon became pointless for they heard a noise from the bathroom and discovered that the man had jumped from a window to a building opposite and made his escape into the back streets of Marseilles.

Immediately after Cole's escape, the business of the organization took O'Leary to the north of France and he seized the opportunity of slipping across the frontier and paying a clandestine visit to his parents in Brussels. He stayed with them for a few hours and then slipped away again as unobtrusively as he had arrived.

A few weeks later he had news that no less than ten of his agents in the north had been arrested. They included two British officers and a French Abbé. He hurried to Paris to investigate the situation on the spot and was quickly given undisputable evidence of the fact that they had been betrayed by Cole.

He made an unsuccessful attempt to track down the traitor and then turned his attentions to the difficult task of replacing the men he had lost. He spent some time in Paris, interviewing potential agents and organizing fresh hideouts for escaping airmen and the work was urgent, for the efforts of Bomber Command were on the increase and so were the casualties to their machines. Often, whilst this process of re-organization was going on, he found it necessary to escort parties of pilots to the south himself.

He had scarcely completed the job of replacing the casualties in the ranks of the organization when there was a fresh disaster. Somehow, a German deserter had found his way into the escape channels. He was a genuine deserter and O'Leary decided that the only safe course was to get him to England. Unfortunately, he and his escort were arrested when they were trying to cross into the unoccupied zone and, under pressure, the German gave away vital information. As a result, six more agents were arrested and O'Leary had, once again, to make a fresh start on the weary work of reconstruction. But, despite all these setbacks, the organization went from strength to strength and the number of escapes that it handled increased every month.

In the middle of 1942 O'Leary was summoned to Gibraltar for discussions with representatives of M.I.9, the War Office department responsible for escape organizations. He went over the Pyrenees by the same route that many of the men he had helped to escape had taken and then he crossed the frontier to the British fortress in the boot of a car driven by the First Secretary of the British Embassy at Madrid.

In Gibraltar he made a full report on the activities of his organization and succeeded in persuading the War Office representatives to let him have a wireless operator. Then, a few days later, he made his way back into France again in a small boat, taking his new recruit with him. Unfortunately this man, also a Belgian, turned out to have insufficient nerve for the dangerous work and had only volunteered for the job in the hope of being re-united with his wife who was living in the south of France. In the end, O'Leary sent the pair of them back to England but, shortly afterwards, he found a French operator to take the place of the man who had let him down.

Paul Cole was not the only traitor to cross O'Leary's path. Early in 1942 a young Frenchman named Dulais made contact with the organization and offered to supply details of German counter-resistance operations in the north. His antecedents were carefully looked into and it was proved beyond doubt that he was, in fact, a German agent.

O'Leary arranged a meeting between himself, Dulais, and

two other members of the organization in a desolate spot on the Spanish frontier. There the Frenchman was accused of being a German spy and broke down and pleaded for mercy. But O'Leary was mindful of what had happened when he had last allowed himself to be influenced by pleas for mercy. He was not prepared to take a second risk of this sort and the young man was shot through the head and, after all means of identity had been removed, his body was thrown into a mountain ravine.

By the end of 1942 the operations of the organization were becoming more daring. Not only were they helping crashed airmen and prisoners who had managed to find their own way out of prison camps but they started to organize the actual escapes. The services of prison guards and visiting priests were recruited and several parties of British prisoners of war were helped out of detention in this way. Many of them had to be smuggled out of the south of France by sea, for sometimes their numbers were too great to use the route over the Pyrenees.

Twice parties of thirty or more were taken off in trawler operations but, on the second occasion, something went wrong and thirty-two men were cooped up in a small seaside villa for several days in grave discomfort. They had to take it in turns to sleep on the floor.

Money for the organization was supplied by wealthy Frenchmen against credit in London but, in time, this source began to dry up and things became difficult. O'Leary decided to cross the frontier into Switzerland and try to enlist the aid of the British Consul in Geneva and he succeeded in doing this, although his journey involved a climb through a barbed wire entanglement and he finally entered Switzerland with bullets flying around his ears.

The Consul agreed to send a million francs to Lyon by the hand of a trusted agent but, unhappily, the agent was not as trustworthy as he believed and every franc went astray.

Soon after this, news came that Ian Garrow, incarcerated in the French fortress prison at Meauzac, was to be moved to Germany and O'Leary decided that his escape must be arranged. He bribed a prison guard to smuggle a French gendarme's uniform to the Scot who succeeded in walking out at a time when the sentries were changing. O'Leary met him outside the prison and drove him off in a car. Three weeks later he escorted him to the Spanish frontier and the former head of the organization made his way to safety over the Pyrenees.

A week or two later O'Leary organized the escape of eight prisoners from another prison. They included one of his agents who had been captured earlier in the year, and again he enlisted the aid of one of the jailors. He doped a number of his comrades with sleeping powders and lead the escapees to a point where a large furniture van waited to take them to safety. The party eventually left France by the overland route, through Spain to Gibraltar.

Things were going well for the organization but, when things went well, O'Leary always suffered from an inner feeling that they were too good to last and now his forebodings were justified. In March 1943, news reached him of the arrest of more of his agents in the north and then, a few days later, when he went to a small café to meet one of his assistants, he suddenly felt cold steel in the nape of his neck and found himself surrounded by half a dozen men whose French-style civilian clothes did little to disguise their Teutonic bearing. The Gestapo had cornered him at last.

From this point forward Pat O'Leary's story has much in common with others that have already been told. The Gestapo's only interest in him was the desire to make him disclose the details of his organization and the identity and whereabouts of its members. To achieve these ends they were ready to stop at nothing and, for a start, he was beaten up until he became unconscious and then thrown into an unlit cell with some of his agents who had been captured with him and had suffered similar treatment.

When he had more or less recovered he was taken before his tormentors for a second time and, for a while, he staved off further punishment by giving false information. He used the ingenious but simple ruse of describing people with the opposite of the truth, calling a fat man thin and a blond one dark. His deception worked for a time but, in the end, the Gestapo discovered that he had been deceiving them and he was again beaten into unconsciousness, this time with an iron bar.

Next O'Leary was put naked into a refrigerator and tied to a chair. After a few hours he was removed and an electric fire was played on his frozen body. Then he was subjected to a long period of questioning but remained silent.

For some months he was moved from one prison to another and his treatment varied between further beatings and tortures, and periods of generous treatment. At times he was well fed and at others he suffered near starvation. He was interrogated almost daily. Eventually he was taken to the notorious prison at Fresnes, near Paris.

There he was held in solitary confinement for five months and then, one day, without any warning, he was bundled into an overcrowded prison van and then into an equally over-crowded train, eastbound for Germany. The journey ended at Saarbrucken and O'Leary suffered three weeks in a camp there, cruelly treated and half starved. There followed a spell in a grossly overcrowded camp at Mauthausen where he was for-tunate to contract no worse infection than scabies. Many of the inmates died of other diseases including typhoid.

From Mauthausen, O'Leary was moved to Natzwieler and then to the terrible camp at Dachau, built to house ten thousand prisoners and now overflowing with three and a half times that number. Every day scores of them went to the gas chamber but, for many, the trip was unnecessary for the release of death came through disease or starvation. The conditions in Dachau broke many of the stoutest hearts but they never broke O'Leary's. He rose above them and the courage and leadership that he displayed in the face of the horrors of that concentration camp, above all else, qualified him for the George Cross that he was awarded.

Typhus broke out and he helped to treat the victims. Symp-toms of the dread disease appeared on him and he had to lie in his bunk with a high fever for two days and then, miracu-lously, he recovered. But others died like flies and O'Leary decided that the time had come for the prisoners to set up some sort of an organization with the aim of giving themselves such protection as they were able. Under the eyes of the S.S. he organized the International Prisoners' Committee, I.P.C. for short.

Within a week every block in the camp was represented on the committee and it set to work with such activities as putting dead and dying men in the bunks of others who were due to go to the gas chamber and falsifying prison records. All the members of the committee carried arms, normally only the legs of stools but, somehow, four pistols were stolen from the S.S. guards.

When plans to kill all the prisoners and burn their bodies in great pits were made, and leaked out, the men of the I.P.C. cornered the Commandant's deputy and threatened him with death, or worse, if they were not stopped. Then, in April 1945, when news came that the Americans were on the way, it was the I.P.C. that took command of the situation in Dachau and ordered all the prisoners to remain in their huts. And when, a few days later, an American tank arrived at the camp, it was O'Leary and the members of his I.P.C. who provided the reception committee that greeted its crew.

One would have thought that Dr Albert Guerisse had seen enough of war but, remarkably, through some feat of wire-pulling, he succeeded in getting himself seconded from the Belgian Army and turned up as a Medical Officer with a British Infantry Brigade in Korea. There he was decorated for saving the life of a soldier under fire. This remarkable Belgian doctor is a worthy holder of one of Britain's premier awards for gallantry.

The resistance movement was not, of course, confined to France. It was particularly strong in some of the Balkan countries and S.O.E. Headquarters spared no effort to succour and encourage the bands of partisans that formed themselves together in this wild and inaccessible part of Europe, with the common aim of throwing out their erstwhile masters. Whenever it was known that a guerilla formation of any size had established itself, efforts were made to send a British Military Mission to join it with the object of training the partisans, directing their activities towards the common end, organizing the supply of such arms and other equipment as could be made available.

The delivery of military supplies to the resistance groups in the Balkans was no easy task for it involved long flights by unarmed transport aircraft and flying conditions were far from easy in the mountainous country in which many of these bands operated. Thus, the equipment was frequently slow to arrive and inadequate and, as a result, the members of the Missions often had to withstand harsh criticism from disappointed Balkan warriors. But they were quick to forgive and, at heart, they were full of admiration for these men—many of them little more than boys—who came to share the dangers and hardships of their rough way of life. Behind a façade that often seemed bitter, a deep bond of fellowship existed between the members of the Missions and the tough fighters with whom they lived.

One of the wildest and most inhospitable territories in which the resistance movement took shape was Albania and several British Missions were introduced into that rugged country to join different groups there, groups that were made up of wild tribesmen who had experienced less of the impact of civilization than the people of any other part of Europe. Their way of life was probably closer to that of the Arab than anything else and they had the Arab's resentment of being ruled by foreigners.

By the middle of 1943 large areas of Albania were controlled by the partisans and German communications through the country had been severely curtailed. But the Germans were not prepared to remain inactive in such a situation and they moved several fresh formations into the country with the aim of restoring the situation. Their plan was to seek out and destroy the principal resistance groups, and particular targets were the British Missions that they knew to be operating with them.

They were given information that one of the Missions was established in the mountains east of Tirane and, in December, they launched a drive against the area with several strong columns converging from different directions. The weather was bitter, with several feet of snow covering the precipitous mountain tracks and blizzards blowing almost daily. Despite these conditions, the Germans achieved the greater part of their aim and, aided by collaborators, they dispersed the partisans and brought resistance in the area to a standstill.

They reached the small hamlet where the British Mission had been established but, before they arrived, the staff had broken up into small parties, each trying to slip through the German cordon before it closed. Unhappily, the party with the wireless sets and most of the equipment was ambushed with all its mules, but the others escaped, though communication with the outside world had ended.

The Commander of the Mission managed to get clear of the area and he was accompanied by three other British officers, two British N.C.O.s and several Albanian and Italian partisans. One of these officers, the principal Staff Officer, was Brigadier Arthur Frederick Crane Nicholls of the Coldstream Guards, a young man in his thirties who had been in the Supplementary Reserve before the war and, after serving as an Intelligence Officer with the 1st Division in the Dunkirk campaign, had been sent to the Staff College and, thereafter, been transferred to S.O.E. He had achieved rapid promotion in this field of work.

Although the little party had succeeded in avoiding the main German thrusts, it had failed to break out of the German cordon and spent several days playing hide and seek with their enemy amongst the rugged and unfriendly mountains. A day or so before Christmas it looked as though a group of the attackers was making straight towards its camp and it was decided to make a hurried move up the course of a mountain stream. Soaked boots was added to the list of miseries that everyone had to suffer and several of the party developed bad frostbite of the feet. Brigadier Nicholls, particularly, had to bear a great deal of pain from his condition but he refused to remove his boots for fear that he would never be able to get them on again.

Eventually, after almost a fortnight of wandering through the mountains, the party reached what they believed to be comparative safety in a sheepfold above Kostenjge. Here they settled down to try to recover their strength but, unhappily, they had miscalculated the situation and next day they were fired on by a small detachment of pro-German Albanians that had established itself on higher ground during the night.

The only possible escape route was up a bare snow-covered hillside that was under long-range fire from the Albanians' rifles and the tired men had the alternative of following the route or inevitable capture. They chose the former.

Several members of the party, including the Commander of the Mission, were hit during the climb and either killed or wounded so that, when the survivors reached comparative safety at the top of the hill, it had been reduced to Nicholls, one other officer and three Albanian partisans.

Nicholls decided that, at all costs, they must escape and make contact with the nearest British Mission so that he could give a full report of events. Some of the rest of the party were in favour of stopping and setting up a fresh camp where they could rest but Nicholls virtually drove them on for sixteen hours until he was certain that pursuit had been shaken off. Then they halted in another sheepfold.

Nicholls sank to the ground exhausted and when, some time later, he tried to rise again he found that he could not stand. Both of his feet were badly poisoned and gangrene had set in. The one other officer who remained with the party was also in trouble with his feet but only one was badly frost-bitten and he could still walk after a fashion.

Nicholls was still determined to make contact with the nearest British Mission and he believed that there were two of them located at some distance to the south. He ordered the other officer to set off to try and contact one of them and to take with him the only one of the three Albanians who spoke English. It was going to be a difficult journey involving a crossing of the deep and fast flowing Skhumbini River but his companion obeyed the order without hesitation.

The Brigadier decided that he himself must try to reach another Mission that he believed to be to the north. He wrapped his poisoned feet in goat skins and then made the two remaining Albanians tow him along the ground on his duffle coat. This method of progress was slow and uncomfortable and, all the time, he was in great pain. To add to his discomfort, at one point, he fell over a bank and dislocated a shoulder.

After some days of journeying in this manner, the little party came across a friendly Albanian who knew where the Mission that they were seeking was and agreed to deliver a message there. Nicholls scribbled it on a piece of paper saying, merely, that he was in trouble with his feet and asking if someone could be sent out to meet him.

The message was delivered safely but, unfortunately, just as the Germans were launching an attack that drove the members of the Mission away from the direction in which Nicholls was coming. As a result, it was several days before an officer was able to go out and meet him.

By now, Brigadier Nicholls was in a very poor condition for, apart from his injuries, he was on the point of collapse from starvation. In three weeks he had eaten nothing but a handful of maize meal, a little sour cheese and some goat's milk.

A litter was improvised and, for five more days, he journeyed in this until he reached a point where a car could collect him. Despite his condition he remained cheerful and talked of little else but reorganizing the resistance forces and resuming the offensive against the Germans. When he eventually reached his destination he insisted on making a full report on the situation in the territory where he had been operating before he would discuss the matter of his own future. Then he was taken to the house of an Albanian patriot who lived outside Tirane and there a doctor amputated his feet.

Everything possible was done for him but Brigadier Nicholls was in no condition to withstand so severe an operation. For some days it was hoped that he would recover but there was little strength left in his tired body. On 11th February 1944, a very brave man died peacefully in bed. He had suffered great hardship with almost unbelievable fortitude. He had gone on doing his duty and, in the end, he had given his life for his country.

The officer who went out to meet this gallant man and brought him in from the mountains was so impressed by his indomitable spirit and determination in the face of great suffering that, as soon as he was able, he wrote a full account of the

events and recommended that Brigadier Nicholls' gallantry
should be appropriately recognized. As a result, he received
the posthumous award of the George Cross.

One of the last areas of Europe in which a resistance movement developed was Italy. The Italians were never whole-
heartedly behind their ambitious leader and this was one of
the reasons for the lack of spirit that was displayed by their
field army on several occasions. As the war wore on and defeat
followed defeat Italian enthusiasm was reduced virtually to nil.
In July 1943, the dictator was ousted and replaced by Marshal
Badoglio and, a few weeks later, Italy signed an armistice with
the Allies.

There were many who favoured a change of sides and were
ready to fight against the Germans and, after the fall of Naples,
Badoglio, contrary to the King's wishes, declared war on them.
Italian formations on the south of Italy joined the Allies as
co-belligerents but, in the north, the situation was confused.
The Germans were pouring thousands of extra troops into the
country and Mussolini, who had been rescued from Italian
captivity in a daring airborne raid carried out by S.S. troops,
had set up a Fascist Republic at Salo. Faced by German
oppression and conflict of loyalties, and out of touch with responsible government, the army disintegrated and many of its
members made their way to their homes. Over half a million,
however, were interned in Germany and put to forced labour.

Despite this situation it was the army that was first into the
field of resistance. In Rome, Colonel Giuseppe, one time Chief
of the Operations Bureau of the High Command, formed an
underground force whose aim was to save the capital if the
Germans tried to destroy it. Into his organization he enlisted
large numbers of Carabinieri and no less than a thousand of
them lived in the cellars of the Palace of Justice, under the very
noses of the Germans. Further to the north, as well, the army
provided the backbone of a movement which had soon recruited close on 30,000 members. Again, the Carabinieri played
an important part in the organization as, also, did the Communist Party.

Outside the cities the resistance movement consisted, in the main, of small groups, established in remote valleys and mountain strongholds where they were fed and supported by the local civil populations. Whenever opportunity offered they would come out of their lairs to ambush small German columns and disrupt their communications. Initially, each of these groups operated independently but, in time, a centralized command was set up and a marked degree of co-ordination was achieved.

One of the effects of the withdrawal of Italy from the Axis was, for a while, hiatus in the security arrangements in some of the camps where British prisoners of war were held, and many of them were able to escape. Some made their way out of Italy by sea but many more found refuge in the hide-outs of resistance groups and, before long, there were few of them that did not have British officers and men amongst their numbers and, in more than one case, they assumed command. Another source of recruits came from the crews of Allied aircraft that had crashed or made forced landings behind the German lines.

One such airman was Sergeant Arthur Banks of the R.A.F.V.R. who, on the 29th August 1944, was one of the crew of an aircraft that was on an armed reconnaissance sortie in the Ravenna-Ferrara area when it came under heavy fire and was so badly damaged that it had to make a forced landing. Banks got away from the machine and tried to find his way back through the enemy lines to his base. He made several attempts but ran into parties of Germans each time and, in the end, he finished up with one of the Italian resistance groups.

The partisans were brave men with a strong hatred of the Germans but they were badly handicapped by a shortage of weapons, ammunition and even serviceable clothing. Early in December Banks offered to lead an attempt to reach the Allied lines by sea. His aim was to try to organize an air drop of supplies to the rest of the group.

Under cover of darkness he led his party to a point where a small boat had been hidden but, just as he and his followers were preparing to board it, they were surrounded and captured. In the confusion, Banks somehow managed to seize a light machine gun and was on the point of opening fire on their captors when one of the partisans took fright and rushed at him from behind and pinned his arms.

The Sergeant was beaten up, tortured, and then questioned about the activities of the resistance men, but without avail. Then he was thrown into a prison at Adria that was staffed by members of the notorious Fascist Black Brigade. Shortly after that he was moved to another prison at Ariano Polesini, where the Fascists stripped and tortured him in a fresh effort to make him talk.

All their attempts failed and, in the end, he was bound and thrown into the River Po. Somehow Banks managed to reach the far side of the river where he was recaptured and taken back to prison. There he was shot through the head.

Throughout all his suffering the Sergeant refused to tell his captors anything more than his name and number. His courage and fortitude were so remarkable that they made an indelible impression even on the Fascists who had tortured him and the account that some of them gave of his behaviour, when hostilities ended, resulted in the posthumous award of the George Cross.

A Lance-Corporal of the New Zealand Army was similarly decorated for his activities in Italy. He was David Russell who was born in Scotland in 1911 and died at the hands of a Fascist firing squad at Ponte de Piave on 28th February 1945.

After surviving the 8th Army campaign in the Middle East, he was eventually taken prisoner in Italy but escaped again soon afterwards. For two and a half years he was at large in Italy, living with an Italian peasant and in contact with other escaped prisoners and partisans. In February 1945, he was recaptured by members of a mixed German-Italian Fascist police regiment.

His captors were convinced that Russell was in a position to give away information that would help them and he was beaten up, chained to a stable wall for three days, and then beaten again. He refused to give away anything and was shot. According to a German Warrant Officer who was present at the time, he died in the bravest possible way.

++

CHAPTER VI

THE ISLAND OF FIRE

DURING the Second World War the George Cross went to all manner of people: young and old, men and women, servicemen and civilians. On 15th April 1942, however, a most unusual award of the decoration was announced. King George VI had decided to confer it on the island of Malta in recognition of the bravery of its people during the second siege of the fortress; a siege that began with the entry of Italy into the war, in the summer of 1940, and was not lifted until the end of 1942, when Allied victories in North Africa made it possible for the Royal Navy to run convoys through the Mediterranean, in comparative safety, for the first time for two and a half years.

Awards for gallantry have, several times, been conferred upon whole regiments and battalions—the French and the Americans are particularly given to this—but never before had one been given to a whole nation. The nearest parallel was the award of the Distinguished Service Cross to the city of Dunkirk during the First World War.

The proximity of Malta to the mainland of Italy, and occasional demands for the adoption of the Italian language, have probably given an impression that the people of Malta are of Italian stock. In fact, Mussolini, although his subsequent actions were hardly maternal, more than once referred to Italy as the mother of Malta. This is not so, however, for the island was originally colonized by Phoenicians from the Eastern Mediterranean, the ancestors of the Cornishman and the race that founded Carthage and came near to overthrowing the Roman Empire. The Maltese language is a Semitic tongue, quite unlike Italian, and closely related to Arabic and Hebrew.

In her time, Malta has come under the rule of Carthage, Rome, Normandy and the Holy Roman Empire. In 1530, Charles V of Spain granted it to the Knights of the Order of

St John of Jerusalem, often called the Knights of Malta. This Order was originally founded as a society of hospitallers, dedicated to the care of sick and wounded pilgrims. At a later date it was expanded to include a noble order of Knights, sworn to defend Christendom against the infidel in all parts of the world.

The Order was homeless and in low straits when it was offered a refuge in Malta. The Turks had driven it from the Holy Land and, more recently, from Rhodes. But, in its new home, it quickly regained its old vigour and most of the colour and richness of Malta's history, tradition and architecture had its origins in the three-hundred-year era of the rule of the Grand Masters of the Order of St John.

The first siege of Malta took place during this period and from May 1565, until the following September, the island was invested by a Turkish fleet of over two hundred ships carrying an army of forty thousand men. The defending army, less than a quarter of the strength of the enemy, was commanded by the Grand Master La Valette and fought back with great bravery. The Turks made many landings but never conquered the island and, in the end, they were thrown back into the sea. Victory was complete but, as in the second siege, it was only won at the price of great hardship and privation.

At the end of the eighteenth century the Knights of Malta, deprived of the large part of their revenues that came from France, capitulated to Napoleon but, within three months he was defeated by Nelson at Abukir Bay, and the Maltese placed themselves under the protection of the British fleet. In 1801 they sent a petition to London asking to become free subjects of the King.

The island fortress was invaluable to British naval control of the Mediterranean. It had a fine natural anchorage and gave the British Fleet a base from which it could dominate the vital narrow sea corridor that split the Mediterranean in two. Its fortifications were improved and a great dockyard was developed and this gave work to many thousands of Maltese people. Thousands more were given employment in other shore establishments or were enlisted into the Royal Navy and the Royal Malta Artillery.

For almost a century and a half the security of the island was unchallenged and an ideal partnership existed, for Malta has never been self sufficient and British financial support was as vital to Malta as was control of the fortress to Britain. But, between the wars, came new developments and views on the impregnability, or even the value, of Malta had to be revised. With Italy fast becoming one of the world's great air powers, it soon became clear that the island could no longer be regarded as a safe base for the Mediterranean Fleet.

When, in June 1940, France was knocked out of the war, and Italy entered it, Malta's situation was gravely changed overnight. It seemed doubtful whether it was either practical, or important, to continue to hold it. In a minute to the First Lord of the Admiralty, the First Sea Lord said:

'I am not at all sure that the risk of passing ships through the Mediterranean is not too great.'

But, by now, Mr Winston Churchill had become Prime Minister and Minister of Defence and this far-seeing statesman quickly appreciated the fact that the little island of Malta could play a vital role in the battles that were about to break in the North African desert. There, the scales were heavily loaded against the British Army which had to be maintained by means of the long sea haul around the Cape. The Axis forces, on the other hand, could be supplied through the port of Tripoli, which involved a sea trip of only two or three days from Italy. If the Axis was given the uninterrupted use of this route, Britain's position in North Africa would soon become untenable. In the view of the British Prime Minister, the key to the situation lay in Malta. Admittedly a whole fleet could no longer be based there but submarines and aircraft, light torpedo craft and possibly even destroyers could, and from there, they would wreak havoc in the enemy's shipping lanes. He minuted the First Sea Lord in characteristic terms:

'Anyone can see the risk from air attack which we run in the Central Mediterranean. From time to time and for sufficient objects this risk will have to be faced. Warships are meant to go under fire.'

Churchill went on:

'It becomes of high and immediate importance to build up a very strong anti-aircraft defence at Malta, and to base several squadrons of our best fighter aircraft there. This will have to be done under the fire of the enemy.'

The suggestion that Malta should be abandoned was never made again. Instead, as and when circumstance allowed, the garrison was reinforced with infantry and anti-aircraft artillery and squadrons of fighters and other aircraft were moved to the island. It became a base from which the Axis supply routes to North Africa were harried until the German and Italian forces met final and complete defeat in Tunisia and the road to victory in Italy was opened up. Credit for the desert victory has only gone to men of the Eighth Army, and to the sailors and airmen who fought beside them, but it should never be forgotten that, without the courage and fortitude of the peasant farmers, the dock-workers, the shop-keepers, the priests and, above all, the women of Malta, that victory might never have been won. They suffered constant bombardment, hardship and privation of greater severity than many of the people of our own islands knew and they never weakened. They put their faith in God and the Royal Navy and they went quietly and bravely about their work.

Italy entered the war at midnight on 10th June 1940, and the first sirens wailed in Malta at half past six on the following morning. Shortly afterwards a formation of Italian bombers and fighters, taking no chances, crossed the island at fifteen thousand feet and dropped their bombs. There were seven further raids that day and in the last, and heaviest, twenty-five bombers took part.

The island's anti-aircraft batteries were active all day and Malta's only three fighters took the air: three rather elderly two-seater Gladiators that were familiarly known as Faith, Hope and Charity. And the intrepid young R.A.F. pilots who took them up to face Mussolini's Regia Aeronautica had not even been trained as fighter pilots but had been sent overseas to fly Sunderland flying boats.

At the end of a gruelling day, Faith, Hope and Charity were lodged safely in their hangars but three of the enemy bombers had been brought down and the people of Malta took stock of the damage that had been inflicted on their little island. It was widespread but not heavy. A few small bombs had landed in the dockyard and a newly built, but as yet unoccupied, hospital had been badly hit; so had an hotel and a cemetery. Twenty-three civilians and seven soldiers had been killed.

What was most heartening was that there was no serious panic amongst the civil population. The people had moved quietly into the catacombs and tunnels that have existed in Malta for generations and into the newly built shelters that had been dug into the soft limestone of the island. Next morning the men stayed at home, unwilling to be parted from their families, and most of the shops and offices remained closed. The streets of the towns were empty and there were no buses on the roads. Then, whole families from the towns, particularly from the crowded area around the Grand Harbour, moved out into the surrounding countryside and were taken into the already overcrowded houses of cousins, brothers and uncles.

Only one enemy plane appeared over Malta on 12th June and that was shot down. Next day, however, there were eight more raids and, by the end of the week, the sirens had sounded thirty times.

But, despite it all, the men drifted back to work and the ordinary routine of the island was resumed. Shops re-opened. The fishing boats put out to sea and the dockyard was soon working at full pressure again.

The Maltese tend to be of a somewhat mercurial temperament and the calm with which they accepted their new and terrifying experience is not easy to understand, but several explanations of this have been offered and there is probably some truth in them all. For a start, they are intensely religious and undoubtedly drew strength from their faith. Other factors were the existence of so many underground shelters of one sort or another and the deep contempt in which the Maltese had always held the Italian race. Finally, there was the character and example of the Governor and Commander-in-Chief.

Lieutenant-General Sir William George Sheddon Dobbie KCB, CMG, DSO, has been described by the adjective 'Cromwellian' by a score of writers, from Churchill downwards. The term is completely apt and there is none other that could sum up the man so completely. He was a simple, unaffected, unspectacular, sincere Scot; inflexible, narrow and, in some ways, perhaps even naïve, but imbued with a deep sense of purpose. He stood solidly by his convictions and his honesty was forthright. He put on no airs but, when he entered a room in the Governor's Palace, his wife and daughter were expected to rise—not to William Dobbie but to the Governor and Commander-in-Chief. Above all, he was devoutly religious, a member of the Plymouth Brethren.

Dobbie was held in high esteem, even reverence, by the whole population of Malta (the Roman Catholic Archbishop once said of Dobbie that he was the only man he had ever met who had the mystic radiance of true saintliness), and his lead was followed and his orders obeyed. He was able to bolster morale by going to the microphone and, in simple terms, praising the people for their courage and assuring them that delivery would come in God's good time. He told them that more shelters must be built and they set to work with a will and bored out a dozen miles of tunnel so that, before the end of the year, every man, woman and child was able to go below ground when the sirens sounded and the red warning flags were hoisted.

Dobbie's greatest fear was the fear of invasion. He felt that there was every chance that Italy would try to remove the Maltese threat to her supply route to North Africa by means of a sea-borne attack. As a soldier he realized, only too well, that the forces that he had at his disposal were utterly inadequate to repel a determined invasion. These forces consisted of a few coast defence batteries, four battalions of British infantry, all well below strength, and one newly formed and half trained Maltese battalion. Each battalion was deployed on a frontage of fifteen miles and there were no reserves.

The Governor appealed to London for reinforcements and Churchill pressed the War Office to find them. But Britain herself was facing the threat of invasion and there were urgent calls for help from the Middle East. Added to this there was the problem of moving troopships through waters where the Royal Navy had lost command of the sea. So reinforcements were not, for the moment, forthcoming and Dobbie introduced conscription.

It would be idle to pretend that this step was popular. There were, in fact, strong protests but the Governor stood firm and the measure was accepted, obediently if not cheerfully, and by this means, additional regiments of anti-aircraft artillery and battalions of infantry were produced.

The main burden of raising a citizen army fell on the shoulders of the British officers and N.C.O.s of the garrison and they discovered that their young recruits were cheerful, quick witted and keen to learn. There were also difficulties, however, for they found that the Maltese did not take kindly to spit and polish and other outward symbols of military discipline. More serious still, it proved very hard to find junior leaders from the rank and file of a race that was essentially democratic in out-look and, since the dawn of history, had become accustomed to serving foreign masters.

Nevertheless these difficulties were overcome and fresh regiments of artillery that were soon to prove themselves in battle were produced and there is little doubt that the newly raised battalions of the King's Own Regiment of Malta would have fought with equal distinction if the call had ever come. The tasks that came their way were the unglamorous ones of repairing runways, helping to service aircraft and unloading ships. All too frequently they were performed under the fire of the enemy.

Whilst fresh military units were being formed, a few fighter reinforcements began to arrive from England. They were Hurricanes, far faster than the Gladiators, and, a month after Italy entered the war, one of them shot down its first bomber. A few days later one of the original Gladiators was shot down and its pilot, Flying Officer Keeble, lost his life. Everyone in Malta experienced a feeling of personal loss.

The presence of Hurricanes in the skies over Malta made the Italian raiders more wary and, for the next few months, the bombing was not severe and there were reports of complete bomb-loads being jettisoned into the sea. But, if aerial assault was diminished, radio propaganda was stepped up and the islanders were subjected to a barrage of scorn and threats. This miscarried completely but provided a certain measure of comic relief, particularly the news that the shore establishment, H.M.S. *St Angelo*, had been sunk, and attempts to convince the inhabitants of an island devoid of mineral resources that their coal mines had been destroyed.

Later in the year British forces based on Malta were able to play a part in the mounting of the most devastating single blow that was struck against Italy in the whole course of the war.

One of the sharpest thorns in the side of British Mediterranean strategy was the existence of the powerful Italian Fleet. Whilst it was able to put to sea it represented a severe menace to the security of our communications even though, in practice, it seemed to prefer to skulk behind the impenetrable defences of Taranto. Admiral Cunningham decided therefore, that, as it seemed to be impossible to engage it on the water, it must be attacked from the air.

But first he wanted aerial photographs and these were provided by Royal Air Force machines based on Malta. Day after day they flew over the Italian naval base, singly or in pairs, until a complete picture of the place had been built up. Then, on 11th November, the aircraft carrier *Illustrious* was moved into range and the blow was struck.

All the carrier's planes went in and all but one returned. An oil storage depot and the Taranto seaplane base were set on fire and half the Italian fleet was crippled and put out of action for over six months. Next morning reconnaissance planes from Malta again flew over the toe of Italy and photographed the devastation.

The successful British raid on Taranto came at a moment when we stood alone and fortune was at a low ebb: throughout the Empire it gave fresh heart and a fresh will to fight but nowhere was the news received with greater joy than in the island of Malta. The morale of the people went straight up and it was kept up by the continuing successes of the Hurricane pilots who, by the end of the year, had almost driven the Regia Aeronautica from the skies.

Italian losses mounted steadily until, one day, early in January 1941, the Royal Air Force achieved its greatest success and shot down nineteen Italian bombers and fighters between dawn and dusk.

But later in January there was grave news. Hitler had become impatient with the failures of his Axis partner and decided to move the Luftwaffe to Sicily. Two hundred and fifty operational German aircraft had arrived by the end of the month and as the people of Malta were soon to discover, when the Junkers dived from the clouds, they were piloted by men of far greater skill and determination than the Italians.

On January 10th the carrier *Illustrious* was at sea with the British Fleet, some hundred miles west of Malta, ferrying Fulmars and Swordfish to the island when, from the north, a formation of some fifty dive-bombers with swastika markings on their wings appeared in the sky. Then they screamed down towards the fleet. Two torpedoes narrowly missed the great carrier but she survived the first wave of attack unscathed and the German bombers were chased back to Sicily by naval fighters.

But further waves of dive bombers came in and, this time, they concentrated their attacks on *Illustrious*. Over the course of three hours she suffered six separate attacks and, at the end of it all, the great vessel was still afloat but her bows were split, her steering gear crippled and fires were burning in several parts of her hull.

That evening, under cover of darkness, Admiralty tugs from Malta slipped out of port and towed *Illustrious* into the Grand Harbour.

For some remarkable reason the Luftwaffe gave the ship a breathing space of five days and, during those days, an army of workmen strove furiously to repair the stricken vessel. Then, on the sixth day, a hundred dive bombers tore down on the Grand Harbour to deliver the *coup de grace* and were met by the full force of the island's anti-aircraft barrage.

No attack was made on the following day but wave after

wave of bombers came in on the next two days, though it was noticeable, as time went on, that the Junkers pilots grew less inclined to dive so low as at the start of the attacks. Then the raids were called off and, for almost a week, the sirens remained mute, the red warning flags were not seen and the islanders were able to take stock of the situation.

Only a few small bombs had hit *Illustrious* and she had been little damaged, but the dockyard had suffered severely and was not put back into proper working order again for over two years. An ammunition ship, carrying four thousand tons of explosive cargo, had received a direct hit in the engine room without exploding. The damage to public buildings and private property was grievous. Large areas of Valletta were flattened. The beautiful Church of Our Lady of the Victories, built at Senglea by La Vallette, to commemorate his victory over the Turks, was a heap of crumbled stone and twisted metal. The runways on the island's three main airfields were badly cratered.

The Maltese, however, were not the only people with wounds to lick, for the Royal Air Force and the anti-aircraft batteries of the Royal Artillery and the Royal Malta Artillery had fought back like tigers. Estimates of the Luftwaffe's casualties vary but there is reason for believing that during the ten days that followed the first attack on *Illustrious*, something like half the German aircraft based on Sicily were put out of action.

The story of the German attempt to sink the carrier had a happy ending. The feverish activity of a thousand workmen had borne fruit and the great ship was patched up sufficiently to let her sail for Alexandria and, as darkness fell on the evening of 23rd January, she slipped her moorings and moved quietly out of the Grand Harbour.

Almost within days of the first raid on Malta the families that had evacuated themselves from the populous area around the Grand Harbour began to drift back to their homes but, with the arrival of the Luftwaffe, they quickly moved out into the countryside again—many had no option for their homes lay in ruins—and there they stayed, often twenty or thirty souls in a two-roomed dwelling, until the end of the siege. This was a good thing, for the Luftwaffe was quickly reinforced and the raids went on unabated until, by the end of May, there had been fifty-eight separate attacks in the year, sometimes three or four in a single day.

An unfortunate result of the Luftwaffe's activities was that the Royal Air Force was kept so busy and the airfields were so badly damaged that plans to attack Tripoli, with Malta-based light bombers and fighter-bombers, had to be abandoned. The Royal Navy, however, was not prevented from making an active contribution to the campaign in North Africa and Malta-based destroyers and submarines wreaked havoc amongst Mussolini's shipping. In March alone, a single flotilla of destroyers sunk 14,000 tons of Axis shipping.

The importance of Malta was a matter that was constantly uppermost in Churchill's mind and, in the early part of 1941, he issued a directive that said:

'In order to control sea communications across the Mediterranean, sufficient suitable naval forces must be based on Malta and protection must be afforded to these forces by the Royal Air Force at Malta, which must be kept to the highest strength in fighters.'

His directive was not ignored and, between January and June, carriers, operating from Gibraltar under the command of Admiral Somerville, brought 224 Hurricanes to within flying range of Malta. And, by midsummer, the first Spitfires arrived and, in some miraculous way, the people of the island seemed to know that they were on the way and they lined rooftops and cheered them in as they flew low over the coast. But sometimes the cheering was premature and the newly arrived machines had scarcely touched down before the Luftwaffe appeared upon the scene and strafed them on the ground.

Other new activities of the Luftwaffe were the dropping, in the Grand Harbour and around the coast, of magnetic and acoustic mines and, over the land, delayed action mines. In April, night raiding began for the first time. Life on the island had become very unpleasant again.

Then, on 22nd June, Hitler sent his armies into Russia and,

to support them, he withdrew the Luftwaffe from Sicily, and Malta breathed a sigh of relief.

The Italians tried to plug the gap but, on the first occasion on which the Regia Aeronautica reappeared over the island, the anti-aircraft batteries pounded them so hard that ten of their planes were shot down and the remainder chased back to their motherland, many with full bomb-racks.

The Regia Aeronautica was no match for the Royal Air Force but Mussolini was determined that the destruction of his transports to North Africa by submarine and destroyer must be stopped and he tried again, but he used a fresh method. In the early hours of the morning of 26th July the sirens sounded and the Maltese people rose from their beds and started to make their way towards the shelters. Within minutes guns were barking but they barked with a different note and the people who still lived near Valletta realized that, this time, it was the coast defence batteries that were in action and they went, instead of below ground, to the bastions around the Grand Harbour.

There were no aircraft in the attacking force that day. It consisted of eight E Boats—tiny one-man suicide craft with a large explosive charge in the bows, two midget two-man sub-marines and two motor torpedo boats. Their target was the shipping in the Grand Harbour—merchantmen and men-of-war.

The coastal batteries of the Royal Malta Artillery had never fired in anger before but they fired with remarkable accuracy. One of the midget submarines blew itself up against a break-water and one of the motor torpedo boats was captured. All the remaining attacking vessels were destroyed before they penetrated the Grand Harbour. Not one of the British ships that lay there was even scratched.

Whilst a strong force of Luftwaffe had been based on Sicily the passage of merchant shipping through the Mediterranean had been a difficult problem and, so far as possible, the islanders had been allowed to draw on reserve stocks of food and fuel. As a result, by the middle of the year, the supply situation was becoming serious. The withdrawal of the Luft-waffe came just in time and, as soon as it was realized that they

had gone, arrangements were made to start convoying merchantmen to the island. In July six ships were brought in and
seven empty ones were taken out without loss.

The process went on and, between July and September,
thirty-four ships left Gibraltar for Malta and only two of them
were lost. During the same period, light British naval forces
based on Malta sunk 150,000 tons of Axis shipping and, in
October, sixty per cent of Mussolini's supply ships went to the
bottom of the sea. And the Royal Air Force, as well, went over
to the offensive, attacking shipping and even the Italian mainland. Naples, for example, was raided five times in the last
quarter of 1941.

The islanders were delighted and their most popular pastime
became climbing onto the house tops, hillsides and harbour
walls to cheer and wave to the returning ships and aircraft.
But their delight was short lived. The Eastern front was soon
in the grip of winter and the Russian and German armies there
were halted. Luftwaffe squadrons that had been urgently
needed could be spared once more and Hitler was becoming
daily more impatient with Mussolini's North African failures.
In December he withdrew a whole Air Corps from Russia and
sent it to Sicily and North Africa. The part that went to Sicily
was placed under the direct command of Kesselring and he
was ordered, once and for all, to subdue Malta, the British
bastion that, by now, the Axis pilots had christened 'the island
of fire.'

++

CHAPTER VII

TO HONOUR HER BRAVE PEOPLE

FOR the people of Malta, 1940 and 1941 had been years of trial but the supreme test of their courage and endurance lay ahead. There were 1,170 air-raid alerts during the first eighteen months of the siege but there were over 1,300 in the first five months of 1942. There was not a raidless day and, during the month of April, a greater weight of bombs fell on Malta than on London during the worst three months of the blitz.

Casualties were lighter than in London and there were several reasons for this. The most important was the fact that, by the beginning of 1942, there were enough underground shelters for the entire population of the island—well over a quarter of a million—to go to whenever the sirens sounded. Many of the larger of these were well furnished with tiers of bunks and they all had their own little shrines with a flickering lamp before a picture of the Virgin.

Another life-saver was the shortage of trees for, as a result, very little timber was used in building and bombing was never followed by the fire that in London, and particularly in Hamburg, did far more damage than the blast of high explosives. Finally, the ordered regularity of the Teutonic mind contributed to the people's safety for, just as on the Western Front, in World War I, it was possible to set a watch by the opening round of the daily German barrage, a regular routine was adopted in the Luftwaffe's effort to flatten Malta. Not only did the Maltese know when to expect the four principal raids of the day but they also knew which part of the island was due to be attacked. As a result they were usually safely in their shelters by the time the bombs began to fall.

Though loss of life was not as terrible as it might have been, damage to property mounted grievously. Literally thousands of humble homes were destroyed until over half of the buildings

in Valletta and Floriana were either flat or unusable. The
Royal Opera House was reduced to a heap of rubble and scores
of churches, convents, schools and hospitals were destroyed.
The Governor's Palace was heavily hit and the Great Market
and the Court of Justice shared the fate of the Opera House.

The Court of Justice was originally the Auberge d'Auvergne,
one of the seven Auberges—or homes—of the seven Langues
of the Order of St John. They were amongst the loveliest and
most historically important buildings in the island and nearly
all of them suffered in some degree. The finest of them all, the
Auberge de Castille et de Leon, was left as little more than a
shell, its lovely interior lost for ever.

The building in which the people of modern Malta have
most pride, the Parish Church of Mosta, escaped miraculously.
This remarkable basilica, built by the free labour of the people
of a small township, boasts one of the largest domes in Europe
and it received a direct hit by a heavy bomb that failed to
detonate.

The islanders accepted the gradual destruction of Malta
philosophically but there were a number of incidents that
aroused their fury. Outstanding amongst these were two devastating attacks on hospitals that were clearly marked with
gigantic red crosses. But, angry though the Maltese were,
nobody condemned these attacks more bitterly than a wounded
German officer who was a patient in one of the hospitals and
worked heroically amongst the ruins.

In the other there was an English Colonel who had been so
badly wounded in an earlier raid that it was impossible to
move him. When the raid began, two nurses moved one to
each side of him and sat quietly holding his hands whilst the
building disintegrated around them.

Another act of barbarism that aroused the bitter ire of the
people was a savage bombing and machine-gun attack on
s.s. *Franco* and *Royal Lady*, the two unarmed little steamers
that provided the ferry service between Malta and her small
sister island, Gozo. The *Royal Lady* went to the bottom of the
sea.

This was by no means the only attack on small unarmed

coastal craft. Several fishing boats were similarly treated and there were many cases of rescue launches, sometimes engaged in picking up Axis pilots, being attacked. One British Flying Officer was riddled with machine-gun bullets within seconds of being dragged from the sea. As he lay dead in the bottom of the launch, his young Maltese wife was delivering their first child.

The remarkable thing was that, despite all the bombing, the work of the island went on. The peasant farmers worked unconcernedly in the fields and, when the sirens sounded, they walked briskly to their shelters where they sat smoking their pipes and chatting to their friends until they heard the note of the all clear. Then they went quietly back to their fields, picked up their rakes or hoes and started again where they had left off.

The shopkeepers had to contend with the fact that few of their shops remained standing, but they displayed remarkable initiative in the construction of outdoor booths and stalls from materials salvaged from bombed buildings, and business went on as usual.

Schools were rarely closed for long. As soon as one was razed to the ground, it would open again a few days later in some church, barn or shed. And two, three or even four times in a single day, when the red flags were hoisted, the classes would form themselves into orderly crocodiles and move to a nearby shelter where lessons were continued.

The priests, as well as the teachers, were undeterred by the bombing and Mass was celebrated regularly, often before a makeshift altar and in the midst of a heap of rubble that was scarcely recognizable as the remains of a church.

Needless to say the constant bombing caused havoc to the island's telephone and telegraph system. At a time when rapid communications were often vital, overhead wires and underground cables were constantly being cut. This brought the Boy Scout movement into prominence and many important messages were passed by their semaphore signallers. One fifteen-year-old lad, David Archer, was decorated with the British Empire Medal for his exploits. He insisted on remaining at his post, on a roof-top, throughout a particularly heavy raid on the capital, despite the fact that more than one bomb struck the building on which he stood. Two other Boy Scouts employed as coast watchers were awarded M.B.E.s for outstanding devotion to duty.

Malta's Police Force, as well, has good reason to be proud of the part it played. It was no unusual sight, during heavy raids, just as in the London blitz, to see a beefy blue-clad policeman standing imperturbably at a cross-roads, quietly directing people to the nearest shelters and, at the same time, creating confidence by his own apparent calm.

The Police Force had many other duties to perform. They regularly had to help in the clearance of debris and the rapid unloading of the few ships that reached Malta during the worst part of the siege. Their hardest and least enviable task was the enforcement of large numbers of unpopular regulations.

Individual acts of heroism were daily events. Typical was the action of 48-year-old Anthony Borg, a flour merchant, who set off one day in April 1942, to try to find flour to replenish the exhausted stocks of his village bakehouse. With him went his nineteen-year-old son George. As they went on their way, German Stukas dived out of the clouds and a hail of bombs fell around them. The boy threw himself to the ground and his father lay on top of him and sheltered his son with his own body. A moment later a bomb fell in the roadway a few feet off. Anthony Borg was mortally wounded and, as he lay dying, his last words to his son were:

'I am dying to save you.'

George Borg survived and, soon afterwards, he qualified as a doctor. Today he practises in Luqa.

It is hard, and probably wrong, to apportion credit at a time of universal suffering and courage but, if any particular section of the Maltese people deserve to be singled out for special mention, it must surely be the women of the island. Many of them, nurses and nuns particularly, devoted themselves selflessly to the care of the wounded and maimed. But the Maltese are a much married race and they raise large families. Thus, it was the lot of most Maltese women to try to clothe, feed and house these families under truly appalling conditions. To this almost impossible task they devoted themselves without complaint and without losing their faith. Somehow they produced meals when there was practically no food and they patched and mended clothes that were only fit for the rag bag. They patrolled the gutters in their search for bread and cigarette-ends for their menfolk, and they went regularly to Mass and prayed.

It was lack of food that nearly brought the Maltese to their knees. The highly populated island has insufficient room to grow enough for the needs of the people and, amongst many other things, wheat, meat, sugar, dairy produce and edible oils all have to be imported in large quantities. By the end of 1941 stocks of everything were very low and General Dobbie sent a desperate cable to London:

'The very worst may happen if we cannot replenish our vital needs: especially flour and ammunition. It is a question of survival.'

Everything possible was done to meet the Governor's call for help. In January 1942, four merchantmen reached Malta from Alexandria. Next month, three left from Gibraltar and the Luftwaffe sunk them all. In March, another attempt was made. Admiral Vian left Alexandria with a convoy of four merchant ships escorted by four light cruisers.

For two days the convoy ran the gauntlet of constant Luftwaffe attack and then, when it was a hundred and fifty miles north of the Gulf of Sirte, four strange vessels were spotted on the northern horizon. They came closer and were recognized as Italian cruisers, ships that outgunned the British light cruisers. But worse was to follow. A short while later a 35,000 ton Littorio class battleship, the *Littorio* itself in fact, attended by two more cruisers and a flotilla of destroyers, joined the other Italian ships. For the first time in a year an Italian naval task force had ventured out of port.

British naval history is full of examples of victory in the face of overwhelming odds, but it is doubtful whether there has ever been a finer example of this than the battle that followed on that day—the Second Battle of Sirte.

The British cruisers were now hopelessly outgunned and the Italian fleet should have been capable of shelling them all day whilst keeping out of range of the British guns themselves. Vian decided, therefore, that his only chance lay in getting to within range of his enemy and he laid a smoke screen to his front. The Italians expected that his next move would be to try to escape and they steamed towards the smoke. Instead, he ordered full steam ahead and, within minutes, he was within range of his adversary.

For four hours a confused battle raged. Then it became dusk and it was the Italian fleet that broke off the engagement and sailed away, with several fires burning in the *Littorio* and one of the cruisers badly crippled. By some miracle, none of the British light cruisers had suffered more than slight damage.

But the fate of the four merchantmen was less happy. Two of them were sunk within eight miles of Malta and the other two reached Valletta and were sunk by the Luftwaffe whilst they were being unloaded. Only 5,000 of the 26,000 tons of supplies that had left Alexandria were landed in Malta.

One of the ships that was sunk in the harbour was the s.s. *Talbot*, carrying a cargo of petroleum products and heavy bombs—the heaviest bombs that had so far reached Malta. It was sunk not by the Luftwaffe but by the Royal Navy.

She was set on fire by the Luftwaffe and the fuel burned so furiously that her whole hull became red hot with her framework remaining black, so that the vessel seemed to be transparent with her skeleton visible. But, strangely, though some ammunition in the cargo was going off, her bombs did not explode. However, the danger was enormous and it was decided to sink her where she lay.

Lieutenant Dennis Arthur Copperwheat, Torpedo Officer of the famous cruiser *Penelope*, volunteered to conduct this operation. With a small party of ratings, he placed charges around the hull of the stricken *Talbot* and then, having sent his men to safety, he fired the fuses and sunk the ship. It had been his intention to climb over a breakwater to safety behind it before the charges went off but, when the time arrived, due to either the physical or mental strain, he had not the strength

5

to pull himself from the water. Despite his exposed position he survived the blast of the explosion.

For this exploit, Lieutenant Copperwheat was decorated with the George Cross.

The position was becoming desperate. Rations had to be cut by half and the troops of the garrison were given no more food than the islanders. There were signs of malnutrition. Men were finding that they could do less work, and this was a serious thing when, already, many working hours were being spent in shelters. Bread had to be made of a mixture of flour and potato.

Other things as well as food were running out. Tobacco became almost unobtainable and, in its place, the enterprising Maltese smoked a mixture of dried fig, lemon and strawberry leaves and pronounced it excellent. But, more serious, stocks of anti-aircraft ammunition were short and supplies to the batteries had to be rationed at a time when the activities of the Royal Air Force were also being restricted by damaged runways and shortage of machines.

Finally, very little petrol and kerosene was left. Petrol was kept for essential military traffic and, to reduce this, the Army requisitioned five hundred mule carts. The shortage of kerosene presented a great problem for, in an island that is without coal and almost without wood, all cooking is done on primus stoves. To conserve supplies of fuel, communal cooking centres were set up and, for several months, almost the entire population of the island ate their main meal of the day in one of these.

Fresh efforts to get food and other urgently needed supplies to Malta were made in June and August. Seventeen merchantmen sailed for Malta in June—six from Gibraltar and eleven from Alexandria. The two convoys started simultaneously and, of the eastbound one, only two ships reached their destination. None of the other convoy got through at all, all eleven vessels being forced back to the shores of Africa. And, in this operation, the cruisers *Liverpool* and *Hermione* were both badly damaged.

The August attempt was called *Operation Portcullis* and, this time, fourteen merchantmen entered the Mediterranean from the west escorted by the battleships *Nelson* and *Rodney*, three carriers and a mixed force of cruisers, anti-aircraft ships and no less than thirty-two destroyers. The convoy was attacked continuously by the Luftwaffe and over half the merchant ships were sunk. The carrier *Eagle* went down as well and, with it, a cruiser, an anti-aircraft ship and one of the destroyers. The carrier *Indomitable* was badly damaged.

Three of the merchantmen reached Malta safely—*Melbourne Castle, Rochester Castle* and *Port Chalmers*. The *Brisbane Star*, badly damaged, limped into the Grand Harbour a day behind the others and, a day later still, the British crewed American tanker *Ohio* was towed in by a destroyer. She had left the Clyde on 2nd August with a cargo of 13,000 tons of gas oil and kerosene and, 70 miles N.N.W. of Cape Bon, she had been holed in the pump room by a torpedo. The kerosene tanks had caught fire and for the next five days she had struggled towards Malta with her crew fighting the flames and firing back at the hostile aircraft that hunted the ship continuously in an all out effort to finish her off. Submarines, as well, stalked the *Ohio* like animals of prey.

The ship's master, Captain Dudley William Mason, was determined that, whilst his tanker remained afloat, he would not relax his efforts to get his precious cargo to Malta and the fact that he achieved his aim was due entirely to his remarkable determination and the magnificent example that he set the remainder of his crew. His gallantry was recognized by the award of the George Cross which he received from King George VI six weeks later.

Following the miraculous escape of the *Ohio*, the Admiralty decided that, for the time being, it was too dangerous to try to run tankers of motor and aircraft spirit through the Mediterranean and, for several months, the only supplies to reach the island came by submarine or fast mine-layer. The submarine *Porpoise* and the mine-layers *Manxman* and *Welchman* each made several trips carrying this vital cargo.

Another serious problem, in the first half of 1942, was the moving of fresh aircraft to Malta, for the ill fated *Eagle* was laid up in April and no other carrier was available in the Western Mediterranean. But Churchill was determined that fresh fighters would be sent to replace the losses of the Royal

Air Force. When the Admiralty convinced him that nothing could be spared for the job, he cabled Roosevelt to ask for help. Characteristically, the American President immediately sent the carrier *Wasp* and it made two trips to Malta in April and May, delivering 126 aircraft.

When Churchill heard of the success of the second trip he made an immediate signal to the ship's captain:

'Who said a wasp couldn't sting twice?'

Having survived two trips through the Mediterranean, *Wasp* sailed to join the American fleet in the Pacific and, there, she had the ill fortune to be sunk by the Japanese.

Whilst the people of Malta were suffering constant bombardment from the air and slow starvation, as well as every other hardship, the fear of invasion was constantly with them. The coast had to be watched day and night and the garrison stayed at their battle stations.

It was Admiral Raeder who was the advocate of the theory that Malta must be invaded. Like Churchill, he was convinced that the fortress was the key to the Middle East and, whenever the opportunity was favourable, he pressed the point home with Hitler and, in the end, convinced him. The Fuhrer discussed the matter with Il Duce and the two dictators decided that the Italian Army would take on the task with the assistance of units of the German Army.

The Italians must have regarded the job as a formidable one for when, in April 1942, they began to plan it, they gave it the appropriate name *Operation Herculese.* Mussolini earmarked two parachute regiments, a battalion of engineers and five batteries of artillery for the assault and Hitler promised to provide additional parachute troops and engineers as well as transport aircraft and barges. He had large numbers of these that had lain idle since the abandonment of his plan to invade England.

In the event, the operation was never launched. In the early days, Kesselring convinced Mussolini that his air assault was so effective that the capitulation of Malta was expected hourly. Then Rommel's offensive in the desert seemed to be going so well that it looked as though the battle for the Middle East would be won without diverting troops to Malta. In the end, the war went against the Axis again but then it was too late to make the attack, for air and naval superiority over the central Mediterranean had been lost. Nevertheless, in Malta, the invasion was expected daily and the fear of it added to the tribulations of the islanders.

On 17th April 1942, the King's decision to decorate the people of the island with the George Cross was front page news. The *Times of Malta* announced the award below banner headlines and, alongside a photograph of His Majesty, was the text of his message to the Governor:

BUCKINGHAM PALACE

The Governor,
Malta.

To honour her brave people I award the George Cross to the Island Fortress of Malta to bear witness of a heroism and devotion that will long be famous in History.

GEORGE R.I.
15th April 1942.

The announcement had an electrifying effect. The main reactions were an upsurge of loyalty to the Crown and a determination to be worthy of the award, though one hungry Maltese saw fit to chalk 'Hobz, mux George Cross' (Bread, not George Cross) on a wall.

On the evening of the 17th, General Dobbie broadcast to the island and everyone who was able listened to his words and was stirred by them. Messages of congratulation poured in from all over the world: from the leaders of the Maltese communities in Egypt, Palestine and America, from Lord Gort on behalf of the people of Gibraltar, Prince Peter of Greece, the Royal Empire Society, the Commander-in-Chief of the Mediterranean Fleet, the Commander-in-Chief, Middle East Land Forces, the United States Consul in Tunisia and a host of other people.

The unique award of a decoration for gallantry to a nation was the occasion for a flood of letters to the newspapers of Britain as well as Malta. The first suggestion that the George Cross should be embodied in the arms of Malta was made in the London *Times*, although this suggestion was not adopted until 1946 when the College of Heralds issued a warrant authorizing the use of the Cross upon the 'Seals, Shields, Banners or otherwise according to the Law of Arms.'[1] The *Times of Malta* published no less than six letters suggesting that the Cross should be incorporated in the Maltese stamps as well as a proposal that it should be used as a post-mark. Other ideas were that it should be incorporated in the island's currency notes, that a national shrine should be built to house the Cross, that it should be housed in the Cathedral of St Peter and St Paul in the old inland capital of Mdina, and that the letters G.C. should be used after the name Malta.

Many of these suggestions were adopted and possibly the most appropriate of them was the last. The significance of an emblem or insignia in a coat of arms, or on a stamp or currency note, tends to be lost with familiarity. The written word has a more lasting value and the use of the letters G.C. in the postal address of every inhabitant of the island is more personal to the ordinary man in the street. It was, after all, the bravery of the ordinary people of Malta, people without armorial bearings or seals or banners, that merited the award.

Whilst the inclusion of the George Cross into such things as the arms of Malta and the island's postage stamps was very proper, its use in such things as trade marks was officially frowned upon and, in 1943, the Government thought it necessary to issue an Ordinance forbidding this sort of thing.[2] However, fourteen years later the Maltese Government exposed itself to the accusation of commercializing the award by issuing three different sets of 'George Cross Postage Stamps' in the course of two years. The latest issue incorporates a facsimile of the original citation, as well as the George Cross, the Maltese Cross, the Queen's head and a royal crown. It is too elaborate to be artistic.

Malta's George Cross was brought to the island on 7th May 1942, by General Viscount Gort—himself a holder of the Victoria Cross—when he arrived from Gibraltar to replace General Dobbie as Governor and Commander-in-Chief. The

[1] *Appendix* IV   [2] *Appendix* V

change of Governors was made suddenly and unexpectedly with the minimum of publicity. It aroused much speculation for several years afterwards but the mystery was cleared up in Churchill's war memoirs where he explains that, in April, he had had disturbing news about Dobbie. It was reported that the strain of events in Malta was proving too much for him. Churchill immediately warned Lord Gort to be ready to replace him.

Later reports confirmed the earlier ones and the Prime Minister advised the King to make the change. The reports were true, for it was a grey, haggard and sick looking man who climbed into the aircraft that had brought his successor. But it was not only the strain of his terrible task that had reduced Dobbie to this low state. When he reached London he was received by the King and invested with the GCMG. Immediately afterwards he underwent an abdominal operation.

Dobbie's name will stand, in the history of Malta, alongside that of La Valette. Gort was an appropriate successor. Though less outwardly devout he had high spiritual values and was a born leader. He was the holder of the Distinguished Service Order and the Military Cross, as well as the Victoria Cross, and had been mentioned in despatches no less than nine times. His personal bravery was in no doubt. He differed from Dobbie in that he was less stiff and reserved, more approachable and easy going.

One of his first acts was to make the public presentation of the George Cross. This event took place against a background of bomb-blasted buildings but with a great display of pomp and ceremony. The award was received, on behalf of the people, by the Chief Justice, Sir George Borg.

Gort then arranged to have the Cross taken round the island and displayed in every township. With it he sent a military band.

For five months, Gort had the task of leading the islanders in what was, certainly from the point of view of privation, the worst period of the siege. Because of the shortage of petrol, he rode around Valletta on a bicycle. He lived on the same meagre rations as the rest of the population and he lost a great deal of weight in the process. He also made a point of being the first person to board and welcome each of the few supply ships that managed to fight their way through to the island.

Once, when he had gone down to the Grand Harbour to make sure that he was in good time to meet an expected ship, fire broke out in a dump of kerosene that had just been landed. He helped the Harbour Fire Brigade to fight the blaze until it was under control. Then he made his way quietly back to his house and sent an orderly to find a doctor. He had been severely burnt.

On 23rd October, Montgomery launched his long awaited attack at El Alemein and, after some days of desperate fighting, the Axis armies fled to the westward. A fortnight later the First Army landed at Algiers and pushed Blade Force to the plains of Tunisia, virtually unopposed. The net was closing. Rommel's forces were driven onto the defensive and, before long, his main preoccupation was a desperate attempt to extricate his men from the continent of Africa. In the Mediterranean, the Axis air and naval forces were diverted to the immediate protection of the Africa Korps' lines of communication. The priority task of the bombers of the Luftwaffe was to delay the advance of the First and Eighth Armies. Malta, that had suffered so much and for so long, was given its first respite for two and a half years.

The last attempt to get a convoy through to Malta had been in August, when nine out of fourteen merchant ships had been sunk and the carrier *Eagle* had been lost. In mid-November a fresh convoy operation was mounted—*Operation Stonehenge*—and four merchantmen reached the island safely. There were further convoys in December and January and thirteen more ships were brought into the Grand Harbour without loss.

The second siege of Malta had been raised. Once again Malta had stood firm against aggression; in the words of President Roosevelt, 'one tiny bright flame in the darkness, a beacon of hope for the clearer days that had to come.' But the Maltese people had had to pay a heavy price for their freedom. Almost 1,500 civilians had been killed and over twice that number were wounded, Valletta and its suburbs lay in ruins and several other parts of the island had fared little better. In all, seven thousand buildings had been flattened or badly hit.

The siege raised, the island was re-armed and re-victualled and soon became an advanced base for Allied advances into Europe. In May 1943, it was very nearly visited by Churchill. He reviewed the victorious Eighth Army in Tripoli and planned to fly over to Malta in a light aircraft with an escort of Spitfires. Montgomery reckoned that the idea was foolhardy and persuaded his political master to abandon it.

In September, Italy capitulated and her fleet was brought into the Grand Harbour. Cunningham signalled the Admiralty:

'The Italian fleet now lies at anchor under the guns of Malta.'

Later in the month, Malta was the scene of Italy's capitulation. The instrument of surrender was signed in H.M.S. *Nelson*, as she lay at anchor in the Grand Harbour, by Marshal Badoglio in the presence of Lord Gort, Eisenhower and Alexander.

Eighteen years after the end of the siege the scars remain. Thousands of buildings have been rebuilt and repaired. Many fine new buildings have been put up, including the wonderfully positioned Phoenicia Hotel, high above Valletta overlooking Marsamsett Harbour. But close to it the Royal Opera House still remains a heap of rubble and the scarred and pock marked façade of the Auberge de Castille et de Leon is a constant reminder of the fury of the onslaught of the Luftwaffe and the Regia Aeronautica.

In a place of honour in the Armoury of the Governor's Palace is a glass case that contains Malta's most treasured possession, a little silver cross and, below it, the original citation that awarded the Cross to the brave people of the island, in the handwriting of King George VI.

CHAPTER VIII

BOMBS AND MINES

ALTHOUGH the task of raising Bomb Disposal Sections was given to the Royal Engineers, that Corps was by no means the only branch of the services that had the job of dealing with unexploded bombs and mines, and many more George Crosses were won by other members of the fighting services for this dangerous work. It is, indeed, rather surprising that the job was given to the Royal Engineers at all, for the Army's experts in explosives and fuses are, in fact, the Royal Army Ordnance Corps, and a proportion of their officers attend an advanced course in the chemistry and science of explosives, fuse design, metallurgy and other allied subjects, to qualify as what are known as Inspecting Ordnance Officers. Some of their non-commissioned officers are similarly trained as Ammunition Examiners.

The truth is probably that, when the Bomb Disposal Organization was first set up, it was never appreciated that it would develop into anything as highly specialized as it did and the Sappers were selected as the experts at burrowing into the ground and blowing things up. However, despite the fact that someone else was given a job that could properly have been theirs, the men of the Royal Army Ordnance Corps did, in the event, play a large part in the task of dealing with unexploded bombs and two of their officers were decorated with the George Cross for this work.

In the early days of the war, before the Bomb Disposal Sections were formed, their experts handled a number of German bombs in England and at least one Inspecting Ordnance Officer was killed. At this time they dismantled several of the original German fuses and they were able to hand over a good deal of information about them to the Sappers when they took over responsibility for this duty. They also bore the brunt of the bomb disposal work in several overseas theatres, before Royal Engineer Sections were drafted abroad. This applied particularly to the island of Malta where, for many months during the siege, sole responsibility for bomb disposal was in the hands of two young Ordnance officers. Both of them were decorated with the George Cross.

For the first seven months of the war there was, in fact, only one Inspecting Ordnance Officer on the island, Captain Robert Llewellyn Jephson-Jones. Jephson-Jones had originally been an infantry officer in the Duke of Wellington's Regiment but, some years before the war when he was under thirty years of age, he decided to get married. In those days, infantry and cavalry officers were not encouraged to marry below the age of thirty and, if they insisted on following this unpopular course they were usually expected either to retire from the Army or transfer to one of the corps. Jephson-Jones elected to transfer to the Royal Army Ordnance Corps and was chosen for training as an Inspecting Ordnance Officer. It is interesting to reflect that, although he transferred from a fighting regiment to what was then a non-combatant corps, when war came he had to face far greater hazards than many infantry officers.

At the outbreak of the war he was living quietly in Malta with his wife and young family, carrying out what was very much of a routine job. And, for a time, the war made relatively little difference either to life in Malta or to his job. Then, in March 1940, three months before Italy entered the war and unleashed her fury on Malta, the War Office posted a second Inspecting Ordnance Officer to the island. His name was Lieutenant William Marsden Eastman. Prior to September 1939 he had been engaged in the dry cleaning business and was a member of the family that owned the well-known London firm that bears his name. When war seemed likely he joined the reserve of officers and, when it started, he was called up and rushed through a shortened war-time course in ammunition duties.

The story of the assault on Malta by the Regia Aeronautica and the Luftwaffe is told elsewhere in this book. It was a story of savage and relentless bombardment of a tiny island and, needless to say, it produced a major problem of bomb disposal. And the problem had to be tackled by two young officers who had no special equipment, no trained staff and no knowledge of the intricacies of Italian and German bombs. Their assets were a basic knowledge of the theory of explosives and fuses and limitless courage.

Over the next few months, one or other of them answered over three hundred separate calls for assistance and, though some of them turned out to be false alarms, a high proportion ended in the disarming or removal of live bombs. Time and again, when one of them was actually engaged on a job of work, a message would arrive ordering him to go to another as soon as he had finished with his present one.

As Malta consists of solid limestone, with only the thinnest covering of soil, they were not faced with the digging problem that bedevilled the work of bomb disposers in England and most of the unexploded bombs lay on the ground. But this was a mixed blessing from the point of view of the two officers who had to deal with them, for it also meant that they were called to deal with virtually every bomb that fell and failed to detonate. It was very rare for an unexploded bomb to be hidden below some unsuspecting house owner's property as often happened in England.

There was rarely time for disarming bomb fuses, but they did remove a proportion with the object of finding out how they worked, for little or no information about enemy bombs filtered through from London. Normally, however, they loaded the bombs into a truck and either pitched them into the sea or exploded them in the country. A particularly large and obstinate one that the pair of them tried to deal with in this fashion had to be detonated no less than three times before it went off. Each time that a fresh charge had to be attached to it, the operation became potentially more dangerous, for it was probable that the weapon had been made more sensitive by the previous explosions.

The fact that it was hardly ever necessary to dig for unexploded bombs in Malta did not mean that there were never any problems in their removal and Captain Jephson-Jones and

Lieutenant Eastman, working together once more, had one particularly difficult job when a four hundred pound bomb fell into one of the water catchment wells that lie below nearly all houses in Malta. First the well had to be pumped free of water and a derrick erected over it. Then the two officers had to work in many inches of filth, slime and dead cats that had accumulated over several generations, fitting slings to the bomb. Finally, when they managed to hoist the thing to the well mouth, which was narrower than the rest of the well, they discovered that the diameter of the bomb was only a bare inch less than the diameter of the mouth. They had a long and grim struggle in persuading it to come through and there was a constant danger that the harness would slip and the bomb fall back to the foot of the well again and detonate.

The citation that announced the award of the George Cross to Captain Jephson-Jones and Lieutenant Eastman was unique in that it was a joint one. The awards were given for their constant bravery over many months, although specific mention was also made of the bomb that they removed from the catchment well.

Twenty years after the event, Colonel Eastman, recalling those hectic days, made the comment that he felt that Brigadier Jephson-Jones deserved more credit than he did for, whilst he was then a single man, his superior was not only married but, throughout the period of his bomb disposal work in Malta, he was actually living at home with his wife and family and the dangers of his job must have played more heavily on his mind. There is truth in this point of view but it was a generous comment and it does not alter the fact that his own decoration was richly deserved.

It is interesting to record that, whilst bomb disposal has remained the responsibility of the Royal Engineers, Inspecting Ordnance Officers of the Royal Army Ordnance Corps still have to perform duties of an equally hazardous nature, particularly overseas, where they are often called in by the local police who rarely employ civilian explosives experts. In recent years this type of work has been particularly arduous in Cyprus where, over a period of four years, during the emergency, a small team of Ordnance experts dealt with some ten thousand bombs, grenades and explosive devices. Two of their number were killed and several more injured, whilst seven of them were decorated for bravery and these decorations included four George Medals.

One other army officer who did not belong to the Bomb Disposal Organization won a George Cross for dealing with an unexploded bomb. He was Lieutenant John MacMillan Stevenson Patton of the Royal Canadian Engineers; a man with a reputation for fearlessness that sometimes amounted to foolhardiness.

The bomb, a 500 pounder, fell just outside the erecting shed of the Hawker aircraft factory at Weybridge in Surrey. Work in the factory had to be stopped and an urgent call was sent for help, but news came back that no Bomb Disposal Sections were available and it seemed unlikely that one could be spared for several days. Then somebody remembered that there was a Canadian Engineer unit in Weybridge and a message was sent to their Commanding Officer to ask if he was able to help.

Nobody in the unit had any training in bomb disposal work but Lieutenant Patton volunteered to see what could be done. He found that the bomb had landed on a hard surface and was lying there in a badly distorted condition. He examined it carefully to see if he could discover any method of making it safe but, in the end, decided that it would be wisest not to tamper with it but to remove it to a safer spot as quickly as possible.

Patton did not want to lift the bomb any more than he could help and so he slid it gently onto a large sheet of corrugated iron and secured it to this. Then, using the corrugated iron as a skid, he towed it slowly away behind a truck. His next problem was to find somewhere to dump it and he remembered passing a large bomb crater in an open field not far off and decided that this would be as good a spot as any. He drove to the place and, towing the bomb up to the side of the crater, pushed it in. Some hours later it went off, presumably under the influence of a delayed action mechanism.

There were also two officers of the Royal Navy who were untrained in this sort of work and had no responsibility for it but were decorated with the George Cross for dealing with mines. One of them was Sub-Lieutenant Richard Valentine Moore and, although he had had no practical training, he had picked up a little theoretical knowledge through working in the Admiralty. In a moment of emergency he volunteered to help deal with some of the large number of German mines that had either been accidentally dropped on land or had floated on to beaches. He disarmed five and, on one occasion, a clock started to tick as he was trying to remove a fuse casing but he went on coolly with the job and succeeded in withdrawing it. He did this just in time, for the detonator exploded a few seconds after it was clear of the mine.

Sub-Lieutenant Peter Victor Dankwerts had not even the advantage of a theoretical knowledge of mine disposal and, at a time when there were a large number of mines lying about in dangerous places and insufficient experts to deal with them all, he discovered where some of them were and, without any orders, he set off to do what he could to help. During forty-eight hours continuous work he disarmed no less than sixteen.

He found two in a large warehouse, hanging from their parachute cords, with their noses just touching the floor and their parachutes caught in the rafters. As he approached them the vibration of his footsteps started up the clock in one. Wisely, he withdrew from the scene. He waited for some time and as nothing happened he went back into the building. This time he found that the clock had stopped again so he went up to the mine and withdrew the fuse. Then he dealt with the other one.

Although this daring pair of officers had had no training in mine disposal, a number of naval officers had and, although the Bomb Disposal Sappers sometimes tackled mines, this was really a naval responsibility.

The Royal Navy's experts in mine disposal came from H.M.S. *Vernon* which, of course, was not a ship at all but the official title of the Torpedo and Anti-Submarine School at Portsmouth. Here a large number of officers and ratings were given specialized training in dealing with all kinds of nautical explosive weapons including mines, torpedoes and depth charges. Demands for assistance in the disposal of mines went to the Admiralty and were relayed to H.M.S. *Vernon* and, from there, the experts were sent all over the country.

Not all the mines that had to be dealt with were enemy ones. Sometimes British mines broke adrift from their moorings and were washed up onto the shore but they presented few problems to men who had been trained in handling them. German mines, on the other hand, had many complications and hazards for, apart from the fact that they were often dropped on dry land and had a habit of falling in the most inaccessible places, the Germans developed a number of different methods of detonation and most of their mines incorporated two, if not three, of them. These systems included an acoustic detonator that was fired by the engine noise of a passing ship, a magnetic detonator, fired by the magnetic influence of a ship's hull, and a pressure mechanism that went off as a result of the pressure wave that is set up by a moving vessel. Other firing mechanisms went off on impact or some with a time device. On some mines, however, the acoustic or magnetic mechanism did not come into operation for a period that was governed by a delay device and one particularly cunning type of pressure mine was designed to allow five ships to pass over it and then detonate when the sixth went by. Needless to say, many of these mechanisms were fitted with anti-handling devices. In a nutshell, the Germans' mines were as devilish and dangerous as their bombs and a number of George Crosses were awarded to the naval officers and ratings who had to handle them.

The fact that they were dropped by parachute often presented difficult problems, for they had a habit of getting hung up in the air and the disarming of a dangerous weapon can be just as difficult when it is dangling ten feet above the ground as when it has penetrated ten feet into it. One George Cross winner, Lieutenant Robert Selby Armitage RNVR, had to face this problem when he was sent for to deal with a mine that was found swinging gently in the breeze, suspended from a high branch of a tree in Orpington, Kent. He removed the fuse standing on the top of a long ladder.

Shortly afterwards he went to deal with another mine in the

same part of the country and he had not been working on it for long when the mechanism began to tick. He did the only sensible thing and, dropping his tools, sprinted harder than he had ever sprinted before. He had covered exactly thirty yards when the thing went off and he was thrown violently to the ground. He was badly shaken and bruised but this did not prevent him from reporting for duty next morning to see if there was any more work for him.

Another hero of this period was Sub-Lieutenant William Horace Taylor who dealt with ten mines in as many days. Once he had to use a hammer to remove a fuse. His recommendation for the George Cross was actually made by the Air Ministry and was the result of a particularly dangerous piece of mine-disposal work that he undertook at the Royal Air Force Depot at Uxbridge.

The same award was given to Lieutenant Hugh Randall Syme who dealt with nineteen mines up and down the coast between Portland and Liverpool. Five of these were acoustic, eight magnetic and two were a combination of both. On one occasion he had to work hanging upside down in a hole in the mud whilst he handled a live wire that was giving him painful electric shocks as he tried to earth it without letting it touch the side of the mine.

Two other sailors, Sub-Lieutenant Jack Maynard Cholmondeley Easton and Ordinary Seaman Bennett Southwell, won the George Cross for, amongst other exploits, dealing with a mine that lodged in a passage on the third floor of a block of London flats. There would have been no quick means of retreat for either man if anything had gone wrong.

Later on these two men had to deal with another mine in some flats in Clifton Street, Shoreditch. Whilst they were working on it they heard the hydrostatic valve close and then ran from the place as hard as they could but failed to put sufficient distance between themselves and the weapon before it went off. Easton sustained a fractured skull and pelvis as well as severe bruising and shock, whilst the less fortunate Southwell was literally blown to pieces.

It is doubtful whether any German mine chose a more

inaccessible place to rest than one of nine that fell in Liverpool during a heavy raid on the night of 28th November 1940. It went straight through the top of a huge gasometer in Garston Gas Works. The parachute caught in the jagged hole in the roof, however, and the thing finished its flight hanging several feet above the floor of the gasometer, which contained some two million cubic feet of coal gas. The Gas Works is in the centre of a highly populated area and it was necessary to evacuate over six thousand people from their homes until the mine could be made safe. In addition, the nearby docks and railway sidings were completely closed down.

Next morning a naval party under the command of Lieutenant Harold Reginald Newgass RNVR arrived in Liverpool, but it was clear that nothing could be done about the mine in the gasometer until the vessel had been cleared of gas. So, whilst the Gas Works staff began to pump it into other containers, Lieutenant Newgass and his party set to work dealing with the other eight mines that were scattered about the city. They disarmed and removed them all.

Then the sailors returned to Garston and Newgass had a look at the gasometer. The chief engineer had cut an entry hole in the side of the great tank and Newgass looked inside. The place still smelt strongly of gas and the atmosphere was still highly inflammable. There were a couple of feet of water on the floor and it was pitch black. He asked the chief engineer to pump away the water and this was done but several inches of sickly smelling slime remained.

Newgass started by having the mine gently lowered onto the slime and then, wearing breathing apparatus, he went in to examine the weapon. He insisted on going in alone. Using an electric torch, he discovered that the mine was now lying with the fuse casing in contact with the floor and the first thing that he had to do was to roll it over to expose it. Then, working alone, he carefully removed the fuse, a task that took him over two hours. When the mine was safe, he allowed other sailors into the gasometer to help remove it.

Lieutenant Newgass was decorated with the George Cross on the recommendation of the Officer Commanding H.M.S.

Vernon but, in addition to this official recommendation, the Admiralty received letters from several people, including Lord Derby, the Chief Constable of Liverpool and the Chief Engineer of Garston Gas Works, all loud in their praise of the work of the naval party. They all made special reference to the outstanding work of Lieutenant Newgass and urged that his bravery should be suitably rewarded. (The Admiralty were kind enough to allow me to read all their confidential files concerning George Cross awards and it is fair to say that no other recommendation was supported by such a wealth of evidence and commendation.)

A few months after this incident, a mine that had been intended to drop in the Thames finished up sitting in the middle of the Hungerford Bridge, the railway bridge that crosses the Thames and carries most of the traffic in and out of Waterloo station. Lieutenant Ernest Oliver Gidden RNVR was sent to deal with it and when he arrived on the scene he found a considerable degree of chaos. All around, buildings were on fire and some of them, including the Charing Cross Hotel, were blazing fiercely. Many of the wooden sleepers on the bridge and a number of parked railway carriages were burning as well, and the flames were creeping closer to the mine. Rail traffic to and from Waterloo station was at a standstill and underground trains on the Bakerloo line, that crosses the Thames below the bridge, had been stopped. A number of large buildings in the vicinity, including the War Office, had been evacuated and, although several humorists suggested that this might well help the war effort, this was, in reality, a serious matter.

The mine was lying with the fuse casing downwards in contact with a live electric rail and sparks were flying from it. Their heat had melted some of the metal around the fuse housing.

Gidden's first job was to turn over the mine and expose the fuse and then he had to prise off lumps of molten metal. Next he fitted an instrument that was designed to withdraw a fuse by remote control, and, whilst some of his party operated it from a distance, he stood about fifty yards away to watch what happened. Whilst this was going on he had to send the firemen, who were trying to extinguish the fire in the sleepers, off the bridge, and the flames began to creep closer to the bomb again.

After several minutes it became clear that the melting of the metal had jammed the fuse casing and it could not be withdrawn by remote control. Gidden, therefore, attacked it with a hammer and a cold chisel but he had not been working at it for long when he heard a clock ticking and he made off at top speed, leaping from one burning sleeper to another as he went. He, and everyone else, took cover but nothing happened. After a while he approached the mine again and found that the clock was no longer ticking. He attacked the fuse once more and, this time, the clock remained silent. Six hours after his arrival on the scene he managed to withdraw the fuse.

Lieutenant Gidden's George Cross was announced in the London Gazette of 9th June 1942, for some reason more than a year after the event.

Another particularly inaccessible mine was one that crashed through the deck of the firefloat, *Firefly*, on the Manchester Ship Canal and finished up firmly wedged in the deck locker alongside the engine room. The officer who rendered it safe, Sub-Lieutenant Francis Haffey Brook-Smith RNR, managed to fix to it a new device for neutralizing the fuse mechanism, despite the fact that he had never used one of these instruments before and had to fit it entirely by feel, for the fuse casing was out of sight. He was awarded the George Cross for dealing with this as well as fifteen other mines.

Another naval winner of the George Cross, Sub-Lieutenant Geoffrey Gledhill Turner RNVR, made quite a habit of dealing with inaccessible mines. One was wedged so tightly inside a small house that he found it impossible to make use of a remote control apparatus and had to withdraw the fuses by hand. Another somehow finished its journey from the sky sitting underneath a railway carriage in Sheffield station. Yet a third he found hanging from its parachute cords several feet above the floor of a wool factory in Liverpool. He arranged several large bags of wool on the floor below it and then cut the cords.

The mine fell onto the sacks without going off and he was able to disarm it there.

Turner's luck held for a long time but, in the end, he was badly injured and narrowly escaped with his life. He was tackling a particularly obstinate mine in Liverpool that refused to respond to the remote control apparatus and had to work on the fuse by hand. After a while the clock started and he ran quickly from the scene. For a time nothing happened and he returned again. He had hardly picked up his tools for a second time when the clock started once more. Again he ran but, this time, the thing exploded before he had gone far and he was blown to the ground and severely wounded and shocked.

Lieutenant-Commander Richard John Hammersley Ryan RN was less fortunate. He had a high reputation amongst the men of H.M.S. *Vernon* and it was he who earned distinction in the early days of the war for dismantling the first magnetic mine that was found. It was in a German aircraft that crashed on the sands at Clacton and it is widely recognized that when he exposed the secrets of the first of Hitler's secret weapons he helped to save the lives of thousands of Allied sailors.

After his encounter with the magnetic mine, Lieutenant-Commander Ryan disarmed a number of others in London and the London area until, one day, he was called from a job at Hornchurch to tackle a mine in a warehouse at Dagenham. It exploded whilst he was working on it and killed him instantly.

On all his exploits, Ryan was accompanied by Chief Petty Officer Reginald Vincent Ellingworth. The two men faced many dangers together and they were killed by the same explosion. Their posthumous awards of the George Cross were announced in the same issue of the London Gazette.

Another naval officer who was decorated with the George Cross for tackling a new type of German mine was Sub-Lieutenant John Herbert Babington RNVR. The Germans were not slow to introduce anti-handling devices into their mines and one of the first people to handle a mine that had this fitting was an officer of the Royal Air Force. He recognized the mine as being a new type but he did not suspect its secret. He unscrewed the locking ring that held the fuse casing into position but, as soon as he tried to withdraw it, the device detonated and the bomb went off and killed him.

A few days later a similar mine fell in Chatham Dockyard and Babington went to deal with it. He decided to move it to a safer place before he tackled it and had it put into the bottom of a sixteen-foot pit. Then he climbed in beside it and carefully unscrewed the locking ring. When this was free, he was careful not to try to withdraw the fuse but tied the end of a long length of cord to it. Then he climbed out of the pit with the other end and, from a point some distance from the mouth of the pit, he gave a sharp tug. Nothing happened and the fixed end of the cord held firm so he tried again but once more without result. He tried several times but the fuse always refused to come out.

Babington was determined to confirm the fact that the fuse case of this particular type of mine was booby trapped so he went down into the pit again and tried to withdraw it by hand. It was probably fortunate that all his efforts failed and in the end he hauled the weapon out of the pit again and took it elsewhere for destruction.

It is interesting to record that, some years after this event, Babington was appointed Headmaster of the Royal Hospital School at Holbrook. This is a school for the sons of deceased officers and men of the Royal Navy and the Merchant Navy and it seems particularly appropriate that these lads should have been offered the inspiration of being led by a holder of the George Cross.

Of course, not all the mines that had to be disarmed lay on dry land. Many of them fell or drifted into mud or shallow water, in places where it was not possible to tackle them with minesweepers. These were often very unpleasant to handle and, not infrequently, officers and ratings were forced to work on them for many hours standing chest deep in icy water or estuary mud. Sometimes it was necessary for the mine disposers to go below the water in diving suits and this was a particularly dangerous operation for, whilst someone dealing with a mine that gives warning that it is likely to go off has some prospect of survival if he runs and gets behind some cover, a diver has little chance of making a swift get-away and the blast effect of an underwater explosion is far more severe than in the case of an explosion in air.

A mine that fell in the Roding River that runs into Barking Creek was removed by Sub-Lieutenant John Bryan Peter Miller and Able Seaman Stephen John Tuckwell. These two men waded out into the filth of one of London's main sewers and, after removing the fuse and primer, lifted the thing with a crane and then completed its disablement. In all, they worked together on ten mines and received the George Cross for their continuous gallantry over a considerable period. Later on Miller, whose civilian occupation was that of a County Director of Education, was in charge of a party that disabled fifteen mines in Coventry.

A particular exponent of the art of dealing with underwater mines was Lieutenant Leon Verdi Goldsworthy RNVR. On one occasion he made three dives, each lasting for over twenty minutes, to tackle a mine that was so corroded that it was unusually difficult to withdraw the fuse. Shortly after that he disarmed a mine that the crew of a fishing drifter had found in the North Sea. They decided that it was a menace where it was and so they hauled it aboard their boat and, to the horror of the harbour authorities, sailed proudly into West Hartlepool with it.

After that, he disposed of underwater mines at Sheerness and in the Thames. Then he went to Southampton and dived to a couple more there. They were badly distorted and gave him a good deal of trouble and, as a result of this feat, he was decorated with the George Medal.

Six months later, in April 1944, he disarmed an acoustic mine that had lain in deep water off Milford Haven for over two and a half years and had refused to respond to efforts at conventional mine sweeping. Following this exploit he was given the George Cross and became one of the very few who are entitled to wear both decorations.

Another officer who can wear both the George Cross and the George Medal is Lieutenant John Bridge RNVR. He was given the latter award for handling mines in 1940 and was decorated with the George Cross for underwater work at Messina in 1944. But what is particularly interesting is that he was actually recommended for the George Cross when he was given the Medal. Actually, Lieutenant Bridge might well discover that he was recommended for the G.C. in 1940 from this book, for although, in practice, people are sometimes told that they have been recommended for an award, this is generally regarded unethical and is contrary to service regulations. In this particular case the Admiralty felt that there was no harm in releasing the information in view of the fact that he eventually received the award. At the time, however, the blitz was at its height and acts of great gallantry were being performed almost daily. The George Cross had been newly instituted and recommendations for its award were being received in large numbers. But the King was anxious that it should be as highly cherished as the Victoria Cross and there were fears in official quarters that it might lose its value through being awarded too liberally. As a result, recommendations were very carefully screened and many acts of gallantry that might well have been recognized by the award of the George Cross at other times were only rewarded with the lesser award.

Lieutenant Bridge's work at Messina was made necessary by a dramatic change in the war situation. The Allies were advancing and Hitler and Mussolini were on the run. Ports and harbours that had been in enemy hands for three years were falling to the British and American armies. But the Germans and the Italians were not running so fast that they did not have time to make things difficult for the advancing Allies and they paid particular attention to the matter of rendering ports and harbours as difficult to use as possible. Cranes and other dock operating machinery were smashed with explosives, barges and lighters were holed, ships that were of no value, or could not be removed, were sunk alongside quays and in harbour mouths, and every variety of mine was strategically placed to produce as much dislocation as possible.

The Americans entered Messina on 16th August 1943, and, in accordance with a prearranged plan, they handed it over to the Royal Navy on the following day. A quick reconnaissance of the area revealed the fact that there were no less than two hundred and fifty explosive charges of one sort or another scattered around the area of the quays, forty of them below water. Two naval parties were sent to deal with the situation and, almost within hours, every member of the first party had either been killed or wounded. The trouble was a new and unknown type of mine.

Lieutenant Bridge arrived in charge of the second party and, despite the heavy casualties that had been suffered by the first, he immediately set to work on clearing the mines. He tackled a group of six of the new type himself and, after making no less than twenty-eight dives, he not only rendered them all safe but salvaged several of their fuse mechanisms. Whilst this work was going on Messina harbour was being shelled from the mainland of Italy.

By the day before the date planned for the assault on the mainland, Messina harbour had been cleaned up and made safe for shipping, the area of the quays had been thoroughly surveyed, and eight hards for Tank Landing Ships had been built.

The naval parties that had gone into Messina had had no specialized training in harbour clearance or in disarming mines under water and, in fact, no parties that specialized in this type of work existed at this stage of the war. However, experience there, and in some of the North African ports, convinced some members of the Admiralty that there was an urgent need to set up and train such parties before the Allies went into France.

Brains were applied to the problem and thought focused on devising some mechanical method of clearing underwater mines from harbour basins. However, all these efforts failed and, in the end, the people who had been studying the problem became convinced that it was a job that could only be done by divers and that the training of these divers was a matter of consider-able urgency. But the job was obviously going to be a very dangerous one and there were several senior officers in the Admiralty who thought that it was too much to ask of men. Thus, it was in the face of strong opposition that permission was eventually given to set up a school for the training of what eventually came to be known as 'P' Parties.

The first essential in this new enterprise was to find a Chief Instructor and it is doubtful whether a more suitable one could have been found than the man that the Admiralty picked. His name was Lieutenant-Commander John Stuart Mould RNVR and he was yet another holder of both the George Cross and the George Medal. He was, in fact, the very first man to win both awards.

Mouldie, as he was familiarly called, was an Australian architect and he was particularly well suited to his dangerous war-time occupation. In the first place, he was highly intelligent and thought out everything he did with great care. He combined this quality with a particularly placid and cheerful personality and an unassuming self-confidence. He had great powers of leadership and was able to persuade men to follow him into anything.

He had been awarded his decorations for outstanding work on the disarming of new types of mines and his George Cross citation made special reference to some that he had to deal with in particularly filthy, arduous and exacting conditions in the Hamble River.

It was essential that the 'P' Parties should be trained to do more than deal with mines that happened to be stumbled upon. They must be able to give an assurance that a captured harbour was free of mines and safe for shipping, and this involved a thorough search of the whole sea bed within the area of a harbour. Mould, together with experts from the Admiralty, made a thorough examination of the problems and it was eventually decided that the only method would be to lay a complete grid of ropes over the area to be searched and then to get divers, wearing non-magnetic diving suits and carrying their own air supplies, to work up and down the grid, feeling every inch of ground with their hands, until the whole of it had been covered.

The first parties were trained in the London Docks but when the flying bombs started to arrive it was decided that the underwater blast effect from any that landed in the river would be lethal to divers working there. Hasty arrangements had to be made to find an alternative training area and this was no easy

matter, for every stretch of water that was suggested turned out
either to be too deep, too shallow or too clear, for it was
thought essential that the conditions likely to be found in the
harbours of the north coast of the Continent should be simulated
as far as possible. In the end the school moved to Barrow-in-
Furness where it stayed for several months until a more suitable
site for it was found at Brixham in Devon.

It was at Brixham that another Australian officer turned up
to be trained in underwater mine clearance, George Gosse, a
bearded Lieutenant of the R.A.N.V.R. with a strong bent for
anything mechanical, and completely fearless. Before he came
to England he had been clearing Japanese mines at Calcutta.
He decided that the Admiralty had probably had no experience
of these and so he brought one home with him and, afterwards,
took delight in recounting the story of the speed with which
it helped him through customs barriers.

George Gosse loved to experiment and he set up his own
workshop in a cellar at Brixham and there he produced many
useful improvements to diving gear and tools for the handling
of mines underwater.

The time and effort devoted to the training of the 'P' Parties
was not wasted and two of them sailed with the British con-
tingent in the Normandy landing. They cleared the little port
of Ouistreham at the mouth of the Caen Canal, and then went
on to the inland port of Caen, which they were able to report
as being safe. Two more went with the Americans and made a
thorough examination of Cherbourg, where they only found one
underwater mine but had to deal with a large number that
had been left on a quayside. These parties followed the Allied
advance eastward and were able to report that Dieppe had
not been mined but they had some work to do in Boulogne.
At the inland port of Rouen they found twenty-one mines and
also had to help in the clearing of wrecks.

When Antwerp, once the world's third largest port, was
captured four 'P' Parties went in and they had a miserable
time, for winter was approaching and the water was icy cold.
The sailors had not even the satisfaction of finding many mines
but, as always, they had plenty to do in helping with the

clearance of sunken ships. They also had to deal with an unexploded flying-bomb that had landed in the water. Whilst
the work at Antwerp was going on a further party went to
search Zeebrugge but found nothing but wrecks.

V.E. Day brought no respite and parties went into Hamburg
and Bremen and, although they found no mines in the former
port, this was not the case at Bremen, and it was here that
George Gosse, now commanding one of the parties, won a
George Cross.

The locating of many of the mines there was not difficult,
for more than one German was ready to say where they were,
but they also supplied the alarming information that several
of them were of a new type that they called Oyster mines, and
they claimed that they were fitted with devices that would
make it impossible for any diver to touch them. Gosse decided
to investigate this matter personally.

He experienced two difficulties when he dived to examine
one. In the first place the water was so muddy that he could
not see what he was doing and had to work almost entirely by
touch. Secondly, for some reason, he had difficulty with his
buoyancy so he overcame this problem by tying himself to the
mine and then gave his full attention to the job. He had made
a very careful study of all known types of mines and, putting
faith in the methodical ways of the Germans, he had formed a
preconceived idea of the principles that would be employed in
this new weapon, and he had also worked out a plan to beat
them if his guess was correct. It was and, after a short while,
he surfaced with the mine's primer in his hand.

Next morning he lashed a rope to the mine and dragged it
out of the water to make a thorough examination of it. He
found that it was booby trapped and would have exploded
either if he had tried to remove the fuse mechanism in the
orthodox way, or if any attempt had been made to raise the
mine without first rendering it safe. After that he dealt with
two more Oyster mines and the remainder were detonated
under water. Altogether, forty-eight mines were accounted for
in Bremen.

After that, Mould flew off to the Far East to make arrangements for 'P' Parties to operate in harbours that were being won back from the retreating Japanese. Gosse stood by to take the first party there, but the sudden and unexpected arrival of V.J. Day made this unnecessary.

A few weeks later the training establishment at Brixham was closed down and the men of the 'P' Parties went back to less dangerous peace-time occupations. But they had the satisfaction of knowing that, on the continent of Europe, they had accounted for 159 mines and 171 other types of explosive charges. Miraculously, their only fatal casualty had been one man killed when a V1 struck a cinema in Antwerp.

Two other naval officers won the George Cross for disarming explosive weapons and, in both citations, reference was made to their gallantry in dealing with the torpedo machines in which the Italians specialized. One of these weapons finished up in fifteen feet of water in St. George's Bay, Malta. The nature of its mechanism was quite unknown but it was eventually found that it was fitted with four different impact and hydrostatic firing devices and it also had a time fuse. The main charge weighed six hundred and fifty pounds. It was disarmed by Lieutenant William Ewart Hiscock RN who went on with his task despite the fact that a clock started to tick in the middle of the operation.

Lieutenant George Herbert Goodman MBE, RNVR, disarmed a similar weapon on the North African coast in spite of the fact that, a few days earlier, two officers of H.M.S. *Medway*, the submarine depot ship, had been killed attempting the same thing. In addition, Goodman disarmed fifty-three parachute and moored mines at different times.

The responsibility of the Royal Air Force in the field of bomb disposal was for the clearance of airfields and other R.A.F. establishments, and six awards of the George Cross were made to members of the junior service for work of this kind. One of them was the first member of the R.A.F. to be decorated with the new distinction—albeit posthumously.

He was Squadron Leader Eric Lawrence Moxey, who was employed as a Technical Intelligence Officer at the Air Ministry. He went out to deal with many of the German bombs that fell on British airfields in the summer of 1940 and risked his life many times. Then, on 27th August 1940, he was called to deal with two that had fallen on the important Battle of Britain airfield at Biggin Hill and one of them went off when he was examining it. The London Gazette that announced his decoration was dated 17th December 1940.

Strangely, the next R.A.F. officer to be decorated with the George Cross won the award for removing bombs from ships. (The official citation does not explain why an R.A.F. officer should have been dealing with bombs in ships and I have failed to discover the answer to this. However, it should be realized that, whilst the spheres of responsibility of the three services for bomb disposal work were laid down, in moments of emergency they were by no means strictly adhered to, and often unexploded missiles of all sorts were dealt with by the nearest expert rather than the person designated in regulations.) He was Squadron Leader John Noel Dowland. In February 1940 he disposed of a bomb that had landed on the deck of the steamship *Kildare* and become wedged there with its nose projecting below the planks. Four months later another bomb became similarly wedged in the deck of a trawler and again Squadron Leader Dowland removed it.

Each of these dangerous operations was successful and Dowland escaped the death that so many of his comrades met. But fate is often cruel and this brave officer died before he received his George Cross.

Squadron Leader Dowland was helped in the dangerous task of removing the bomb from the *Kildare* by Leonard Harrison, a civilian Armament Instructor stationed at R.A.F. Manby. Mr Harrison, who had previously served for twelve years in the ranks of the R.A.F., was also concerned in the handling of several other unexploded bombs and his bravery was also recognized by the award of the George Cross.

Another member of the R.A.F. to be similarly decorated was Flight Lieutenant Hodgson Charlton who was concerned in the disposal of over two hundred bombs. He must have borne a charmed life for he survived the staggering number of risks he ran and lived to receive his award from the King.

Another officer who survived a very large number of bomb disposal incidents and also received the award was Wing Commander John Samuel Rowlands MBE, who was continuously engaged in this work for a period of over two years.

The last member of the R.A.F. to be decorated with the Cross for bravery in handling bombs did not perform his act of gallantry until after the end of the war. During the clearing up operations in Germany one of the tasks of the R.A.F. was the dumping at sea of stocks of Luftwaffe bombs, and one day in August 1946, some of these were being moved from a railway truck to a barge at Lubeck, when one of a batch of twelve exploded.

By some stroke of good fortune the other eleven did not detonate but there seemed to be little doubt that their electric fuses had been rendered shock-sensitive and there was grave danger that they might go off at the least movement. Close by, there was a train with a further hundred tons of German bombs in it.

Squadron Leader Hubert Dinwoodie OBE, MC, in charge of the operation, decided that the safest line of action would be to disarm the fuses of the eleven bombs and, helped by a corporal and an aircraftsman, he worked for several hours at this difficult and dangerous task, accomplishing it successfully. His two companions were also decorated, one with the George Medal and one with the British Empire Medal.

++

CHAPTER IX

AIRCRAFT IN DISTRESS

SEVERAL George Crosses have been awarded to members of the Royal Air Force and the Royal Canadian Air Force for acts of gallantry in connection with crashed or burning aircraft since the outbreak of the Second World War. In addition, one has gone to a civilian member of the Air Ministry Works Department, one to a farm labourer, and one to a woman, a corporal in the Women's Auxiliary Air Force.

The first member of the service to be decorated in this way at the beginning of the war was Flying Officer Reginald Cubitt Graveley, who received the E.G.M. in November 1939. Two years later, it was replaced by the George Cross, and according to an article that appeared in the January 1951 issue of *Aeronautics*, Flying Officer Graveley somehow managed to retain his original E.G.M. when he received his G.C.

He must have been one of the first Royal Air Force casualties of the war, for it was only seventeen days after it began that the aircraft he piloted was shot down by a German fighter over France. As the aircraft struck the ground its fuel tanks caught fire and, within seconds, it was enveloped in flames. Graveley, although badly burned, managed to scramble clear and then he realized that the other two members of the crew were still inside the aircraft. Despite his injuries he went back through the flames and managed to extricate his observer. Then he went back a second time to get the air gunner.

He found the man strapped in his seat, dead. He decided, however, that it was his duty to get him out and, for some seconds, he struggled to release the dead man. His efforts were in vain and eventually Flying Officer Graveley was forced to make his way to safety alone, his clothing blazing. By some miracle and thanks to the skill of the surgeons he lived to receive his George Cross.

The next award went to Mr Harold Francis Charrington, Assistant Civil Engineer at Middle East Air Headquarters who, in the early days of the war, was flying as a passenger in an R.A.F. plane over Palestine when it ran into bad weather and suddenly went into a spin at 7,500 feet. The pilot did everything possible to regain control of the machine but failed. Then he ordered his passengers, Mr Charrington and another man, to bail out.

Mr Charrington was just about to climb from the aircraft when he noticed that his companion was in difficulties and unable to get out. Immediately, he returned to his side to help him. He struggled furiously to release the man and, as he did so, the plane plunged steadily down towards the rugged Palestine hilltops below. It was a desperate fight against time but Harold Charrington won it. Eventually he managed to heave the other man clear of the falling plane. Then, with barely a second to spare, he climbed out of the machine himself, pulled the release cord of his parachute, and floated to the ground below. If his jump had been delayed another moment he would undoubtedly have been killed.

A few months after this incident two further E.G.M.s, later converted to George Crosses, were awarded to two junior ranks of the R.A.F., Leading Aircraftsman Michael Campion and Aircraftsman Ernest Ralph Clyde Frost. Both these men were members of 90 Bomber Squadron, operating from Upwood.

One evening, as the Blenheims of the Squadron were taking off for a bombing mission, two of them collided on the ground and one of them heeled over and burst into flames. All the members of the crew except the pilot climbed out to safety, but he had been knocked unconscious and lay helpless in his cockpit. The danger of the aircraft's full petrol tanks exploding was great, but the two airmen, who had rushed onto the scene, ignored it and climbed into the machine and pulled the injured man to safety. They had scarcely dragged him clear when the flames reached the fuel tanks and the wreckage was burnt out completely in little more than seconds. Unfortunately the pilot died a short while later.

A few days later Corporal Joan Daphne Pearson of the

6

Women's Auxiliary Air Force was looking from the window of the W.A.A.F.'s quarters at Detling, in Kent, watching the bombers returning from a night mission. She noticed that the engine of one of them was coughing slightly as it approached the runway but thought little of it until she noticed flames coming from one wing and she saw the machine crash on the edge of the airfield.

Corporal Pearson dashed from her hut to the scene of the crash and was the first person to reach it. Accounts of what took place then differ: according to one report she climbed onto the plane and helped the badly injured pilot to escape, whereas another eye-witness has said that the pilot was actually clear of the machine when she arrived and being helped along by two other members of the crew. Whichever is the truth, it is established that her next action was to tell the other two men to make their own way to the station sick bay to have their burns dressed whilst she took charge of the pilot.

He could not walk and was in very severe pain, but between his moans, he told her that his machine had a full bomb load and that the bombs were liable to go off at any moment. The girl acted quickly and, spotting a low bank some yards off, she dragged the man to the other side of it. She had no sooner moved him there than the first bomb went off and Corporal Pearson threw herself on top of the man and shielded him with her own body. She remained on top of him until it seemed clear that there were no more bombs to explode.

She comforted the pilot until a stretcher party arrived and he was taken off. Then she returned to the burning aircraft to look for the fourth member of the crew. She found him—the wireless operator—dead inside the bomber.

A month later the Corporal was commissioned and became an Assistant Section Officer. She served throughout the remainder of the war as an officer with Bomber Command.

There were few more dull and generally unexciting duties in the war-time R.A.F. than those that came the way of the several thousand Auxiliary Airmen who manned Britain's balloon barrage system. Not unnaturally, very few aircraft, either friendly or hostile, came near them and their day was largely taken up with unvarying routine. One corporal of this service, however, was decorated with the George Cross for entering a burning crashed aircraft. His name was John McIntosh McClymont.

In January 1940, McClymont was serving with 18 Balloon Centre at Bishopriggs, near Glasgow. The winter of 1939-40 was a very bitter one and in Scotland there was not a day in January when the ground was not covered with snow. On the 18th, there was a particularly heavy blizzard in the Glasgow area and whilst it was at its height the men of 18 Balloon Centre, struggling to keep warm, suddenly heard the note of a low flying aircraft, and then a dull crash.

Several of the Auxiliary Airmen made their way towards the area from which the sound came and the first man to find the plane was Corporal McClymont. It was a Blenheim bomber and it was on fire. The Corporal went up close to it to try to find out if there were any of the crew still on board and through the flames he saw something that looked like a man. Without hesitation he climbed up into the burning fuselage, reached the man, and began to pull him clear of the wreckage. As he did so, he saw a second man lying close by.

Corporal McClymont succeeded in getting the first man clear of the blaze and then made a second trip into the plane and dragged out the second one. McClymont was badly burnt and, unhappily, both the men that he pulled from the Blenheim were already dead.

Two months later the pilot of another Blenheim, Flying Officer Anthony Henry Hamilton Tollemache, of 600 Squadron, operating from Manston, struck a tree whilst he was making a night landing. He was thrown clear of the plane and suffered no more than a few scratches and bruises. The remaining members of his crew, however, were imprisoned inside the Blenheim which quickly burst into flames.

Tollemache fought to rescue the trapped men until he was so badly burnt that he was incapable of doing anything more. Unfortunately his efforts were also in vain and he nearly died of his injuries. His bravery was recognized by the award of the E.G.M.

In the same month a farm labourer called Gerald Winter was working in a field in Sussex when an R.A.F. plane crashed on a hilltop named Jeffries Point, which lies to the north of Brighton. It burst into flames, ammunition began to explode, and the gorse bushes around it were set on fire.

Winter hurried to the spot, running through three hundred yards of blazing gorse and scrub, and dived into the plane and pulled an aircraftsman from the after part of the machine. The man told him that the pilot and the navigator were still trapped in the forward cockpit and Winter immediately climbed in again and tried desperately to get the two men clear. This was not possible and, after some moments of struggling, he was eventually forced by the heat to abandon the task. He was decorated with the E.G.M. and, eventually, the George Cross.

In June 1940 another pilot, Pilot Officer Edward Donald Parker, was decorated with the E.G.M. for rescuing his stunned wireless operator after he had crash landed his Hampden bomber shortly after taking off from Scampton where his unit, 40 Squadron, was based. The plane had full fuel tanks and bomb rack and was burning fiercely when Parker re-entered it. He had scarcely pulled the wireless operator clear of the machine when the bombs began to explode.

Pilot Officer Parker was the last member of the R.A.F. to receive the E.G.M. for, a few days after his award was gazetted, the institution of the George Cross was announced. Three years later this brave officer failed to return from a bombing mission.

Although there have been several senior officers who have held the Victoria Cross, only one officer, who later reached the rank of General (or equivalent), holds the George Cross. He is Air Vice-Marshal Sir Laurence Frank Sinclair.

On 30th September 1940, Sir Laurence, then a Wing Commander, was watching a Blenheim bomber take off from the R.A.F. Station at Wattisham when it suddenly burst into flames. The machine carried a full bomb load and, as the Wing Commander ran towards it, one after the other they began to explode. He was undeterred by the detonations, however, and climbed up into the blazing aircraft and pulled out the gunner. Unhappily the man later died.

The circumstances in which Aircraftsman Vivian Hollowday won the same award were unusual in that his citation referred to two entirely separate but remarkable similar incidents.

Hollowday was stationed at Cranfield and, on an evening in July 1940, he had been off duty and was making his way back to the station when he saw an aircraft crash on the airfield not far from where he was walking. The machine caught fire, but the aircraftsman ran to it and, climbing on board, found that the pilot was trapped in his cockpit and his clothing was burning. Hollowday had nothing to fight the fire with except his bare hands and with them he put out the flames and then pulled the pilot from the plane only to find that he was dead.

A month later Hollowday was again returning to the same station when exactly the same thing happened. Again he rushed to the burning plane, but this time the heat was too intense for him to enter it and he was forced back when he tried. Bombs and ammunition were exploding all over the place and adding to his difficulties.

By now, an ambulance had appeared on the scene and Hollowday grabbed some blankets from it and wrapped himself in them. Then he borrowed a gas mask from somebody, put it on, and managed to enter the aircraft. He remained in the inferno for several seconds and then reappeared carrying a man. He made two more trips into the flames and brought out two more of the plane's crew.

Fate can be a cruel thing. Once more this very brave airman's heroism was in vain for all three of the men that he extricated were already dead. To date, nobody has won the George Cross twice, but Vivian Hollowday is one of the few who surely deserved the double award.

Another aircraft captain to be decorated for saving one of his crew was Sergeant Pilot Raymond Mayhew Lewin. On 3rd November 1940, he took off from Malta as pilot and captain of a Wellington bomber but the great machine had scarcely become airborne when it began to lose height again. A moment later it struck a hillside and was soon enveloped in flames.

Lewin climbed clear but he had been badly bruised by the crash and had broken a knee-cap. As he lay on the ground, clear of the burning bomber, he watched two of the three other members of the crew climb out and pull themselves to safety, but there was no sign of the third man, his second pilot. Lewin waited for a few brief seconds but the missing man did not appear and then, in spite of his severe bruising and the intense agony of his broken knee, he ordered the other two members to get clear of the danger of exploding bombs, climbed back into the Wellington himself and pulled to safety his second pilot, who had been trapped inside.

But the two men were only safe from the flames of the burning fuselage. The full fuel tanks in the Wellington's wings, below which Lewin had just crawled, were still intact and there was a full load in the bomb bay. The captain could do no more than crawl and the man he had rescued could not even do that. Somehow, Lewin dragged him across forty yards of rough ground until he found a shallow hole in the ground and he slid into it and pulled the other man in behind him. They had barely reached the spot when a huge sheet of flame lit the night sky and, a second later, the aircraft's bombs went off. Both men survived their ordeal.

The first member of the Royal Canadian Air Force to be decorated with the George Cross was Leading Aircraftsman Karl Mander Gravell who was being trained as a wireless air gunner at 2 Wireless School, Calgary, when the Moth Trainer in which he was flying crashed and caught fire. Despite the fact that he lost an eye and was badly burnt he went back to the plane to help the pilot. He dragged him clear of the machine and then rolled on the ground to extinguish the flames that were leaping from his own clothing. The pilot survived but Gravell died of his burns and the decoration that he earned was posthumous.

Three other R.C.A.F. men won the Cross including Leading Aircraftsman Kenneth Spooner, who was also on an instructional flight as a student navigator when he performed the feat of heroism that was recognized by the award. Shortly after the Anson in which he was flying left the Training School, at West

Freugh, the pilot suddenly collapsed over the controls. There were three others in the machine apart from Spooner and everyone rushed forward to see what had happened. They found that the pilot had fainted and nothing anyone could do would bring him round.

None of the others was capable of handling a plane and Spooner, the senior, took the initiative. He seized the controls himself and ordered the other three men to bail out. After a short argument they obeyed this order and all three of them landed safely. Leading Aircraftsman Spooner tried, for the first time in his life, to land an aeroplane but his attempt was unsuccessful and both he and the unconscious pilot were killed.

Six weeks later an Air Commodore of the R.C.A.F., Arthur Dwight Ross OBE, performed an act of bravery that was also recognized by the award of the George Cross. He was present at Tholthorpe when a Halifax, making a night landing, slewed off the runway and crashed into another bomber that was waiting to take off. The second plane had a full bomb load and, within seconds, both planes were on fire and there was grave danger of the bombs going off.

Air Commodore Ross made a wild rush to the scene and succeeded in extricating the pilot and rear gunner of the Halifax. Whilst he was in the plane one of the bombs went off and he lost an arm from the blast. A flight sergeant, a corporal and two airmen, all of the R.C.A.F., followed him into the burning machines and helped in the work of rescuing members of the two crews and they were decorated with either the George Medal or the British Empire Medal.

The last member of the R.C.A.F. to receive the George Cross was Flying Officer Roderick Borden Gray. He was the navigator of a Wellington that was shot down over the sea by a German U-boat. The bomber crashed on the water and for a moment there was confusion. Gray managed to grab hold of a two-man inflatable dinghy and, although one of his legs was badly hurt he somehow managed to get the tiny craft afloat and to scramble aboard. Then he paddled around to see if he could find any other member of the crew and soon he came on the captain who was floating in the water, badly wounded.

He pulled him into the dinghy and a few minutes later Gray heard cries and made for the place they were coming from. There he found another airman, floating in the sea with a broken arm. The navigator manoeuvred his tiny boat alongside the man and then slipped over the side and helped him on board. There was no room for a third man in the dinghy and so Gray himself clung on to the side of it. Later in the night he died and the body of a brave man floated gently away from the two comrades that he had saved.

Another Wellington navigator, Sergeant Graham Leslie Parish, was also posthumously decorated with the Cross. His bomber was being delivered from the United Kingdom to the Middle East when it crashed on an airfield in the Sudan and Parish lost his life in an attempt to rescue a passenger who had broken his two legs. Both men perished in the burning Wellington.

The first member of the R.A.F. to be awarded the George Cross for a similar act of bravery after the war, also won it in the Middle East. He was Sergeant John Archibald Beckett, a member of the ground staff at Eim Shemer, in the Levant Command. On the 16th December 1947, he was engaged in the task of refuelling a Lancaster when a petrol tanker caught fire and began to blaze fiercely.

Beckett was badly burned by the flames but he immediately jumped into the cab of the burning lorry and drove it four hundred yards away from the Lancaster and some twenty other planes that were parked nearby. The planes were all saved but a fortnight later Sergeant Beckett died of his burns.

Two more George Crosses have been awarded to members of the Royal Air Force since the war and both were posthumous. The first of them was awarded to Aircraftsman Ivor John Gillett, a ground-crew fitter. He was working on a Sunderland flying-boat at its mooring in the R.A.F. Flying-Boat Base at Seltar on 26th March 1950, when a fire broke out on board and the machine blew up. Several men were killed and the survivors were thrown into the water.

Amongst those who escaped instant death were Gillett and an R.A.F. corporal who was a great friend of his. They had not been in the water for long when a rescue launch raced to the scene. Its crew spotted Gillett but failed to notice the corporal who was struggling in the water close by and, as a result, a single lifebelt was thrown into the water before the launch rushed off again to look for other survivors.

The lifebelt landed close to Gillett and he caught hold of it and then passed it to his friend who was badly injured and, at the best of times, was a poor swimmer.

Some while later the launch reappeared and picked up the corporal. But there was no sign of Ivor John Gillett. A couple of days later his body was washed up on the beach. Doctors examined it and it was clear to them that he had been badly injured by the blast of the explosion. Obviously he had been in as much need of the lifebelt as the friend to whom he had thrown it.

In the following year Flight Lieutenant Alan Quinton DFC won the award for an act of self-sacrifice that was very similar in character. On 13th August he was a passenger in the rear compartment of a Wellington bomber that was involved in a mid-air collision. The Wellington broke up and the portion in which Quinton had been seated plunged earthwards, separated from the rest of the machine.

There was one other occupant of the rear compartment, a young cadet of the Air Training Corps. Immediately after the crash, Quinton looked round for some means of escape and he found a single parachute. Grabbing hold of it, he clipped it on to the harness that the cadet was wearing and, pointing to the rip-cord handle, pushed the youngster through a gaping hole that opened up in the side of the compartment.

The cadet pulled the rip-cord and floated down to the ground where he made a safe landing. Flight Lieutenant Quinton stayed in the rear compartment which fell like a stone and he was killed instantly when it hit the earth.

+++

CHAPTER X

EXPLODING AMMUNITION

FEW things can be more terrifying than fire or explosion amongst ammunition, and the natural instinct of any normal man is to put the greatest possible distance between himself and any ammunition or explosives that remain. But often bold action can prevent further catastrophe, and there are brave men who are ready to take such action.

Norman Tunna of Birkenhead was such a man. In 1922, when he was fifteen years of age, he followed in his father's footsteps and found himself a job on the railway. He started as a wagon checker but, by the outbreak of the war, he had worked his way up to the post of first-class shunter.

In the days of the blitz, Merseyside was selected as one of the major targets of the Luftwaffe, and Liverpool and Birkenhead suffered grievously. One evening, at the height of it all, Norman Tunna left his wife and small son and set off for the marshalling area alongside the Birkenhead docks, to work a night shift. At 7 p.m., when he had been on duty for an hour, the sirens wailed and Tunna and his mates put on their steel helmets, dimmed their oil lamps, and carried on with their job of assembling trains.

Searchlights were turned on and narrow pencils of light swept backwards and forwards across the black sky. In the distance the guns began to fire and their flashes were reflected from the clouds. Then the low drone of German bombers could be heard and the sound grew louder. As it reached a crescendo there was a whine, not unlike the sound of flighting duck, and a score or more of incendiary bombs rained down amongst the docks, warehouses and wagons in the marshalling yard. A moment later they were blazing fiercely and a large shed beside the yard was burning in several places. Behind it, other fires were breaking out and, within minutes, flames were rising from all over the area.

Alongside the burning warehouse stood a train of railway wagons loaded with ammunition, explosives, bombs and petrol. Tunna knew what was in those wagons and the danger of the situation. His instinct must surely have been to get as far away as possible but, instead, he shouted to the driver of a shunting-engine to back it up to the train and then he coupled the leading wagon to it. He moved away to signal to the driver and then, to his horror, he saw that a fire was burning under the tarpaulin cover of one of the trucks. It was loaded with 250 pound bombs for delivery to the Royal Air Force.

Tunna kept his head and ran up to the engine, filled a bucket with water, raced back to the burning wagon and threw the water on the flames. Then he untied the cords that held the cover to the wagon and pulled it off. He found that an incendiary was wedged between two of the bombs and that the latter were becoming very hot. He seized hold of something to use as a lever and tried to dislodge the incendiary but it was firmly jammed. He turned his attention to the bombs and, somehow, managed to lever them apart until their grip on the incendiary was relaxed and he was able to knock it clear and throw it over the side of the truck to the ground.

Someone else took charge of the incendiary and Tunna turned his attention back to the truck-load of bombs and found that several of them were very hot indeed. He rushed off to a signal-box for a stirrup pump and a bucket of water and sprayed them until they were cool.

When he was satisfied that the load of bombs was safe he went off and joined a party engaged in fighting one of the fires in the warehouse. An hour or so later, when all the nearby fires had been extinguished, he returned to his job of assembling a train that was due to leave in the morning and he carried on with this task until 6 a.m., when his shift was over.

There can be very little doubt that, but for Norman Tunna's cool-headed and courageous action, the wagon load of bombs would have exploded and, in all probability, all the other trucks of explosives and petrol would have gone off as well. His gallantry was recognized by the award of the George Cross and he went to the Palace to receive it from the late King, dressed in his railwayman's blue uniform, a very appropriate, if unusual, dress for the occasion.

Norman Tunna was not the only railwayman to be decorated with the George Cross. It was given to two others and they also were decorated for bravery in handling a burning ammunition truck.

Quite how this particular truck caught fire has never been revealed and is probably not known. All that is known is that one day, in 1944, Driver Benjamin Gimbert was driving the engine of a goods train made up of some fifty wagons of ammunition and explosives. As he was passing through a station, somewhere near Cambridge, he found that the signals were against him and he stopped his train. Then he glanced behind him to see if all was well and was horrified to find that the wagon immediately behind his engine was burning fiercely. Close by there were the station buildings and, not far away, several houses, shops and other property.

Gimbert sized up the situation quickly and turning to his fireman, James William Nightall, he told him to disconnect the coupling behind the burning truck.

Nightall did as he was told without hesitation and then ran back to rejoin his driver in the cab of the engine. Gimbert released the vacuum brake, opened the steam cock, and headed the engine and the blazing wagon for the open countryside beyond the station.

Some distance out of the station there was a signal-box and there, Gimbert stopped his engine and jumped out of the cab. He shouted to the signalman and told him to stop any other train from entering the section. Then he turned to remount his engine and, as he did so, the wagon exploded. Nightall was killed instantly but, though he was very severely injured, Gimbert survived.

The George Crosses that were awarded to Norman Tunna, Benjamin Gimbert and James Nightall were in recognition of acts of great personal gallantry but all railway workers took pride in them. And it is right that they should have done so for, although these three men were singled out to receive this high distinction, and many more railwaymen received lesser awards, their bravery typified the spirit of the thousands more who were given no reward but faced with fortitude daily hazards and dangers in keeping Britain's railways going during the difficult days of the blitz.

There are probably very few people who know that, on 13th June 1941, a serious underground explosion took place at Loch Laggan in the Scottish Highlands. A vitally needed aluminium plant was being set up close by and it was necessary to dig a tunnel to provide a water supply. Labour was short and, as the job was urgent, the Ministry of Supply was loaned the services of a detachment of No. 1 Tunnelling Company of the Royal Canadian Engineers. The detachment consisted of one officer and fifty-three other ranks, all hard-rock miners.

On the day of the explosion Corporal James Hendry was in charge of an underground working party. Suddenly fire broke out in the powder magazine and Hendry was one of the first men to see what had happened. His immediate thoughts were for the safety of others and he ordered his men and civilians who were working alongside them to take cover. Then, having satisfied himself that everyone else was as safe as possible, he made his way towards the burning magazine to try, single-handed, to get the fire under control.

He never reached the place. As he came near to it the hill-side was shaken by a violent explosion and the brave corporal was killed. One of his men died as well and two others were injured, but the casualties would undoubtedly have been far heavier but for Corporal Hendry's prompt orders to them. His posthumous decoration with the George Cross was not promulgated until April 1943, and even then no details of the circumstances of the award were contained in the London Gazette.

Several other George Crosses have been given to men who displayed great courage when ammunition and explosives were on fire. Two of them belonged to the Royal Army Ordnance Corps and they were Major Kenneth Alfred Biggs and Staff Sergeant Sidney George Rogerson.

In January 1946, Major Biggs was commanding one of the Sub-Depots of the Royal Army Ordnance Corps, Command

Ammunition Depot at Corsham, near Bath. This depot has existed for a long time and its stocks are safely housed in underground tunnels in the nearby hills. During the late war, however, it had to expand and fresh areas for storing ammunition and explosives had to be found. One place that was chosen was the famous beauty spot, Savernake Forest, in Wiltshire. There, in the deep glades of the great forest, it was possible to erect hundreds of little corrugated iron ammunition shelters that were safely hidden from hostile reconnaissance aircraft. This was the Sub-Depot that Major Biggs commanded.

Although the war had been over for nearly six months, Britain still had large forces abroad, and overseas stocks of ammunition had to be replenished. Thus the men of the Sub-Depot were still working hard and regular trainloads of mines, shells, small-arms ammunition and explosives were still leaving the sidings that had been built in the forest.

At 3 p.m. on the afternoon of the 2nd January a train was being loaded there, and, on another line alongside the half empty trucks, stood a full train of ninety-six loaded ammunition wagons. Suddenly there was a violent explosion and a three-ton lorry, used for bringing ammunition from the shelters to the siding, and two railway wagons, literally disappeared. Then fire broke out at a dozen points around the yard. A wagon-load of five-point-five inch shells, some distance off, went up and the fire spread further. Small arms ammunition started to explode in every direction and the scene became more like a battlefield than anything else.

Eight men died in the original explosion and six more were badly hurt. There were, in fact, few of the original working party left to do anything about the terrifying situation. However, the noise of the explosions brought men hurrying from all over the area and one of the first to arrive was Staff Sergeant Rogerson.

Rogerson made a quick survey of the scene and, realizing that he was the senior non-commissioned officer on the spot, he at once took charge. He collected together the few uninjured men who remained and others who had arrived on the siding. With great calmness and a total disregard for danger, he split the men up into small parties and detailed each party to one of the fires that was burning. He gave one party the terrifying task of unloading an explosives truck that was close to a bad blaze and then he climbed under a burning truck full of shells to rescue two badly injured men. As further reinforcements appeared on the scene he gave them the job of carrying the wounded to safety, or sent them to join the fire fighting parties.

Some minutes later Major Biggs arrived and took over command. He remained as cool and calm as Rogerson had done and one of the first things he did, with the help of another officer, was to uncouple a burning wagon full of shells from the rest of the train and push it clear of the other trucks. Then he set to work extinguishing the fire. Next he organized the removal of other wagons to create fire breaks.

At about half past four there was a particularly heavy explosion and Biggs was thrown to the ground by the blast and badly shaken. He picked himself up again, however, and went forward to inspect the site of the latest detonation and to see if any further danger had been caused. He went alone to the spot, refusing to let anyone else go with him.

Soon after this he decided that everything possible had been done to remove unharmed loaded trucks from the burning ones, and that further efforts at fire-fighting could do little good and might well result in more loss of life. He therefore withdrew all his men from the siding and was the last to leave himself. But he did not go far. He stayed within sight of the siding, ready to deal with any fresh situation, until the last fire had burnt itself out, nineteen hours later.

People who saw the scene next morning have described it as a fantastic piece of devastation. No less than twenty-nine wagons had exploded and there was one crater that measured ninety feet across. A second one was nearly as big. Telegraph poles had been snapped like matchsticks and some of them thrown fifty yards. But over a hundred full or partly full wagons had been saved from exploding and there can be little doubt that this was, in large part, the result of the gallantry, determined leadership and high personal example of Major Kenneth Alfred Biggs and Staff Sergeant Sidney George Rogerson.

The award of the George Cross to these two men was announced in the London Gazette of 11th October 1946, together with details of eight other awards, including two George Medals, to eight other members of the Royal Army Ordnance Corps, the Royal Army Service Corps and the Royal Pioneer Corps who had helped to fight the fire in Savernake Forest.

1946 was an unfortunate year for ammunition accidents for, two months after the fire in Savernake Forest, there was a very unpleasant explosion on Hong Kong island in which a driver of the Royal Service Corps, Joseph Hughes, was killed when his three-ton truck, loaded with mixed ammunition, exploded. He was posthumously decorated with the George Cross.

He was delivering his load to the magazine in Lyemun Barracks and had just stopped alongside the doors of the magazine and gone round to the back of his truck to lower the tail board, when he noticed that one of the ammunition boxes was smouldering. He went forward to grab hold of it and pull it from the back of the lorry when it suddenly burst into flames and he found that he could not get his bare hands to it.

He then ran to the cab of his vehicle for his fire extinguisher and, as he was getting this, he heard an explosion in the back of the truck. He ran round behind the lorry again and found that it had only been a fairly minor explosion but that the fire was spreading rapidly. He dragged his blazing camouflage net onto the ground and then played his extinguisher on the blaze but it had little effect and, as he worked, there were several more small explosions.

There were a number of other soldiers and some Chinese in the area and some of them came towards the burning truck, but Hughes shouted to them to take cover and then he went for his second extinguisher and tried again to put out the fire. Again he failed and, as he stood beside his truck, suddenly the whole three tons of ammunition exploded and Driver Hughes was killed. But he did not die in vain for there is little doubt that his efforts delayed the explosion and gave time for everyone else in the vicinity to take cover. Had it not been for his courage, several other soldiers might well have been killed.

A corporal of the Manchester Regiment was also awarded

a posthumous George Cross for his bravery in dealing with exploding ammunition. He was Kenneth Horsfield, who joined a Territorial Battalion of his Regiment in 1939.

When the war broke out it was discovered that he had defective eyesight and, as a result, he was kept in England until 1942. He was employed on fatigues until somebody noticed that he was an intelligent man and he was posted for duty with the Special Air Service. Late in 1942 he was sent out to the Middle East and put in charge of packing explosives, an important commodity for that cloak-and-dagger section of the Army.

For a time he worked in the delightful little North African township of Derna and then his unit moved to Brindisi. There they were billeted alongside a Royal Air Force Squadron, with which they were co-operating, at a place that went by the name of Paradise Camp.

Corporal Horsfield was in charge of a part of the camp known as the 'Demolition Area' where a variety of explosives and other dangerous equipment was stored and packed in readiness for dropping over occupied Europe. One particular building was used to house mortar bombs and mines and it was here, at about lunch-time on 18th August 1944, that there was a violent explosion which killed two Jugoslav civilians and a British soldier who were working inside. Several other men were badly hurt.

Corporal Horsfield was working in another part of the Demolition Area at the time but he raced to the spot and found that fire had broken out in the building. He stopped everyone in the vicinity from approaching the place and went up to it himself. Looking through a window, he saw a man inside trapped by fallen rubble and he climbed in and tried to release him, but was driven back by the heat of the fire. Then he rushed off and fetched a 32-gallon fire extinguisher and, from the doorway, tried to keep the flames back from the trapped man.

Kenneth Horsfield clearly realized the danger of a further explosion but he disregarded it completely and devoted his efforts solely to the task of trying to save the man inside. A few seconds later a second explosion occurred and he was severely wounded by the blast.

He died of his wounds and was buried in a local cemetery. Later, his remains were removed to the British Military Cemetery at Bari. The announcement of his award appeared in a London Gazette in March of the following year.

Five soldiers have been awarded the George Cross for throwing themselves on to bursting hand-grenades to save the lives of their comrades, and it seems hardly necessary to say that these awards were all posthumous. As it is difficult to believe that any of these men thought they stood any chance of survival, they must surely rank amongst the very bravest of the many brave men who have been decorated with the award.

The first of them was Lieutenant William Foster of the 7th Battalion the Wiltshire Home Guard. He was instructing a party of recruits in grenade-throwing from a slit trench when one of the men threw one badly and it struck the parapet in front of the trench instead of going over it. It lodged there for a second or so and then began to roll backwards towards the trench. By the time that it dropped at the feet of the half dozen men in the trench its fuse had a bare second left to burn. Lieutenant Foster reckoned that there was not time for him to pick it up and throw it clear again so he threw himself on the bomb and was killed. There can be little doubt that most, if not all, of the other men who were in the trench owe their lives to his brave action.

In August 1943, Major André Gilbert Kempster of the Royal Armoured Corps, lost his life in precisely the same manner as Lieutenant Foster. The incident happened on a practice range at Philipville, in Algeria.

The third soldier to throw himself on a grenade was Private Charles Alfred Duncan of the Parachute Regiment. He was serving in North Africa at a place called M'Saken and, on 10th July 1943, his battalion should have made a parachute drop. After a long and weary wait on an airfield, however, the operation was postponed for some reason, and the troops returned to the camp. They went back to their billets and started stripping off their equipment and stowing away their arms.

All the paratroopers had live grenades in their pouches and

one of the first jobs that they had to do was to render them safe again by unscrewing the base-plates and removing the primers and fuses. Several of them were engaged in this when there was suddenly a clatter as one of Private Duncan's grenades fell to the floor. There would have been no danger if the safety pin had been in and Duncan stepped unconcernedly across the room to retrieve the thing. But then he noticed that the pin was, in fact, out and the fuse was already burning. He did the only thing that could have saved the lives of his comrades.

Five months later the same brave act was performed by Private Joseph Henry Silk of the Somerset Light Infantry. He was on active service with the 1st Battalion of his Regiment in Burma and was sitting in a jungle clearing with other members of his platoon, cleaning their weapons when, somehow, the pin came out of one of his grenades and it rolled down a short slope in front of him. Silk shouted, 'Look out' and, without a moment's hesitation, he hurled himself after the weapon and clutched it to his body. The grenade exploded almost at once and Private Silk was killed instantly.

It was also in Burma that Lance-Naik (Lance-Corporal) Islam-Ud-Din of D Company, the 6/9th Jat Regiment, gave his life in this way to save his comrades, at Pyawbwe, on 12th April 1945. He, also, was with a party of men who were cleaning their weapons when the pin came out of a grenade. His Company Commander, who rushed to the spot on hearing the explosion, said afterwards that he had found the remains of this brave soldier lying face downwards on the ground with his arms clasped to his chest.

A very similar act was performed by another Indian non-commissioned officer when he threw himself on to an anti-personnel mine. Subedar Subramanian of Queen Victoria's Own Madras Sappers and Miners, had the distinction of being the first member of the Indian Army to win the George Cross. This happened during the Italian campaign, at Cassino, when the Subedar was in charge of a small party that was engaged in mine clearance.

He was walking through the minefield, operating a mine-detector, when a Lance-Naik following behind him stepped on a Schumine. These are detonated by means of a pressure mechanism which fires a small charge which ignites a four-second fuse. The Subedar heard the initial detonation and, in a flash, he swung round and threw his body on to the mine, which went off a moment later. He was killed almost instantly, whilst a British officer and five other soldiers close by were unhurt.

Another Indian soldier who received the Cross posthumously for giving his life to save his comrades was Naik Kirpa Ram of the 8th Battalion, the Frontier Force Rifles. During a field-firing exercise in September 1945, a grenade fired from a discharger by one of his section fell short, landing only about eight yards in front of the troops. Ram shouted to his men to take cover and then he dashed forward and picked up the grenade. Presumably he intended to hurl it as far away as possible, but it went off in his hand.

The force of the explosion was taken by the Naik's body and, as a result, none of his section was more than slightly injured. Kirpa Ram, however, was mortally wounded and he died very soon afterwards.

A Canadian soldier was also decorated posthumously for doing the same thing. He was Sergeant John Rennie of the Argyll and Sutherland Highlanders of Canada, and he was killed at Slough, near Thetford, on 20th November 1943.

Sergeant Rennie was instructing recruits in throwing grenades from a trench when one of his men misthrew one and it rolled back. Rennie ran to the spot to pick up the grenade but, as he leaned down to grasp hold of it, it exploded. His body shielded the blast from three other men who were standing only five yards off.

The circumstances in which Signalman Kenneth Smith of the Royal Corps of Signals won his posthumous decoration were not dissimilar. He was a member of the famous Long Range Desert Group but, on 10th January 1945, he found himself, not in the desert, but on the Adriatic island of Ist.

The place was in a state of confusion and nobody knew who was friend and who was foe. There were many loyal partisans who were ready to risk their lives helping the liberation forces and there were others who still thought that subservience to Hitlerism was, at least for the moment, the safest course to follow. Acts of sabotage were daily events and both the Germans and the British were equally vulnerable.

It was in this general state of confusion that Signalman Smith went to take a breath of fresh air outside the little partisan homestead in which his detachment had set up its headquarters and suddenly heard rifle shots in the neighbourhood. He was not sure who was shooting at whom but he decided that his proper place was beside his wireless set and he dashed into the room where it had been set up. There, close to his wireless he saw an unfamiliar object. He examined it and noticed that there was a ticking noise coming from it and he realized that it was a time-bomb.

In the house there were other members of his detachment, partisans, and several young children, and so far as Smith knew the bomb was liable to go off at any moment. He did not hesitate but picked it up and hurried out of the house and made towards a low wall, presumably with the intention of throwing the thing over it. He had covered half the distance to the wall when the bomb went off and the Signalman was blown to pieces. He did not die in vain for nobody else was even hurt, but those who saw the explosion said that there was little doubt that, but for his gallant act, several of them would have been killed.

One member of the Royal Air Force also died dealing with exploding ammunition. He was Leading Aircraftsman Albert Matthew Osborne who was posthumously decorated with the George Cross for fearless courage in dealing with many fires amongst aircraft and torpedoes during the siege of Malta. He met his end fighting a fire that had broken out amongst a stack of torpedoes when one of their air-vessels detonated when he was pouring water over them.

It is perhaps sometimes forgotten that one of the most dangerous occupations is the manufacture of explosives and, in wartime, this industry has to be much expanded. Thus, it is not surprising that several George Crosses were won by men engaged in this work.

The earliest of these awards went to three workers in the Royal Gunpowder Factory at Waltham Abbey, in Essex. These men were originally decorated with the E.G.M. On 18th January 1940, Leo Francis O'Hagen and Stanley William Sewell were engaged in a particularly dangerous task, the nitration of glycerine, when there was an explosion in another part of the factory and this caused a failure in the supply of hot water and air needed to complete this stage in the manufacture of nitro-glycerine, a stage in which the explosive is in its most unstable state, liable to detonate at the smallest disturbance. There was over a thousand pounds of material in this highly dangerous condition.

News came that efforts were being made to restore the air and water supplies and O'Hagen and Sewell decided to stay at their post ready to stabilize the nitro-glycerine at the earliest possible moment. But it took over two hours to repair the ruptured pipes and throughout that time O'Hagen and Sewell remained at their workplace, doing what they could to prevent the nitro-glycerine from detonating. Then as soon as the air and water came through they went on with their task and rendered the explosive stable.

Equally dangerous is the task of purifying the high explosive and, in another part of the factory, William George Sylvester was busy on this job when the explosion occurred. He also needed air and water but found himself without either and there was grave danger of the nitro-glycerine freezing and detonating.

He also remained at his post until the services were restored and was decorated with an E.G.M. that was subsequently replaced by a George Cross.

Two months after these events another explosives worker was similarly decorated but, this time, posthumously. He was John McCabe, Assistant Foreman in a Royal Ordnance Factory. On 2nd April 1940, he was on duty in a section of the works when he realized that the explosives that were being manufactured were not behaving normally. He did what he could to restore the situation but fire broke out in one of the mixing vessels. He at once tried to empty the contents of the vessel into the 'drowning pit' but he failed and the fire began to spread to other vessels.

The danger of a serious explosion was now acute and he ordered everyone else to leave the building. Then he returned to the task of trying to empty the blazing tank of chemicals. A moment later there was a violent explosion and John McCabe was killed instantly.

Later in the war another member of the staff of a Royal Ordnance Factory, a factory Development Officer named Richard Arthur Samuel Bywaters, also won the George Cross. He was employed at a factory at Kirkby, near Liverpool, which, amongst other things, was turning out 150,000 anti-tank mine fuses a week.

Fuses of all sorts are essentially sensitive things but, in addition, the fuse of an anti-tank mine incorporates an unusually powerful explosive charge. Thus when, at 8.20 on the morning of 22nd February 1944, one of these fuses was accidentally detonated and caused twenty-four others to go off as well, it was not surprising that the results were devastating. Two girls were killed and another wounded, whilst the part of the factory in which the incident happened was badly damaged. But the danger had not passed, for in addition to the twenty-five fuses that had exploded, there were over twelve thousand there that had not gone off but were in a highly sensitive state.

There was only one thing to do and that was to remove them all to a place of safety where they could be destroyed. Richard Bywaters volunteered to take charge of this highly dangerous operation and, assisted by three other men, he removed 12,724 fuses from the factory. These gallant men worked at this job for two full days and they finished it in the late afternoon of the second day.

During the course of the operation no less than twenty-three fuses were found to be in a critically sensitive condition and, as each of them was discovered, Bywaters ordered the other men to take cover whilst he removed them himself. One of them was so near to the point of detonation that it was thought that it would go off at the slightest movement. Bywaters moved it from the building with the utmost care, and to avoid the necessity of carrying it too far, he arranged for a steel box and sandbags to be placed at a short distance from the factory. Using these to muffle the explosion he detonated the thing there.

Richard Bywaters' George Cross was well merited, for explosives experts subsequently calculated that his chances of surviving the task that he undertook were insignificant. However, remarkable heroism was rewarded by remarkable good fortune and this young man survived and, seven months later, he again displayed great pluck when he was concerned in another even more serious explosion in the same factory, and was decorated with the George Medal. (Several holders of the George Medal have subsequently been decorated with the George Cross but Richard Bywaters is unique in having received the two decorations in the reverse order.)

Whilst many of those who have won the George Cross have previously had a reputation for fearlessness—sometimes to the point of recklessness—and their award has come as no great surprise, this is by no means true of everyone who has received that high distinction. The story of Nora Inayat-Khan, who wrote fairy stories for children, has already been told and another equally unlikely candidate was Simmon Latutin, a sensitive professional musician of Russian-Jewish extraction.

His father was born in Riga and bore the same name as General Vatutin, the hero of Kiev. As a young man, he emigrated to England and, in translating his name, the 'V' became an 'L'. In London, he met and married a Polish girl, Simmon Latutin's mother.

Simmon had an artistic temperament and his parents sent him to study at the Royal Academy of Music. At the age of twenty he achieved the unusual distinction of being selected as a member of the London Symphony Orchestra. Then came the war and he was called up.

He suffered from poor eyesight and was drafted into the Royal Pioneer Corps. Eventually he was selected for training at an Officer Cadet Training Unit and was commissioned into the Somerset Light Infantry. In 1943 he was selected for service as an instructor in East Africa and, soon afterwards, he was made O.C. of the Somaliland Gendarmerie Training School,

at Mogadischu. The climate there did not treat him kindly
and he developed ulcers that refused to heal. He was sent to
the Military Hospital in Nairobi and, after treatment there,
was flown back to Mogadischu again, still wearing plaster.

He arrived back there in December 1944, and one day soon
afterwards he went to a storeroom where another officer, a
sergeant-major and a native boy were selecting rockets and
explosives for a New Year entertainment. For some unknown
reason, as he was standing in the doorway, fire broke out in the
store and hundreds of rockets began to explode. Within seconds
the place became a white-hot inferno and the three men inside
fell to the ground, torn by the blast and badly burned by the
hot flames.

Without hesitation, Captain Latutin dashed through the
bursting rockets into the store and succeeded in dragging out
the officer. Then, his clothing blazing, he returned and came
out again with the sergeant-major, who was by then quite
naked with every stitch of clothing burnt from his body. Had
he been able, he would undoubtedly have gone in a third time
for the native boy but the heat had become too intense and
Captain Latutin was too badly burned for him to take any
further part in the incident. He lived throughout the following
night but his injuries were mortal and, next day, he died.
Simmon Latutin may not have been physically strong, but he
more than made up for this in toughness of spirit and, in the
final test, that short-sighted, sensitive musician died as gallantly
as any other man.

The most recent award for dealing with exploding ammunition was made posthumously to Sub-Officer George Campbell
Henderson of the Gibraltar Dockyard Fire Brigade on 20th
November 1951. He died directing fire-fighting operations
when a lighter loaded with ammunition and explosives caught
fire in the harbour. It lay alongside the Naval Armament Vessel
Bedenham which had had to be abandoned on account of the
risk of explosion.

The fire was virtually out of control, the heat intense, and
the grave danger of the situation obvious to all, but single-
handed, George Henderson climbed aboard the *Bedenham* with

a hose and succeeded in directing a jet of water into the burning lighter. For some moments the tongues of flame seemed to leap less fiercely into the air and it began to look as though there was some faint chance of getting the fire under control. But they were also creeping amongst the boxes and cases that held the ammunition and hope was ended when the whole island was shaken by a violent explosion. The entire cargo had detonated and Sub-Officer Henderson was killed instantly.

++

CHAPTER XI

BRAVERY AT SEA

F E W men live closer to danger than sailors, and in times of war their perils are increased. During World War II the activities of enemy aircraft, submarines and surface raiders caused the loss of thousands of brave lives throughout the oceans of the world. Our losses were tragically severe amongst the ships of the epic Malta and Russian convoys. There can be little doubt that this situation must have produced almost daily acts of supreme heroism, and it seems surprising, therefore, that only ten George Crosses have been awarded for bravery at sea. (This number does not include a small number of G.C.s that have been given in replacement of E.G.M.s.) Probably it was because gallant deeds were daily events and were accepted as a normal standard of conduct that few were singled out for special recognition.

The first war-time award of the George Cross to a sailor was made posthumously to Commander Richard Frank Jolly RN, who originally received the posthumous award of the E.G.M.

Soon after the outbreak he was patrolling thirty-five miles off the east coast, in command of the Tribal-Class Destroyer *Mohawk*, when the vessel was attacked by German aircraft that dived on it and sprayed the decks with machine-gun fire. Possibly the sailors had yet to learn the need to take cover quickly when enemy planes appeared, or perhaps they were just unlucky. Whatever the reason, casualties were heavy and, as the planes banked and roared away into the distance, followed by anti-aircraft fire, a score of men lay on the deck badly wounded.

Commander Jolly had been on the destroyer's bridge and he was struck by several bullets, a number of them entering his stomach. One of his officers moved to his side and suggested he should leave the bridge and go for medical aid, but he refused and gave orders for the *Mohawk* to head for harbour.

For the next hour and twenty minutes the Commander remained on the bridge and continued to direct his ship. At intervals his officers tried to persuade him to leave but always he refused. They made his Surgeon-Lieutenant try to get him below and Jolly answered, sharply:

'Leave me alone. Go back and look after the others.'

Eventually the Commander's voice became so weak that he was unable to make his orders heard and had to whisper them to his Navigating Officer who relayed them. But he stayed on at his post until he had taken the *Mohawk* into harbour and given the order to shut down the main engines. Then he collapsed and was carried from the bridge. Five hours later he died.

The award of the E.G.M. to Commander Richard Jolly was announced in the London Gazette of 23rd December 1939, and it was one of the very few posthumous awards of this decoration that was subsequently converted to the George Cross.

Another naval officer who received the E.G.M. in the early days of the war was Sub-Lieutenant Alexander Mitchell Hodge RNVR. He was serving in an aircraft carrier when there was an explosion in the bomb-room. Smoke rose from the room to the main deck and it looked as though there was a serious fire below.

Sub-Lieutenant Hodge was one of the first people to notice the smoke and he realized where it was coming from. Immediately he raced to the bomb-room and tore open the door. Inside, the place was in darkness and it was very hot and full of fumes. Several badly injured men were lying on the floor.

Hodge was far from clear about what had happened but one thing was fairly obvious, and that was that the bomb-room, and possibly the ship as well, was liable to go sky high at any moment. He was undeterred by this prospect, however, and one by one he dragged the injured men outside. Then he found two more men trapped beneath heavy bombs and he struggled to free them. He failed in this and rushed away for assistance, returning with some ratings and eventually getting the men clear.

Although there was no further explosion this did not make Sub-Lieutenant Hodge's valour any less conspicuous for, throughout the time that he spent getting the injured sailors from the bomb-room, all the indications pointed to the probability of a violent detonation at any moment.

Four other members of the Royal Navy were posthumously decorated for acts of gallantry at sea and these acts were practically identical. The awards were made as the result of two incidents and, in each, an officer and a rating lost their lives because they placed devotion to duty before personal safety. On each occasion two men remained on board a sinking submarine until it was too late to escape. Each time both knew the danger that they faced and could have made their escape if they had been so minded. The two incidents differed only in that one of the submarines was British and the other was a captured German U-boat.

The men who lost their lives in the British vessel were Lieutenant Niven Angus Low RN, and Able Seaman Henry James Miller, both of the British submarine *Unity*. *Unity* left her berth in the small Northumberland port of Blyth for patrol duty in the North Sea on 29th April 1940. The harbour was shrouded in fog when she slipped her moorings and, as she sailed slowly away from the land, it grew denser. But, in wartime, fog had certain advantages and *Unity*'s Captain knew that, although he had to face its inevitable hazard, at least he was safe from spotter aircraft and, in any event, he would soon be able to submerge and the fog would trouble him no longer. But, unhappily, he was never given the chance.

At 7 o'clock in the evening *Unity* was still moving slowly through the fog, in relatively shallow water, when a siren sounded directly ahead. Her Captain at once gave the order, 'Hard to starboard,' but the submarine had hardly started to move from her original course when a second siren sounded, closer than the first, on the fine starboard bow. He gave the only command that was possible in the circumstances: 'Full speed astern; shut the watertight door.'

Slowly *Unity*'s speed slackened as her propellers threshed the water but it was too late. She was still moving forward when the bows of a large freighter loomed up out of the darkness. It was the Norwegian *Atle Jarl* and the submarine lay right in her course. A look-out in the freighter spotted her and shouted an alarmed warning to the bridge, but before the Norwegian's Captain could give an order, there was a sickening jolt and the noise of tearing metal. The *Atle Jarl* had torn a gaping hole in *Unity*'s port side and the sea was pouring through it.

Within a minute she was lying at an angle of twenty-five degrees and water rushed through the open conning-tower hatch. Orders were rapped out in both vessels and the *Atle Jarl*'s boats were lowered. In the submarine, the command was, 'Stop the engines! Abandon ship!'

At the time of the accident there were two men on duty in the submarine's control room, Lieutenant Low and Able Seaman Miller. When the order to close the water-tight doors was given, Low at once dashed off to obey it and had just succeeded in shutting one of the engine-room doors when the order came to stop the engines and abandon ship.

Sailors moved quickly from all parts of the submarine and made for the conning tower. There was a good deal of confusion and congestion in the restricted entrance, for it was clear from the steep angle at which the vessel lay and the noise of water rushing in through her side, that she was not likely to stay afloat for long. It was hardly surprising that some of the sailors were frightened and there were shouts of alarm and men began to struggle for position.

Low immediately took command of the situation. He shouted:

'Steady up, boys! There's no need to panic. There's plenty of time, so take it easy.'

His words had an immediate effect and signs of panic vanished. The men queued up to make their escape and Low, aided by Miller, helped them up the sloping exit route to safety. Then, as the last man was on his way, the young officer turned to the able seaman and said:

'Come on now, quickly! Get that door closed whilst I shut down the engines.'

Miller went off to close a door and Low returned to the

engine-room. As the last man to leave the ship went by he noticed that he had just succeeded in shutting down one of the main engines and was calling to Miller to help him with the other one.

All these events took place within the space of three minutes. Then *Unity* vanished below the water taking two brave men with her. Every other member of the crew got clear before she went down and all but those two were picked up by the *Atle Jarl's* boats.

It is sad to reflect that Lieutenant Low and Able Seaman Miller could have made their way to safety as well and that there was no real value in their remaining behind to shut down the engines. But that is unimportant. What matters is that in accordance with the highest traditions of the Royal Navy, they stayed behind to carry out their Captain's orders without any thought for their own safety.

The German submarine that sank with a British officer and rating in her was the U 559. In October 1942, she was on patrol in the Mediterranean and, under cover of darkness on the night of the 29th, she surfaced to charge her batteries and take in fresh air. As the first rays of the sun began to creep above the horizon her commander gave orders to prepare to dive, but he was unlucky and had left his command too late for, far away, the look-out noticed a tiny speck in the sky. It was a British aircraft on a dawn patrol, and the U 559 was just the kind of target it was seeking.

The U-boat crash dived and the pilot of the aircraft signalled back to his base. His information was at once relayed to the commander of No. 12 Destroyer Flotilla and, within a short time of the submarine submerging, His Majesty's Ships *Packenham*, *Hero*, *Dulverton*, *Hurworth* and *Petard* were racing to the spot that the pilot had indicated.

The destroyers were soon in the area and making a wide sweep of it in an effort to locate the U-boat on their instruments. For well over an hour no trace of the vessel was recorded and the destroyers separated to sweep a wider area. Then one of them signalled that she had picked up something and the Flotilla commander closed up the other ships. Then the recordings were lost and the destroyers fanned out once more.

This desperate game of hide-and-seek went on all through the day. Most of the destroyers, at one time or another, picked up faint signals on their instruments but always they lost the U-boat again. But gradually, from this information, it was possible for the Flotilla commander to form an idea of her approximate position and course, and to close his destroyers around her.

Eleven hours after the message from the aircraft had been received, *Dulverton*'s instruments showed that the U-boat was lying close by. She raced towards the spot followed by great spouts of water as her depth charges exploded behind her. A few moments later the U-boat surfaced between *Petard* and *Hurworth* and both ships opened up with their 4-inch guns. The U 559 was holed on the water line forward of the conning tower and a moment later, her crew came out on deck and her commander signalled a message of surrender.

Petard and *Hurworth* lowered their boats and took off the Germans, for the U-boat was beginning to sink. Then *Petard* came alongside and passed lines around her, fore and aft, to try to keep her afloat. One of them snapped like a piece of string under the weight of the water-logged vessel and another attempt was made to support her with a stronger line but it seemed certain that she was doomed.

It was at this point the First Lieutenant of *Petard*, Lieutenant Francis Anthony Blair Fasson shouted, 'Come on, for God's sake, someone! She's going down. We must get her papers and instruments.' Then he jumped from the forecastle of his own ship on to the deck of the U-boat and climbed into the top of the already half submerged conning tower. He was immediately followed by Able Seaman Colin Grazier. Another officer and a couple of ratings went after them.

When Fasson reached the control room he was already waist deep in water and it was practically pitch dark but he seized hold of some books and papers and handed them to somebody to take on board the *Petard*. Next he found a large and heavy metal document box and managed to get it up the conning tower, in spite of the fact that, by now, water was beginning to pour down it.

From the bridge of the destroyer it was clear that the U-boat could not stay afloat for more than seconds longer and the Captain ordered everyone to get clear of her. A Petty Officer climbed down the conning tower and shouted:

'Come on, sir. She's going down fast. Captain says everyone must come off.'

In the dim light of an electric torch he had a brief view of Lieutenant Fasson, struggling with an axe to break some instruments from a bulkhead in the control room. Grazier was doing something somewhere in the gloom of the background. Fasson answered:

'O.K. I won't be long. I must just get these things. I think they could be important.'

The Petty Officer climbed out of the U-boat and hauled himself back on to the forecastle of H.M.S. *Petard* and, as he did so, the lines that were supporting the U 559 snapped and she disappeared like a stone below the waters of the Mediterranean.

One soldier was decorated with the George Cross for bravery at sea. He was Jenkins Robert Oswald Thompson, a Captain of the Royal Army Medical Corps. He was one of the Army's many seagoing soldiers and he spent most of the Second World War as a Medical Officer in H.M. Hospital Carriers, more commonly known as 'Hospital Ships.'

In May 1940, he was serving in the Hospital Carrier *Paris* and, when the evacuation of Dunkirk began, *Paris* was sent across the Channel to help with the removal of sick and wounded. At that time the most unpleasant place this side of hell was the foreshore and the sea that lay off the little strip of coast between La Panne and Dunkirk for the area, thick with weary soldiers and ships of all sizes, was under constant artillery and air attack whilst, later on, German heavy machine guns added their contribution to the general beastliness as their bullets spattered the water with an effect like showers of pebbles thrown from the shore.

A Hospital Carrier might have been a relatively safe haven for it was adorned with Geneva Crosses that could be recognized from a distance of several miles. But, either by design or as the

7

result of criminal carelessness, the device proved to be without significance and the *Paris* received no less attention from the enemy than any other of the thousands of vessels that were engaged in the task of removing the British Expeditionary Force from the continent of Europe.

Conditions in the carrier were far from pleasant but there was a job to be done and the crew, doctors and nursing staff went on with it quietly, doing their best to turn deaf ears to the roar of battle going on around them. Their only defence lay in their somewhat inadequate tin hats, slightly hysterical little jokes when something dropped particularly close, and occasional tots of rum and brandy from the hospital store.

The only sign of panic came from one or two of the shell-shocked patients who, having come so far, found these last hours of waiting more than they could bear. Amongst the crew and the staff of the carrier there was nothing but calm efficiency, as more and more wounded men were brought on board and given such treatment as was possible.

In conditions such as these it seems surprising that the conduct of any one man should have earned particular notice. The complete disregard of all danger that was displayed by Captain Thompson was, however, noticed by many people and, in particular, by his superiors. They also noticed that, in addition to having nerves of steel, he also seemed to be tireless and, when there were patients to be treated, he simply went on and on without a break for sleep or meals.

From the *Paris*, Thompson was drafted to the *St David*, and in her he served in the Sicily, Salerno and Anzio landings and on each occasion the Hospital Carrier was shelled and dive bombed. Each time, again, Captain Thompson displayed the same utter disregard of danger that he had shown at Dunkirk.

It was at Anzio, on 24th January 1944, that the *St David* suffered a direct hit from a dive bomber and began to sink. Many of the casualties in the ship were stretcher cases and were unable to make their own way to the boats. Thompson's only thought was for them and he seized hold of everyone who could walk or hobble and organized parties to carry the badly wounded to safety. His conduct was such an inspiration that hardly a fit man gave a further thought for himself and everyone set to work with such energy that every single patient except one was carried to safety.

The one patient who failed to get away had been trapped below decks when the bomb struck the ship and, by the time that it was certain that the *St David* could only remain afloat for seconds more, all efforts to release him had failed. The order 'Abandon Ship' was given and with the exception of Captain Thompson, everyone made their way to safety as best they could. But the doctor went below to make a last attempt to free the trapped patient. The task was a hopeless one and the *St David* took two men to the bottom of the Mediterranean with her.

The Reverend Herbert Cecil Pugh MA, won his George Cross in similar circumstances. On the 5th July 1941, he was one of 1,300 passengers in the Troop Carrier *Anselm*, en route for Takoradi, in West Africa, where he was due to take up his office as a chaplain with the Royal Air Force.

Soon after first light a German U-boat slipped through the screen of destroyers that guarded the convoy and there was a streak of silver on the dark water of the Atlantic and then a deep rumble and a crash somewhere close to the *Anselm*'s water line.

The troopship heaved in the water and it was obvious that she was doomed. Boats and rafts were lowered and frightened men scrambled down ropes or jumped into the water to reach them. But there was one man whose only preoccupation seemed to be to comfort others, and clad only in pyjamas and a dressing gown, he hurried round the decks consoling the frightened and the injured, and helping men over the ship's side. In some remarkable way he seemed to be everywhere and there were few survivors who did not recall meeting him at one stage or another.

When it was clear that the *Anselm* could only remain afloat for a few more moments Padre Pugh discovered that there were a number of airmen trapped in a damaged part of the ship and all efforts to get them out had failed. He asked if it was possible to lower him to them and was told that it was but that there

7A

was not time. If he went down, the chances were that he would never get out again.

The chaplain's reply to this comment was:

'Those men need me. Let me down.'

His mind was clearly made up and, much against his better judgement, one of the ship's officers lowered the chaplain into the damaged hold.

The scene below was illuminated by a pale shaft of light and, in numbed silence, the officer watched the chaplain as he signalled to a small party of frightened men. They gathered round him and he said some words that the officer could not hear but it was not difficult to guess at their meaning. The chaplain sank to his knees on boards that were already inches deep in water and some of the airmen knelt beside him. Others stood silently in the background. Padre Pugh joined his hands together and lifted his face towards his God and, as the water rose around his body, his lips moved in prayer. The water reached his shoulders and he remained on his knees. Then the stricken ship gave a final lurch and a stunned ship's officer made a last second dive to safety.

Behind him he left a Christian leader whose denomination does not matter. What does matter is that he went to his death with his faith unbroken and in communion with his Maker. What is regrettable is that the story of this act of supreme faith is not more widely known.

The first member of the Merchant Navy to receive the George Cross was James Gordon Melville Turner, who was serving as a radio officer in s.s. *Manaar* when, 120 miles west of Cape St Vincent, she was attacked by a U-boat three days after the outbreak of the war. The German vessel surfaced and, without making any signal to the merchantman, fired about ten shells into her at short range. One of them took away the fore part of the wheel house and another damaged the wireless mast, leaving the *Manaar* in the unhappy position of being both out of control and out of radio communication with the outside world. Her master decided to take to the boats and gave the order to abandon ship.

With one exception all the ship's officers went to their

appointed stations for this operation; James Turner, however, remained by the wireless desperately trying to get it to work. In the end he gave up the hopeless task and was making his way to the side of the ship when he found a badly wounded Lascar deck hand who had been left behind. He stopped to try to get him to safety.

Whilst he was doing this he heard a cry for help and, on investigating, he found that a native fireman had also been left on board and he was badly hurt. He carried this second man to the deck and put him in a lifeboat that was still hanging from the davits, and then went back for the first sailor. Whilst he was away, one of the submarine's shells hit the lifeboat and blew it and its occupant to pieces.

Luckily there was still one more boat and Turner managed to get the Lascar into that and to lower the boat into the water. A few moments later two torpedoes were fired into the stricken *Manaar* and she sank rapidly.

For his gallantry, James Turner was given the E.G.M. but, on 23rd November 1943, the King presented him with the George Cross.

It was nine months after the sinking of the *Manaar* before another member of the Merchant Navy won the George Cross and this award went posthumously to Gunner Henry Herbert Reed of s.s. *Cormount*. The vessel was on a voyage from Blyth to London when, at midnight on 20th June 1941, she was attacked from the air with cannon, machine gun fire and bombs. Reed was on duty manning a Hotchkiss gun when the attack began, and each time the German fighter-bomber dived at the *Cormount* he crouched behind his weapon and blazed back at the attacking aircraft. Bullets and cannon shells ripped great pieces of wood and metal from the little raised platform on which his weapon was mounted but the gunner did not flinch and went on pouring lead back into the air. Then, suddenly, out of the corner of his eye, he noticed that the ship's Chief Officer had been hit and was slumped over the deck rails close by.

Reed slid from his perch and picked up the injured man. Somehow he carried him down two ladders and laid him on

the deck in the shelter of a lifeboat. Then Reed himself dropped
on the deck beside him. A sailor ran to his assistance but he
found that Gunner Reed was dead. His stomach was full of
bullets—bullets that must have hit him before he even went to
the rescue of his Chief Officer.

Mrs Reed received her dead husband's award from the late
King on the 17th March 1942.

Shortly after this, Captain Dudley William Mason, Master
of the tanker *Ohio*, won the award for the gallant leadership he
displayed when he took his ship, its cargo on fire, into Valletta
harbour after five days of constant air attack. (Chapter 7.)

Two George Crosses have been awarded to members of the
Merchant Navy for acts of gallantry when their ships were in
harbour, and the first of them was a young apprentice belonging to the ship's company of the Motor Vessel *San Emiliano*.

On 6th May 1941, the *San Emiliano* was lying alongside the
South Dingle oil jetty in Liverpool Docks, discharging a cargo
of petrol, when a bomb struck the jetty and broke the pipeline.
Petrol gushed from the hole and within seconds the jetty was
blazing furiously. There were not many men in the *San Emiliano*
at the time, for discharging a cargo of oil, once the flexible lines
to the jetty have been connected up and the pumps started, is
not an operation that needs many hands. One of the few members of the crew present was the apprentice, Donald Owen
Clarke, and at once he realized the danger of the fire spreading
to the ship, for there was petrol lying on the deck and showers
of sparks were being blown towards her.

Donald Clarke could have been excused if his immediate
action had been to dive overboard and swim for safety. But
this was not what he did; instead he devoted all his energies
to the task of saving his ship and his first act was to cut away
her moorings.

This prompt action did not prevent a number of fires from
breaking out in the tanker but they were quickly attacked by
Clarke and a few other sailors who had rushed to the scene.

More than once it looked as though the fire would spread to
the ship's main storage compartments but none of the men
allowed this to deter them in their efforts to gain control over

it. In the end it was extinguished and this was in no small part due to the bravery and resourcefulness of the young apprentice who was constantly in the forefront of the struggle.

It is tragic that this gallant boy did not live to receive the George Cross himself. A year later the *San Emiliano* was torpedoed and sunk and Donald Clarke was posted as 'missing, presumed drowned.' His father and mother went to Buckingham Palace to receive their dead son's award from the late King.

The circumstances that surrounded the award of the George Cross to George Preston Stronach, Chief Officer of s.s. *Ocean Voyager*, were very similar. This vessel was lying in Tripoli harbour on 19th March 1943, when she was struck by three bombs. Her cargo consisted of a mixture of ammunition and petrol and she quickly caught fire and some of the ammunition began to explode.

For a moment it looked as if her crew was about to panic and jump for safety but the Chief Officer took command of the situation and rallied them. At great personal risk he led a long and determined fight to get the fire under control, but in the end it became clear that the battle was a losing one and he gave the order to abandon ship. Soon afterwards a violent explosion shook the water-front and the *Ocean Voyager* disappeared for ever.

Two years after the end of the war an Able Seaman, Raymond Thomas Kelly, won the first peacetime George Cross to be given to the Merchant Navy. The award was posthumous.

Raymond Kelly was serving in the troopship s.s. *Empire Plover* when, on 18th March 1947, a wireless message was picked up giving the news that the Motor Vessel *Famagusta* was in difficulties in a violent storm in the Bay of Biscay. The *Empire Plover* made full speed towards the area mentioned in the signal, and arrived there on the following day. The *Famagusta* was badly battered and several sailors who had left her were swimming in the heavy sea.

A boat was lowered into the water in the lee of the *Empire Plover* but, as soon as it left the protection of the ship, it overturned. It seemed clear that the storm was too violent for any lifeboat to survive and the Master did the only other thing that was possible and lowered every available rope, ladder and scramble-net over the side of his ship.

Sailors climbed down the nets and ladders to give a helping hand to the struggling men in the water and three of the *Empire Plover*'s crew, including Raymond Kelly, entered the heavy sea and swam out to aid men who seemed to be too weak to support themselves any longer. Kelly swam out twice and brought two men back to safety. Then he went out a third time to a man who seemed to be on the point of drowning. He grasped hold of the man and, as he did so, a great wave surged over him. Men clinging to the nets and ladders strained their eyes towards the spot but all they could see was swirling foam and neither Able Seaman Kelly nor the man he had swum out to save was ever seen again.

The most recent George Cross to be given for bravery at sea was, like almost all post-war awards, posthumous. It was won by David Broadfoot, Radio Officer of the ill-fated Stranraer-Larne cross-channel ferry, *Princess Victoria*, which sank with tragic loss of life on 31st January 1953.

The vessel sailed for Stranraer at 7.45 a.m. and, soon after leaving Loch Ryan, was struck by a violent north-west gale accompanied by sleet and snow. Within minutes the great stern doors that were used for loading cars were buckled and burst open. The car-deck quickly became flooded and the ship took a ten degree list to starboard. All attempts to close the doors failed, as also did the efforts of the Master, Captain Ferguson, to turn the ship around and head back towards the Scottish coast. It was then that David Broadfoot sent out the first of many distress messages. It read:

'Not under command; car deck flooded; need a tug.'

No tug appeared, which was hardly surprising, and the storm grew worse. The next thing that happened was that the cargo shifted and the list became worse. Captain Ferguson decided that his only chance lay in heading through the gale for Larne. As the *Princess Victoria* sailed westwards, Broadfoot remained by his wireless set sending out message after message.

Late in the afternoon the Irish coast was sighted and it seemed as though the battle with the storm would be won, but fate was cruel and the motor vessel suddenly heeled almost on her beam and the order to abandon ship had to be given. The passengers remained calm whilst the crew made desperate efforts to launch the lifeboats, but this was an almost impossible task and they only succeeded in lowering two into the violent sea. One of these was immediately smashed against the ship's side.

In the meanwhile a coaster and a destroyer had reached the scene but neither of them was able to launch a boat and they were unable to give any effective assistance although the destroyer managed to pour some oil on to the water. The next vessel to get to the spot was the Donagadee lifeboat, but long before she arrived the *Princess Victoria* had gone to the bottom of the Irish Channel.

At six o'clock in the evening forty-four survivors were landed at Donagadee. Eighty-seven men, women and children were missing and amongst them were Major J. M. Sinclair, the Northern Ireland Minister of Finance, Sir Walter Smiles, M.P. for North Down, Captain Ferguson, and Radio Officer David Broadfoot. Nobody knew how any of them died with the exception of the radio officer who went down with his ship, still sending calls for help until the wireless mast of the *Princess Victoria* went below the dark water.

✦✦

CHAPTER XII

BEHIND WIRE

HAD all nations seen fit to honour the articles of the Geneva Convention concerning the treatment of prisoners-of-war it is unlikely that any of the inmates of prison camps would have qualified for the award of the George Cross. Unhappily, this was not the case and the decoration has been given to several servicemen and civilians in recognition of the heroic way they faced the dangers of captivity. The gravity of those dangers is evidenced by the fact that most of these awards were posthumous.

When one remembers the utter inhumanity of the Nazi concentration camps, where literally millions of Jews and other internees, including British resistance agents, perished miserably, it is surprising that German prisoner-of-war camps were, in the main, reasonably humane institutions. There were, of course, isolated instances of brutality and unnecessary privation but they were relatively few and far between.

It was in the Japanese prison camps that British servicemen —and civilians as well—had to suffer the severest hardship, brutality and privation though, strangely, to some extent this sprang from a curious form of military chivalry. Under his code the highest honour that can befall a Japanese soldier is to die in battle and the blackest disgrace is to be captured alive. The only honourable escape from this is suicide. Thus, in Japanese eyes, a prisoner-of-war is unworthy of proper treatment, a pitiable object fit only to be used as a target for bayonet practice or a beast of burden.

As a result of this distorted philosophy, many thousands of unhappy Britons were fated to suffer almost unbearable misery and a high proportion were murdered. Under these appalling conditions some lost the will to live but many more accepted their situation with grim stoicism. Others refused to be bowed and set an example of discipline and courage that fortified their comrades in a remarkable way.

One such man was Captain Matreen Ahmed Ansari, of the 7th Rajput Rifles, the second son of the Registrar of Usmenie University. Somehow, in his youth, he survived bubolic plague, cholera, and becoming a victim of the terrible influenza epidemic of 1918. In the mid-thirties he passed his Senior Cambridge examination and was selected for training at the Military School of Dehra Dun.

In the early part of the war Matreen Ansari served for short periods with the West Yorkshire Regiment and the Scottish Rifles and then he joined the 7th Rajputs in Hong Kong. With the fall of the island, Ansari became a prisoner of the Japanese.

For some reason that is not clear, the Japanese believed that he was a close relative of the Nizam of Hyderabad and this belief also persisted elsewhere, for it was repeated in the citation, dated 18th April 1946, that accompanied his award of the George Cross. In fact, it was without foundation and had been denied a year earlier in a letter to the *Times of India*, written by his younger brother, Lt.-Col. Masood Rafat Ansari. However, the Japanese stubbornly insisted in believing that, in Ansari, they had a very important prisoner.

The allegiance of an oriental race to an occidental King-Emperor was beyond Japanese comprehension and they had hopeful ambitions of spreading subversion in India with the aim of causing the collapse of the powerful Indian Army. Ansari, they felt, if properly handled, might be persuaded to bring pressure to bear on his important relative [*sic*]; to persuade him to dissent from loyalty to the British Crown and to take with him his several million subjects.

For a time the Indian Captain was treated well and his captors did everything in their power to persuade him of the wisdom of coming over to their side. His protestations that he was not related to the powerful Nizam resulted in understanding laughter. Then, when it became clear that this approach was fruitless, the Japanese tried to win over Ansari with the whip.

After a time, they realized that this method was proving as

ineffective as the other and, in disgust, the Japanese threw
their important captive into the notorious Stanley Jail. There,
over a period of several months, he was regularly subjected to
the most brutal treatment and prolonged periods of starvation.
As a result, he reached a stage when he was unable to walk and
had to be removed to a hospital, where, for a change, he
received fairly humane treatment.

When he recovered, he was moved to a camp for Indian
soldiers and was refused any of the privileges of an officer.
There, he started an organization for assisting prisoners to
escape and his plans were well advanced when a traitor gave
them away to the camp guards.

Ansari was returned to Stanley and, after a short stay, he
was marched before a Japanese military tribunal and sentenced
to death. A few days later he was beheaded.

Though Captain Ansari was now dead, his name lived on in
Stanley Jail. It became a byword for all the finest qualities in a
captive; refusal to accept defeat or to be intimidated by captors; above all, refusal to be diverted from the course of duty.
When the survivors of this Dachau of the East were eventually
liberated, all who had known Ansari, European and Asian
alike, spoke so highly of his conduct that his name was selected
for the posthumous award of the George Cross.

Ansari was not the only inmate of Stanley Jail to get the
posthumous award of the George Cross. Another was a civilian,
John Alexander Fraser, who had served in the First World War
as a Major in the Machine Gun Corps and had been demobilised with a Military Cross and bar, and a badly shattered leg.
Like another who won the George Cross—the Earl of Sussex—
he was a graduate of the University of Edinburgh.

When, in 1919, he was discharged from hospital, he joined
the Colonial Service and was sent to Hong Kong. In 1931 he
qualified as a barrister and was made Attorney General of the
Colony. With the entry of Japan into the Second World War,
he was appointed Defence Secretary and, a few months later,
he was a prisoner in Stanley Jail.

There John Fraser became involved in plans for communication with the outside world and he actually succeeded in

setting up a concealed wireless station. Because of his intimate knowledge of the country and of several Chinese dialects he was a particularly useful member of the camp escape organization. But, eventually, his part in the scheme was detected and he was subjected to savagely cruel treatment and eventual execution. He withstood everything with courage and fortitude that was particularly praiseworthy in view of the war wounds from which he suffered and the fact that he was well on the way to fifty years of age when he died.

Another officer who was similarly decorated for conspicuous bravery in the face of brutal treatment by the Japanese was Captain Douglas Ford of the Royal Scots and he, also, was captured in the fall of Hong Kong. He was sent to a camp at Shamsuipo and, on arrival there, he immediately set himself the task of establishing an underground organization, and by means that have not been disclosed, he made contact with a secret British organization in China.

At no small risk to himself he continued with this work for several months until the Japanese eventually realized that something was afoot and arrested two of his accomplices. Then, on 10th July 1943, Ford himself was arrested.

The Japanese were determined to uncover the whole organization and he was tortured, locked away in solitary confinement and kept, for weeks on end, on a starvation diet that did little more than keep him alive. Throughout all this he not only refused to give away any information but displayed a degree of cheerfulness and fortitude that not only inspired his fellow prisoners but even invoked the admiration of his captors.

On 1st December he was brought before a Court Martial, charged with espionage, and sentenced to death. For eighteen days after that he was kept in a cell and given no more than water and a few grains of rice, and even then he remained silent and cheerful. Finally this very brave officer was executed.

Although such evidence as exists shows that Captain Ford, a comparatively junior officer, was the ringleader in the organization at Shamsuipo, there were several senior officers in the same camp and several of them were active members of it.

As a result of Ford's silence, the Japanese never discovered who most of them were but a notable exception was Lieutenant-Colonel Lanceray Arthur Newham MC, of the Middlesex Regiment, who was arrested on the same day as Ford.

Newham was one of the leading spirits and the author of a scheme for a mass break-out. He was subjected to the same treatment as Ford and, like him, he refused to give away any information. His courage and self-control remained unbroken to the end when he died the same death and was also given the posthumous award of the George Cross.

Another captain of the Indian Army received the George Cross for bravery as a prisoner in Japanese hands and he was the only Japanese prisoner to be given this award and live to receive it in person. He was Mahmood Khan Durrani of the 1st Bahawalpur Infantry, Indian State Forces.

Durrani was cut off during the retreat in Malaya and succeeded in remaining free for three months until he was betrayed and made a prisoner. He resisted all his captors' efforts to induce him to become a member of the Japanese sponsored Indian National Army and, in fact, took active steps to thwart Japanese efforts to infiltrate members of that organization into India. His efforts were successful but, in the end, the Japanese became suspicious of him and tried to persuade him to admit what he had been doing. Their methods of persuasion included depriving him of food and sleep for ten days and burning his legs with cigarette ends.

Eventually Captain Durrani was sentenced to death by a Court Martial of doubtful authenticity, but this sentence was never carried out and he was subjected to further torture and periods of solitary confinement.

In spite of all his sufferings, Durrani refused to divulge anything about his activities and his consistent bravery was an inspiration to everyone. He was eventually liberated but, to this day, he still bears the marks of the torture that he suffered and his health has been permanently impaired.

The bravery of Major Hugh Paul Seagrim DSO, MBE, MC, of the 17th Hyderabad Regiment, also posthumously decorated with the George Cross, was significant in that, well knowing the horrors of captivity in Japanese hands, he deliberately gave himself up to them.

He was a member of a small patrol that was operating behind the enemy lines in Burma in 1943. It remained undiscovered for almost a year until a day when several members of his party were ambushed and killed. Seagrim, however, got away and was given shelter by Karen villagers, but the Japanese now knew of his existence and made sustained efforts to track him down. Amongst other things, they arrested no less than 270 of the Karens in the area and many of them were tortured and put to death in the most brutal manner.

Despite all this, the Karens who were sheltering Seagrim made no attempt either to get rid of him or even to suggest that he went. However, the Japanese succeeded in getting a message to him to say that, if he gave himself up, they would cease their reprisals. As soon as he heard this he walked out of the village where he was hiding and into the nearest Japanese camp.

He was sent to Rangoon with eight other members of his patrol who had previously been captured and, on 2nd September 1944, they were all court martialled and sentenced to death. As soon as the sentences were announced Seagrim stepped out in front of the Court and addressed the President, saying that he had been in command and anything that the others had done had been done on his orders. He was quite ready to die but asked that the others should be spared.

His pleas were ignored and all the men were returned to prison to await execution. There, Seagrim devoted himself to comforting and inspiring the others and he did this so successfully that each one of them said that if their commander had to die they would prefer to die with him. They did.

Two members of the Royal Air Force were decorated with the George Cross for bravery in Japanese hands. Both awards were posthumous and the first of them went to Flying Officer Hector Gray, who was captured in Hong Kong and imprisoned in a camp on the island.

Apart from the normal hardships that practically every Japanese prisoner had to withstand, Gray was suffering from

a severe stomach disorder that caused him much pain throughout the period of his captivity. But he refused to let this, or
anything else, discourage him and he devoted himself completely to the task of doing what he could to ease the lot of
other prisoners in the camp and helping to sustain their morale.

He was a sick man but there were many in the camp who
were in a worse state of health. Medical treatment was rudi-
mentary and the Japanese were either unable or unwilling to
spare any drugs for their captives. He took on the task, therefore, of setting up an organization to smuggle drugs into the
camp and distribute them where they were most needed.
Precisely how he achieved this has not been disclosed but he
must obviously have made some contacts with the outside
world for his plan was successful and, over the next few months,
many sick prisoners had good reason for being grateful to him.

Gray had not been engaged in this work for long before he
realized that there was another factor, as well as ill health,
that was responsible for the lowering of morale in the prison.
This was the lack of news and, through his outside contacts,
he was one of the few prisoners who knew much about what
was happening outside. He therefore established a second
service—a news service—and he managed to publish a regular
secret news bulletin.

Eventually, the Japanese discovered what Gray was doing
and that he was in touch with people outside the camp. Needless to say they wanted to know who they were and, also, the
names of his accomplices inside. He was thrown into solitary
confinement and, over a period of five and a half months, he
was systematically tortured. Throughout this time Flying
Officer Gray did not divulge a single name and, as a result,
several people escaped death. In the end, the Japanese accepted
the fact that he would never talk and on 18th December 1943,
he was shot.

Sergeant Stanley James Woodbridge fell into Japanese hands
when his Liberator bomber, of 159 Squadron, operating from
Digei, in India, crashed in the Burmese jungle. All six members
of the crew were captured and tortured in an effort to make
them talk about the British bomber organization in India.

Woodbridge, however, was singled out for especially harsh treatment. He was the wireless operator and the Japanese thought that he was in a position to give them information that they were particularly anxious to discover, concerning wireless equipment, codes, and wavelengths.

He refused to say anything and, on 7th February 1945, he was beheaded. The story of his resistance to torture became known to the authorities after the fall of Japan and later that year, as a result of what was said by other prisoners who survived, six Japanese officers and non-commissioned officers were tried by Court Martial. Three of them were sentenced to death and the other three to long terms of imprisonment.

Another prisoner of the Japanese who displayed outstanding tenacity in the face of every form of torture and privation was Captain Lionel Colin Matthews of the Australian Corps of Signals. He must be one of the very few people who have ever been posthumously decorated twice. He was put to death in 1944 and notification of his award of the Military Cross appeared in the London Gazette in January 1946. His posthumous award of the George Cross was announced on 28th November 1947. He received the M.C. for laying signal cable under mortar and artillery fire and air bombardment prior to the fall of Singapore, where he was eventually captured.

In July 1942 he was amongst the 1,500 allied prisoners who were moved from Malaya to the Japanese camp at Sandakan, on the north-east coast of British North Borneo, and he remained a captive there until his death two years later. But perhaps 'captive' was not entirely the correct word for his position, as he was employed as a gardener and seems to have been permitted considerable latitude in his movements and was allowed to go outside the prisoner-of-war compound. He was not slow to take advantage of this situation.

He made contact with friendly Chinese and other Asians in the area and, with their help, he was able to smuggle the necessary parts to build a wireless set in the camp. When this was in operation he established contact with the British civilians who had been rounded up in North Borneo and imprisoned on the small island of Berhala, a few miles distant. Over a period of many months he was able to send them regular weekly news bulletins.

With the assistance of his Asian contacts outside the prison Captain Matthews also succeeded in communicating with Allied forces in the Philippines and, as a result of the information that he passed them, a submarine was sent to Berhala Island to investigate conditions amongst the prisoners there.

Before long Captain Matthews had established an elaborate and efficient intelligence and communication network and he used it several times in connection with attempted escapes from Sandakan. Unfortunately few of these were successful.

A good deal of help was being given to the prisoners in Sandakan by the members of the British North Borneo Armed Constabulary, a British officered force of Sikh, Malayan and Dusun police which the Japanese took over when they arrived. They imprisoned their officers at Berhala and replaced them by Japanese but, not for the first time, they made the mistake of believing that all Asians automatically preferred taking orders from Japanese rather than from the British. In fact, whilst they pretended to accept the control of their new masters, the Constabulary remained loyal to their imprisoned old commander, Major Rice-Oxley, and most of their underground activities were directed by him.

Early in 1943 the civilian internees on Berhala were removed to Kuching and Rice-Oxley and the other officers of the Constabulary went with them. When this happened, Captain Matthews, although a prisoner-of-war, was officially appointed to command the force and he became their commander in more than name, preparing elaborate plans for it to take part in a rising against the Japanese.

This rising never took place for, in July 1943, four Chinese members of the underground were betrayed and, under torture, revealed Matthews' name to the Japanese.

He was arrested by the Kempie Tai—the Japanese Gestapo —who discovered two wireless sets in the camp and uncovered details of the plan for a rising.

They were anxious to find out the names of everyone involved and Matthews was subjected to torture, beatings, and slow starvation over a period of some eight months in an effort to make him reveal them. This he steadfastly refused to do and, in March 1944, he was tried, sentenced to death, and executed.

His posthumous award of the George Cross was made primarily in recognition of his stubborn refusal, throughout his long period of systematic torture and starvation, to betray his associates. But it should not be forgotten that his many activities prior to his arrest, carried out, as they were, under the very noses of the Japanese and knowing that detection meant certain death, were gallant in the extreme.

Tragically, the end of World War II did not mean the end of prisoner-of-war camps, nor of intolerable suffering in them and further examples of heroic conduct. After a few short years of uneasy peace, the Korean war burst like a bombshell in an uneasy world and war weary troops were in action once more.

In theory the Korean War was a conflict between the forces of the United Nations and the aggressive North Koreans. In practice, it was a pilot trial of strength between the forces of Communism and anti-Communism and, although Russia and Communist China never openly declared war, much of the North Korean equipment and not a few technical experts came from Russia, whilst large numbers of Chinese troops openly took part in the operations.

Many of the United Nations soldiers had the misfortune to fall into Chinese hands and it soon became evident that their methods of treating prisoners differed little from those of the Japanese.

One of the most heroic actions of the campaign was fought by the Gloucestershire Regiment and, in it, their Commanding Officer, Lt.-Col. Carne, won the Victoria Cross. But, though the stand of the Gloucesters was an heroic one, their losses were severe and many of their men were killed, wounded or captured.

One of the captured was Lieutenant Terence Edward Waters. He was not a member of the Regiment but belonged to the West Yorkshire Regiment, the Prince of Wales Own, and had been seconded to the Gloucesters to help fill the gaps in their ranks that had been caused by casualties. Terence Waters was a young regular army officer who had passed out of the Royal

Military Academy, Sandhurst, in the middle of 1949. After a short tour of service with his own Regiment, in Austria, he had been drafted to a Reinforcement Unit in Japan.

He was wounded in the battle on the Imjin River, in April 1951 and, when he fell into enemy hands, he was suffering from injuries to his head and his right arm. Despite this, he was made to march with a number of other prisoners, some of them more seriously hurt than he was. During this march he displayed a magnificent example of courage and fortitude and set himself the task of looking after the other wounded as best he could.

After a journey of immeasurable hardship and privation the party arrived at an area west of Pyongyang, known as 'The Caves.' Here the prisoners were held in a tunnel driven into the side of a hill and, through it, there flowed a stream of water that flooded much of the floor on which large numbers of men were forced to live. Into this small space hundreds of South Koreans, as well as European prisoners, were crowded like animals. Many of them were dressed only in filthy rags and their bodies were crawling with lice. There was no medical attention and the food consisted only of two small meals of boiled maize a day. Every morning several prisoners were found to be dead, either from sickness or wounds. Some died simply of malnutrition.

After some days of this torment a Political Officer visited the prisoners and, with offers of better food and medical attention, tried to persuade them to join a pro-Communist formation called the Peace Fighters. Without exception the British soldiers rejected the suggestion out of hand but, in it, Terence Waters thought he saw their only prospect of salvation. He had tried to work out some method of escape from their prison but he could find none and the only future he saw for the British captives was a slow death from wounds and starvation.

He collected them together and ordered the men to pretend to accept the Communists' offer and he told the senior N.C.O., Sergeant Hoper, to take charge of the party and, as soon as an opportunity offered, to try to make an escape.

At this, some of the men looked up at their officer and asked why he was not going to take charge of them himself. Terence Waters smiled faintly and explained that he had thought it all over very carefully and decided that, as the only British officer in the prison, his proper job was to maintain British prestige and refuse even to pretend to give way.

He would not be moved from his decision and the men insisted that, in that case, they would have to remain with him. Sternly, but kindly, Waters pointed out that it was not a matter of what they decided but what he ordered. He was their commander and he expected them to obey his orders without question, even though they were all prisoners.

Lieutenant Waters remained in his terrible prison and the rest of the British soldiers went off to join the Peace Fighters. It disturbed the Communists that the only British officer had refused to join his men, and, for some time, they tried hard to persuade him. He stubbornly refused, however, and their efforts were eventually ended when this young, inexperienced, but very brave officer died from his wounds. His posthumous award of the George Cross was announced in the London Gazette later in the year.

Another very remarkable British soldier was captured in the fighting on the Imjin River: Fusilier Derek Godfrey Kinne of the Royal Northumberland Fusiliers. The story of his constant refusal, over a long period of more than two years, to submit to his Chinese captors is a most remarkable one.

From the first his only aim was to escape, and he succeeded in doing this within twenty-four hours but, unluckily, he was recaptured again a few days later when he was trying to cross over into his own lines. He was then made to join a column that had to march for over a month to a prison camp far to the north of the battle area. It was during this march that he first earned a reputation for being a man of outstanding leadership and high morale. By his conduct he set an example that sustained all the other troops in the column.

As a prisoner, he quickly earned a reputation for refusing to co-operate with his captors and, in July 1952, he was taken before a Chinese officer who lost his temper and struck the Fusilier. He immediately retaliated by returning the blow and,

for this offence, he was subjected to a period of torture. Later
in the month he managed to escape again, but was once
more recaptured and kept in tight handcuffs for the next 81
days.

Even this failed to subdue Kinne's indomitable spirit and he
was made to suffer every kind of hardship which included confinement in a box and a rat infested hole, as well as many
beatings. Often he was prodded with bayonets and, more than
once, he was spared further pain by falling into unconsciousness. Throughout this period Kinne was suffering great pain
from a hernia that had resulted from his second escape. He was
denied all medical attention but his normal form of retaliation
was to spit in the faces of his tormentors.

Fusilier Kinne's final sentence of solitary confinement was
awarded for the double offence of refusing to obey an order
and wearing a rosette on the day of Her Majesty's coronation.
Some time after this his name was put forward for repatriation
exchange and it is not impossible that it was selected because
the Chinese were only too keen to get rid of him. Even at the
eleventh hour he continued to be a thorn in the side of his
captors and, more than once, he was threatened with having
his name removed from the repatriation list for a variety of
offences which included demanding to be interviewed by an
International Red Cross representative who was visiting his
camp. But in the end, on 10th August 1953, Fusilier Kinne
was repatriated at Panmunjon.

Throughout his long period of captivity, under conditions
of degradation and increasing brutality, every possible method,
both physical and mental, had been used to break his spirit.
But they all failed utterly. His powers of resistance were remarkable and he was a high inspiration to every other prisoner who
came into contact with him. Eight months after his release his
award of the George Cross was announced in the London
Gazette and he received the decoration from the hands of the
Queen. It was the last George Cross that was not awarded
posthumously.

A number of Australians were captured by the Chinese
Communists and one of them, Private Horace William Madden

of the 3rd Battalion, the Royal Australian Regiment, was posthumously awarded the George Cross for conduct very similar
to that of Fusilier Kinne.

Madden, a signaller at his regimental headquarters, was
taken at Kapyong on 24th April 1951, after having been con-
cussed. He remained a prisoner until the 6th of November of
the same year when he died of malnutrition.

He defied all efforts to make him collaborate with his captors
and these included beatings, other forms of torture, and slow
starvation. Throughout all this he remained cheerful and his
spirits never flagged. Often, when his rations had been reduced
almost to nothing, he would give part of the pitifully small
portion of rice that he received to sick comrades.

Two other Australians received the award for extreme bravery
in a prison camp but, on that occasion, they were not prisoners
but guards in a camp that housed 1,100 Japanese. They were
Private Ralph Jones and Private Benjamin Gower Hardy of
the 22nd Australian Garrison Battalion.

On the night of 4th August 1944, the Japanese organized a
mass escape and, storming over the perimeter wire, they rushed
the towers in which the duty guards were stationed. Jones and
Hardy were in one of these towers and almost the first they
knew of the breakout was when they found several hundred
fanatical Japanese prisoners bearing down on them with knives,
clubs and other weapons. They opened fire on them with their
Vickers gun and dropped several of the Japanese to the ground
but this had no effect on the remainder of the little yellow men
who surged on, screaming. Obviously nothing that the two
soldiers could do would stop the onward rush of the Japanese
and the most practical course of action would have been to
run for their lives. Instead, Privates Jones and Hardy remained
at their post and continued to fire their machine gun until they
were overpowered and clubbed to death.

++

CHAPTER XIII

IN THE NAME OF THE LAW

A NUMBER of George Crosses have been awarded to men who have displayed unusual gallantry in tackling dangerous criminals; things sometimes as dangerous as, and less predictable than such hazards as bomb, fire or tempest. Not surprisingly most of these men were members of the Police Force, but there has been one exception, a young Bristol man named Robert George Taylor, who lost his life when he tackled two bank robbers.

He was a decent, likeable, clean-living young man of middle-class background who practised judo as a hobby. In 1939, at the age of nineteen, he joined a Territorial Regiment of Artillery and served overseas in North Africa, Sicily and Italy, attaining the rank of sergeant. Then, in 1945, was demobilised and, like many other young men of his age and circumstances, he did not find it easy to settle down in civilian life. He had had no training for any special job and post-war England seemed drab and unexciting after six years of active service in the Gunners.

He found employment selling insurance but he did not enjoy it and changed this job for another as advertising representative of the Bristol *Evening World*. It was whilst he was going about his lawful duties in that capacity that he happened to pass the branch of Lloyds Bank that stands on the corner of Down's Park Road and North View, at 11.37 a.m. on Monday 13th March 1950. About three minutes earlier two men wearing raincoats had strolled into the bank and held up the staff at pistol point.

The raid had not been very cleverly organized, nor was it very effective. One of the men grabbed from a counter what money he could reach—twenty-eight pounds—and then, shouting that nobody was to move for five minutes, the pair had rushed out of the building and jumped on a passing bus. Their warning went unheeded and they were closely followed from the bank by the bank guard, Mr. Bullock, whose cries caused the bus driver to stop his vehicle within seconds of the thugs boarding it.

The two men clambered off again and ran down the street with the driver, the conductor and Bullock after them. Passers-by stood and watched, fascinated, but one of them, Taylor, joined in the chase. He was younger and fleeter of foot than the rest and whilst the others began to lose ground Taylor gained on the men. Someone shouted a warning to him to be careful as the robbers were armed, but he paid no heed and, after a short while, he overtook them and tried to tackle them. As he leapt towards the nearest thief the man turned in his tracks and, raising a pistol, shot Taylor through the head at point blank range.

Robert Taylor was rushed to hospital but his wound had been mortal and he died soon afterwards. The two men were eventually caught and overpowered. The pair of them, both Polish refugees, were eventually tried and executed.

Five years before Robert Taylor received his posthumous award another man was decorated for gallantry in very similar circumstances but on the other side of the world. He was the late Sergeant Eric George Bailey of the New South Wales Police Force. He was not the first Australian to receive the George Cross but was the only man ever to win the award in Australia.

At about 8.30 p.m. on a hot summer evening in January 1945 he was on duty in the town of Blayney when he noticed a man who was behaving in a suspicious manner in Adelaide Street. He watched him for a while and then, convinced that he was not engaged in any lawful pursuit, he went up to him and challenged him. The man's answer was to pull a pistol from his pocket and, at point blank range, to fire a shot into the policeman's stomach.

Bailey closed with the man and he fired two more shots. The policeman was mortally wounded and must have realized the fact, but he was determined that his assassin should not escape. He continued to struggle with him and called out for assistance.

The thug tried desperately to escape but Bailey refused to release his hold and still had him firmly in his grip when other police arrived on the scene and arrested him. Very soon afterwards Sergeant Eric Bailey was dead, but he lived long enough to tell what had taken place.

The circumstances of the award of the George Cross to Detective Constable Henry Williams Stevens of the Metropolitan Police were also similar but, though he was seriously injured, he had the good fortune to escape with his life.

Henry Stevens was a London man and was born in West Ham. He was only eleven years old when the war broke out and was not old enough to join the forces until 1945 when he went into the Royal Navy and served for three years as a Naval Air Artificer Mechanic. He joined the Metropolitan Police in 1953. After his normal period of uniformed duty he was selected for plain clothes work.

It was in the spring of 1958 that he was on plain clothes duty in a police car at Bromley, in Kent, when a radio call was received that sent him and two other police officers to the place where he was to demonstrate his great courage. A burglar alarm had gone off in a private dwelling house and the occupants of the police car were ordered to go and investigate.

When they reached the house the other two officers entered the front garden and Stevens went round to the rear. The back garden was separated from the road by a high fence and he was standing looking up at this when a man suddenly jumped down from it, a few yards from the detective. He tried to apprehend the man but he ran off with Stevens close on his heels. After a short chase the burglar suddenly stopped in his tracks and levelled a pistol at the detective, threatening to fire if he did not stop.

Stevens took no notice and advanced towards the man who was as good as his word. A bullet struck the detective in the face, shattering his teeth and part of his jaw-bone. Although in severe pain, Stevens flung himself at the man and succeeded in taking his weapon from him and pinioning him against some railings. After a moment's struggle the man stopped struggling and agreed to come with the policeman. Stevens released his grip and the moment that he did that the man ran off again.

Despite the pain and with blood flowing profusely from his wound, Stevens set off in pursuit again and managed to close with the man a second time. A desperate struggle followed but the criminal got clear again, leaving his overcoat and jacket behind.

Stevens refused to give up and, once again, he set off after the man but, this time, he only followed a short way before he fell to the ground exhausted. The criminal's escape was only temporary, however, and he was eventually traced and brought to justice. And it was the loss of his overcoat and jacket that contributed to the success of the manhunt that followed the desperate struggle in Bromley.

Few cases of bravery have had so much publicity as the one that resulted in the award of the George Cross to Detective Sergeant Frederick William Fairfax of the Metropolitan Police.

At 9.15 p.m. on the evening of 2nd November 1952, a woman was looking out of a window in Tamworth Road, Croydon, when she noticed two figures moving quietly along in the shadows. There was something suspicious about their behaviour and this was more than confirmed when she saw the pair scramble over a gate. She hesitated for a moment and then, deciding that the men could not possibly be engaged in any lawful pursuit, she telephoned the police.

Her message resulted in the arrival of two separate parties of police. At 9.25 p.m. a van appeared containing Fairfax—then a Police Constable—and Police Constable Harrison. A very short time afterwards a wireless car turned up carrying Police Constables Miles and Macdonald.

In the meantime the two men had temporarily disappeared but they were spotted again on the flat roof of a nearby building. The police decided to go after them and it was Fairfax who led the attack, climbing up a vent-pipe. As he scrambled up onto the roof he could just make out two dim figures crouching behind a chimney stack,

The constable moved to within six feet of the stack and called out:

'I'm a police officer. Come out from behind that stack.'

For a moment there was no reply and then a voice said:

'If you want us, ——ing well come and get us.'

Fairfax did as the voice suggested and dived towards the stack, closing with one of the men. There was a short struggle and the man managed to drag himself free of the constable's clutch, calling out, as he went:

'Let him have it, Chris.'

Then a shot came from the direction of the stack and Fairfax fell with a bullet in his shoulder. Quickly, however, he picked himself up again and made another dive at the man he had tackled and, this time, managed to knock him down. Then he dragged him behind the cover of a ventilator and searched him for weapons. He found a sizeable knife and a wicked looking knuckleduster with a spike on it.

There was a staircase leading onto the roof and, making use of such cover as there was, Fairfax dragged his captive to the doorway and, as he struggled with him, another shot came from the direction of the stack.

In the meantime P.C. Macdonald, a rather portly man and not built for such pursuits, had somehow managed to climb to the top of a vent pipe but was unable to pull himself up onto the roof. Despite his wound and the danger of being fired at again, Fairfax went to his aid and helped him up. Then he turned his attention back to the man behind the chimney stack and shouted:

'Drop that gun.'

The reply came:

'Come and get it.'

This retort was followed by two more shots that whistled close to P.C. Harrison. Then more police, headed by P.C. Miles, arrived at the head of the staircase and a further shot was fired in their direction. It struck Miles between the eyes and he dropped dead.

Next, the man behind the stack stepped out into the open and fired another shot. He shouted:

'I am Craig. You've just given my brother twelve years. Come on you coppers. I'm only sixteen.'

The youth stood, a revolver waving in the direction of the policeman, waiting for someone to make a move. The situation was desperate and the uniformed men hesitated a moment. Then P.C. Fairfax flung his truncheon and followed it with a bottle and a lump of wood. They all missed and the policeman turned round and ran towards the staircase. A moment later he reappeared with a revolver in his hand.

Whilst the other policemen stood motionless, Fairfax rushed towards the youth, firing as he went. The killer tried to return the fire but his weapon clicked harmlessly. It was empty.

Fairfax saw that his chance had come and dived towards the boy who pivoted round and threw himself towards the ground, twenty-five feet below. He survived his fall but appeared in the magistrates' court a few days later on a stretcher.

Christopher Craig was strangely intelligent but possessed a twisted outlook and an absence of any moral balance. Beside him in the dock was his companion, Derek William Bentley, the nineteen-year-old son of a respectable bank official, who had never learned to read or write and suffered from an inferiority complex as a result.

Both boys were sent for trial on a charge of murder and both were convicted. Craig, on account of his age, was sentenced to be detained at Her Majesty's pleasure. Bentley was sentenced to death. At the conclusion of the trial the policemen who took part in the roof-top gun battle were congratulated by the judge on their bravery and devotion to duty. Some weeks later the award of the George Cross to Frederick William Fairfax, now promoted to the rank of Sergeant, was announced in the London Gazette. A few days after this, an appeal by Bentley was dismissed by the Court of Criminal Appeal.

The case evoked a great deal of discussion which revolved around both of the convicted men. Psychologists, psychiatrists and sociologists concerned themselves with the circumstances that had turned a youth of sixteen into a cold-blooded murderer. Many who were interested in the reform of criminal law argued bitterly against a position that permitted conviction on a capital charge of a man who was actually under arrest when the offence was committed.

What is significant is that, although so many people concerned themselves with the welfare of these two young criminals, the name of Fairfax was rarely mentioned. Today, though the names Craig and Bentley are familiar to many, that of the married policeman with two young children who, wounded and in pain, as well as in deadly danger, tackled a desperate gunman on a roof-top in Croydon has been practically forgotten. Fame and notoriety achieve strange priorities.

CHAPTER XIV

UNUSUAL AWARDS

Most of the acts of heroism that have resulted in the award
of the George Cross have had features in common with others
and this has made it possible to group the accounts of them into
chapters with a common theme. Sometimes the circumstances
have been so similar that it has been hard to tell of them without repetition. A few, on the other hand, have taken place in
circumstances that have been exceptional, or even unique, and
this chapter is devoted to these.

One award for extreme gallantry under the most unusual
circumstances was made posthumously to a young National
Service Officer, Michael Paul Benner, who gave his life trying
to save a soldier who had slipped and was falling to almost
certain death, high in the Austrian Alps.

Michael Benner had a deep love of the mountains. As a boy,
at Canford School, he had taken part in all the normal games
and become Captain of Riding, but all his holidays had been
spent walking, ski-ing and climbing. When he left school he
had spent some months in the Bavarian mountains before going
to London University to read German. And, as an under-
graduate, his vacations were spent in the mountains of Switzerland, North Wales and Scotland.

He went to the University of Munich for a term to improve
his German. Whilst he was there he set himself an endurance
test which involved a 120-mile round trip on an ancient motor-
cycle and climbing the Zugaspitz—Germany's highest mountain—on his own, all within twenty-four hours. He failed on
his first attempt but succeeded when he tried again, despite
the fact that the lights of his decrepit machine failed in the
middle of the night.

When he returned to England he had the news that he had
won a place at Merton College, Oxford, and in his first term

there he took up rowing, devoting himself to this sport with such fervour that he had little time for anything else, including his studies.

Michael Benner spent his first Oxford vacation climbing in Scotland and the next one in the Middle East and Asia Minor. He succeeded, somehow, in reaching Baghdad in fourteen days at a cost of £2. Then he returned home via Basrah, Persia, Turkey, Greece and Italy. It was typical of his outlook that he refused to take more than £15 with him when he left England and typical of his determination that he managed to complete his journey on this small sum.

When he left Oxford he asked for an accelerated call-up of his national service but there was some delay and so he looked around to find some way of earning some money to pay off his debts. He found two jobs. By day he worked as a steel erector's mate and, in the evenings, as a barman.

His father was a Brigadier in the Regular Army and, when his call-up came, he chose his father's Corps, the Royal Engineers and, in due course, he was selected for a National Service Commission and was posted to a Field Regiment in Germany. There, he quickly earned the reputation of being a man of outstanding enterprise and resource, described by his Squadron Commander as the best junior officer who had ever passed through his hands. Perhaps he gained some inspiration from the Benner family motto: *Forti et fideli nil dificili* (To the brave and faithful, nothing is difficult).

In Germany he had every opportunity of taking part in his favourite recreation and in 1956 and 1957 he represented his Corps in the Army Ski-ing Championships. It was in 1957 that he evolved the idea of organizing a regimental mountaineering course and he managed to persuade his superiors of the training value of such a venture. 17th June to 6th July was selected as a suitable time and it was decided that Benner would be put in charge of the course. Preliminary arrangements made, he applied for fourteen days leave and, setting himself another endurance test, he disappeared into the Arctic Circle via Sweden, Finland and Norway.

The mountaineering course started in Osnabruck with

lectures and practical training in rope-work in rock quarries. There were also long gruelling route marches with heavy packs and these resulted in a good many blisters and other ailments that were responsible for the rejection of several of the volunteers who seemed to be unlikely to be able to stand up to what was to follow.

On Sunday 23rd June 1957, the fourteen survivors from the course and their trainer and leader, Michael Benner, left Osnabruck by train with their tents, cooking pots, climbing gear, fuel and rations. After an all-night journey, they reached Zell-am-See, in Austria, and two days later the party was high up in the Alps sleeping in huts and bivouacs on the glacier.

They spent five days climbing and training on a number of peaks but the weather was bad, with high winds and blizzards. New soft snow made going difficult and the combined influence of the wind and the reflected glare of the sun gave everyone a good deal of discomfort. Several of the men's faces became badly swollen and blistered but they carried on cheerfully, exhilarated by what was, for most of them, a new and exciting experience.

On Sunday 30th June, after a long trek from the mountain village of Kals, the party reached the Glorer Hut (2,651 metres). Some of the men had flagged on the way up and their leader decided to leave eight of them behind with the heavy packs, whilst he went on with the six fittest to spend the night at the Strudel Hut (2,800 metres). Next day, he planned to climb the Glossglockner (3,792 metres) via the Studelgrat—a difficult route that followed a rocky ridge. Before he left, he sent a post-card to his Commanding Officer saying, 'Sir, Everything is going to plan. All are exhausted but in good spirits.'

Next morning the seven men set off on two ropes. Benner led the first party of four and the most experienced of the soldiers followed, roped to two other men. The second party lagged badly behind and, at about 2 p.m., the subaltern ordered the two ropes to be joined and the seven men slowly resumed the climb as a single team.

Later in the afternoon there was a fierce and prolonged

mountain storm with blinding snow and violent lightning and the party had to halt on an exposed rock face for an hour, until it passed. Then, cold and wet through, they resumed the climb and, at about six in the evening, they successfully negotiated the difficult knife-edge summit with a sheer drop of 2,000 feet on each side.

The Aldersruhe Hut lies about an hour's journey below the peak of the Glossglockner and there is a ridge track that leads down to it. This track is normally relatively safe but, freshly covered with snow that was now well frozen, it was icy and slippery. Benner decided, therefore, to move ahead of the rest of the party and make sure that it was safe for them to follow. He had only gone a few yards when one of his men, Sapper Phillips, suddenly slipped and started to slide sideways off the track down an eighty degree slope towards the precipice below. What happened next is probably best described in the words of the official citation in the London Gazette of 17th June 1958, that announced the posthumous award of the George Cross to Second Lieutenant Michael Paul Benner:

'Seeing this, Michael Benner jumped out of his own secure foothold on to the open slope and caught the falling man, holding him with one hand and endeavouring, with the other, to dig his ice axe into the snow. This he could not succeed in doing. Both men slid down the slope together until they disappeared to their death over the steep face of the mountain.

'In making his attempt to intercept Sapper Phillips, this gallant young officer took, as he well knew, a desperate risk. As the two gathered speed down the slope he must have realized that he could save himself only by releasing his grasp on Sapper Phillips' arm but he did not do so. He held on to the last, struggling to obtain a grip in the snow with his feet and axe.

'With supreme courage and devotion he sacrificed his life endeavouring to save his companion.'

The two bodies were found lying side by side on the glacier, 2,000 feet below the summit. And, at the wish of their parents, they were buried side by side in the churchyard of the village of Kals, in the shadow of the High Peaks. The military funeral was conducted by their Regimental Chaplain and was attended by officers and a bearer party from the Regiment, as well as by leading Austrian officials from the district.

The Parish Priest of Kals gave an address and said:

'One of these two young men died in the course of fulfilling his duty as a soldier; the other by giving his life to save his comrade in the highest traditions of a British Army officer.'

A few days after the funeral, Herr Thomas, Chief Guide of Kals, wrote to Michael Benner's parents with full details of the accident. He had been to the place at daybreak on the following morning and, from the frozen marks in the snow, had been able to reconstruct everything that had taken place. He found the exact point where the young officer had leapt sideways into the path of the falling Sapper and, in his letter, he described this leap as, 'One that I would certainly not have dared to take.' He concluded by saying of the dead officer, 'Because of that gallant jump, his honour stands high with us guides, even more so because he sacrificed his life by so doing.'

Another army officer, Lieutenant St John Graham Young, won his George Cross in very unusual circumstances. His award was also posthumous. Lieutenant Young was a war-time member of the Royal Tank Regiment but he was seconded to the Central India Horse and went, with that Regiment, to Italy on active service.

On 23rd July 1944, he was placed in command of a patrol that was ordered to occupy a hill feature, called Polly Clifton's Hill, in the Arezzo-Perugia area, between Rome and Florence. The operation began at last light and the patrol reached a position close to its objective with little difficulty. Then the advance was interrupted by a number of loud explosions and Lieutenant Young thought that his men had come under mortar fire and he ordered them to withdraw to behind some cover a short distance in the rear.

Whilst the patrol was being pulled back there were several more explosions and Young realized that they were in the middle of an enemy minefield. He ordered everyone to stay where they were until daylight.

His men took such cover as they could but one or two of the soldiers had been hurt and one of them, who was in severe pain,

suffered in silence for about two hours until he could bear
it no longer and then began to cry out for help. Young shouted
to the others to keep still and began to make his way towards
the wounded Indian himself, probing the ground in front of
him with his fingers as he went.

He came on three Schu mines and rendered them harmless,
but his luck did not last and eventually he knelt on another
which blew off his right leg below the knee and shattered the
ankle and calf of his other one. Again this young officer shouted
to his men to remain where they were and he began, once
more, to pull himself towards the man he was trying to help.

Somehow Young reached the wounded Indian, who had by
now become unconscious, and he dressed his badly injured
thigh with a first field-dressing. Then, for the next five hours,
he kept up a continuous flow of words of encouragement to his
men, assuring them that if they stayed quite still until dawn
it would be an easy matter for them to extricate themselves.

At 5.30 a.m. one of Young's Indian soldiers crawled to his
side and managed to carry him out of the minefield. Half an
hour later the Regimental Medical Officer of the Central India
Horse found him. He was sitting on the ground on the edge of
the minefield, calling out orders to the members of his patrol
who were trying to extricate themselves and supervising the
removal of the wounded.

The doctor gave him such treatment as he was able but, very
soon afterwards, Lieutenant Young lost consciousness and,
about twelve hours later, he died of his wounds.

The announcement of his posthumous award appeared in
the London Gazette, like Second Lieutenant Benner's, almost
exactly a year after the event.

One of Lieutenant Young's soldiers was also awarded the
George Cross for his bravery on that occasion and his decoration, as well, was posthumous. He was Sowar Ditto Ram of
the Central India Horse.

This gallant Indian had his left leg blown off soon after the
patrol walked into the minefield. He did not call out for help
but quietly applied his first field-dressing to the stump. Then,
some way off, he heard one of his comrades crying out in pain

and, without hesitating, he dragged himself through the mines to where the other man lay. He spent some time dressing his wounds as best he could and then, exhausted from his efforts and loss of blood, sank backwards, unconscious. A few moments later his heart beats stopped.

Another George Cross that was awarded for gallantry in unique circumstances and was also posthumous went to a boiler-man named Frederick John Craddock, in September 1943.

To understand the extent of this man's bravery it is important to realize the terrible effects of exposure to steam from an industrial boiler. Under pressure, and far hotter than the steam from a kettle, it can produce fatal burns within seconds and this fact is well known by every boiler-man.

Craddock worked in the boiler-house of the Flax Factory at Glemsford in Sussex and, one day, during the winter of 1942-43, he was watching one of his fellow workmen, Albert Sterry, working in a well between a boiler and a furnace, cleaning the plant. Suddenly, for reasons that are not clear, a valve became defective and the well was quickly filled with super-heated steam. Sterry screamed with pain and fell to the ground, writhing in agony.

Craddock had every opportunity of jumping to safety and he must have known that the chances either of Sterry surviving the blast of the hot steam or of anyone else entering the well and escaping with their life were remote in the extreme. In spite of this, he called for a ladder and climbed down into the steam to try and rescue his mate.

He had only descended a few rungs of the ladder when the pain from the burns that he received became so intense that he pulled himself clear and staggered about in agony. Then he seemed to recover and, once again, he started to go down into the pit. Again he only succeeded in descending part of the way before he was overcome but, this time, he collapsed and fell to the floor below. It was some time before anyone else was able to enter the well and when this became possible Sterry and Craddock were found lying together dead. Medical experts believe that Craddock must have died from the shock of his very severe burns at the moment that he collapsed.

8

Amongst the many members of the Commonwealth who have been awarded the George Cross was a solitary Malayan, Awang anak Rawang, a jungle tracker from Jahore. During the operations against the Communist bandits, Rawang was leading a section of the Worcestershire Regiment through thick undergrowth when the party was ambushed by a group of about fifty Chinese.

Another tracker, who was moving ahead, was killed by a burst of fire and Rawang was struck in the thigh by a bullet that penetrated the bone. Close by, a soldier of the Worcesters fell badly hurt by a bullet that smashed his knee. Rawang caught hold of him and dragged him behind cover and then, disregarding his own wound, he seized hold of a rifle and drove off every attempt that the Chinese made to reach his position.

Before long he was hit again and, this time, his right arm was shattered. Unable to use his rifle any longer, he dragged himself to the side of the wounded British soldier and took a hand grenade from his equipment. With this, held above his head in his left hand, he defied any of the bandits to approach him.

They were eventually driven off and, soon afterwards, the position was relieved. Then the gallant Malayan tracker was carried to a field hospital where his wounds were treated. They were severe and, for a while, his life was in the balance. However, through a combination of medical skill and courageous determination, he survived and is still alive.

Only one award of the George Cross has been made to a fireman in peacetime, to Frederick Davies of the Central Fire Station at Willesden, London. The award, like the majority of post-war ones, was posthumous.

Davies, who was thirty-two years old when he died, had been a fireman for nine years and, by one of those unhappy twists of fate, had tired of his occupation and had actually given notice of his intention of leaving the service. If he had lived, he would have started a new job with the London Passenger Transport Board a few days later.

This was not to be, for one day in August 1945, a serious fire broke out in a house in Craven Park Road, Harlesden, and

Frederick Davies went there. By the time the Brigade reached the spot the fire had taken a strong hold and it was felt that the building was in too dangerous a condition for anyone to enter it. However, there were two children trapped in a front room on the second floor and, ignoring all advice, Davies went up a ladder and climbed in. After a short time he reappeared with a limp body of an eight-year-old girl in his arms. He passed her to another fireman who was waiting at the top of a ladder.

Davies then disappeared into the room for a second time to look for the other child. The place was, by then, a blazing inferno and many of the silent watchers thought that he would never reappear. He did, however, though without the child and with his clothing alight and his body terribly burned. He was helped down the ladder and rushed to hospital where he died forty-eight hours later. Unhappily, the girl that he brought out was dead and Frederick Davies gave his life to no avail.

He was buried with full honours in Kensal Green Cemetery and the Union Jack draped his coffin. His award of the George Cross was announced in the London Gazette of 5th February 1946, and his young widow went to Buckingham Palace to receive the decoration.

A disturbing feature of the incident was that the fireman to whom Davies handed the dead girl dropped her body from the top of the ladder and must, for a time, have suffered agony of mind for it was thought that she had died from the fall. However, a post mortem revealed that she had been dead when Davies brought her out.

An Indian soldier also died in a fire and received a post-humous George Cross for his bravery. He was Havildar Abdul Rehman of the 3rd Battalion, the Jat Regiment.

In 1946 his battalion was serving in the Dutch East Indies and, on 22nd February, he was travelling along a road in a jeep when it ran over a mine and the vehicle was thrown into a ditch. The Havildar was thrown clear but three Indian soldiers were pinned under the jeep which caught fire and began to blaze fiercely.

Abdul at once set to work trying to extricate the men and,

at considerable risk to himself, he managed to pull two of them clear. He then turned to the third man and, as he was struggling to get him to safety, one of the petrol tanks exploded and drenched the Havildar with burning fuel.

He took no notice of his own danger and continued with his efforts until an ambulance party arrived on the scene. Then he shouted to them to complete his work and collapsed on top of the jeep. He was carried away at once but it was too late to do anything for him for he was already dead from the shock of his severe burns.

Another man who displayed great bravery in a fire also has the distinction of being the youngest person ever to win the George Cross. When he received the decoration John Bamford, of Newthorpe, Nottinghamshire, was only fifteen years old.

At the time he was living in his father's house with his parents and five brothers and sisters. One night in 1952 fire broke out in the house and, within minutes, the downstairs rooms were blazing fiercely. John Bamford and his father rushed down to investigate the situation and then found themselves unable to get up the stairs again. Still up there were Mrs Bamford and five younger children.

Mr Bamford and his son went outside and climbed up to the window of the front bedroom and, through it, they assisted Mrs Bamford and three of the children. The other two children were in a bedroom at the back of the house, immediately above the seat of the fire. Mr Bamford tried to force his way into this room but was driven back by the heat. In the end, he climbed out of the house again and went round to the back to see what could be done from outside.

His son stayed behind and, crawling on his hands and knees, reached the bed where his two brothers were and, pulling one of them from it, threw him from the window into his father's arms. Then, his clothing ablaze, John Bamford went back into the room to rescue the other boy. The child panicked and John had to chase him round the burning room before he eventually caught hold of him and threw him, as well, from the window.

Finally Bamford, by now terribly burned, managed to lift one leg over the window ledge and fell to safety below.

It is surprising that this youngster survived the shock of the extensive burns that he received but he did and, after skin grafting operations, he was reported, some years later, as being little the worse for his terrible experience, though in the hands of the doctors once more as the result of breaking his leg when on holiday at Lowestoft.

Five years after young John Bamford won his George Cross the same decoration was awarded to a man who must have been one of its oldest recipients. John Axon was fifty-seven years of age when he performed his act of bravery and, like several other men who were similarly decorated, he was a railway worker.

Axon, who lived in Stockport, first joined the railway service at the end of the First World War when he became an engine cleaner at Longsight, in Manchester. Eight years later he became a fireman and, after a further eighteen years, he was made a driver.

Shortly before noon on Saturday 9th February 1957, he was in charge of a goods train that was carrying over five hundred tons of freight between Buxton and Warrington. The train was moving slowly down a steep gradient at Chapel-en-le-Frith when suddenly, and without warning, a steam pipe supplying the braking system fractured and the wagons began to gather speed. Steam from the broken pipe poured into the cab of the engine around the feet and legs of the driver and his fireman, Ronald Scanlon.

Axon was badly burned but he stayed on in his cab and struggled to apply the hand-brake. He threw his full weight onto it but the train merely went faster. Then he shouted to Scanlon to jump from the engine and apply as many wagon brakes as he could. His assistant did this and succeeded, running alongside the train, in forcing down the hand-brake levers of several of the loaded wagons. But he might as well have tried to hold back the heavy train with his own weight for they did little or nothing to check its gathering momentum.

In the cab of the engine the gushing steam had turned to boiling water and, with this driving against his legs, John Axon continued to struggle with his brake. Soon afterwards this brave man's agony was ended in death when his engine ran into the back of another train.

Mrs Axon went with her son to Buckingham Palace to receive the Cross from the Queen. She also received a cheque and a certificate from British Railways at a ceremony held at Euston.

The first story in this chapter concerned a mountain and so does the last: Mount Lamington, a 5,850-foot volcano in the Owen Stanley range in Papua, New Guinea. The range forms part of the great corridor of volcanic activity that sweeps in a vast arc across the Pacific Ocean. In its course there are some eighty volcanoes that have erupted since the dawn of history, but most of them, like Mount Lamington, have been more often dormant than active.

On the night of 18th January 1951, the people who lived in the hamlets and villages around the mountain were awakened by a deep rumbling and slight earth tremors. When the sun rose in the morning they saw steam and ash coming from its cone but the situation did not seem serious and, as people will, almost everyone decided to stay in the area and hope for the best.

For a while it looked as though all would be well; the activity seemed to be subsiding. Then, on 21st January, suddenly and without warning, there was a violent explosion and a great rent was torn in the side of the volcano. Massive pieces of rock were thrown into the air and steam, smoke and white-hot ash belched from the hole. Thousands of acres of countryside were devastated and several people were burned to death in the township of Higaturu, nine miles off.

In settlements beside the mountain some four thousand persons died within a few hours and the plight of the survivors was desperate. A carpet of hot ash made movement impossible, thick sulphurous fumes made it difficult and painful to breathe, and every source of drinking water, including storage tanks and streams, was smothered in fine pumice dust.

Rescue parties with food, water and medical supplies hurried to the area and they toiled, in conditions of the utmost difficulty, to do what they could for the injured and homeless.

Whilst they worked, Mount Lamington continued to breathe fire and steam and the danger of another violent eruption was ever present.

A volcano is an unpredictable thing but a man whose job it was to try to predict fresh eruptions was rushed to the scene and he arrived within twenty-four hours of the disaster. He was George Anthony Taylor, a vulcanologist of the Australian Bureau of Mineral Resources.

The job of rescue and rehabilitation went on for months and, throughout those months, George Taylor remained on the scene, watching, listening and measuring with delicate geophysical recording instruments. Alone and on foot he visited the lip of the crater almost daily and he flew over and around it in a light aircraft on over two hundred occasions. Once, at a critical period in the rescue operation, he spent a whole night on the mountain-side, ready to signal the earliest possible warning of an expected eruption.

Several times George Taylor was able to give information that saved many lives. But he was not always able to predict outbreaks of activity and once, on 5th March, there was a violent eruption that flung huge pieces of the dome for distances of up to two miles, and it came immediately after a period when his instruments had recorded no volcanic activity. If Taylor had been anywhere near the crater then—and he might well have been—he would undoubtedly have been killed.

This brave scientist spent several hundred hours in an area that he would not let anyone else except his native assistant enter. He was constantly in the utmost danger but he was favoured by fortune and became one of the six men to receive a peace-time George Cross that has not been posthumous.

APPENDIX I

++

RECIPIENTS OF THE GEORGE CROSS

PART I

Holders of the Medal of the Order of the British Empire, for Gallantry, whose decoration was subsequently replaced by the George Cross.

Name	Reference	Date of London Gazette
Adamson, George John		1 Feb. 1937
Alder, Lance-Sergeant Thomas Edward, The Green Howards		4 Aug. 1931
Ali Bey, Kaimmakan Yousef Hussein		3 Jan. 1939
Anderson, Chief Engine Room Artificer Frederick John		8 June 1939
Anderson, Flying Officer Walter		12 April 1929
Andrews, Captain Wallace Launcelot, Royal Engineers	Ch. 3	17 Sept. 1940
Arnold, Corporal Walter, Royal Air Force		9 Nov. 1928
Ashraf-un-Nisu, the Begum		1 Feb. 1937
Atkinson, Sergeant Thomas, The Green Howards		25 July 1939
Barnett, Quartermaster Sergeant Instructor William, The Royal Scots Fusiliers		27 Nov. 1936
Barraclough, Sergeant Arnold, Assam and Bengal Railway Battalion		25 Nov. 1930
Bayley, Captain Clive Cyril Anthony BEM, Surma Valley Light Horse		24 July 1931
Beattie, John		3 May 1927
Bhim Singh, Superintendent, Punjab Police Force		1 Jan. 1932

*Posthumous award.

236

Name	*Reference*	*Date of London Gazette*
Bell, John Frederick		2 Dec. 1930
Blackburn, Private Richard, Cheshire Regiment		23 June 1936
Blogg, Henry George		30 June 1924
Bogdanovich, Kaid Theodore		30 June 1939
Bonar, Pilot Officer Eric Watt, Royal Air Force Volunteer Reserve		5 Aug. 1932
Branch, Pilot Officer, Auxiliary Air Force		25 March 1938
Brett, Colonel Douglas Alexander, 9th Jat Regiment		8 May 1934
Brooks, Private Arthur, The Queen's Royal Regiment		19 Nov. 1935
Burke, James		3 June 1925
Burton, Major Herbert Edgar OBE, Royal Engineers		30 June 1924
Button, Sergeant William John, Royal Engineers	Ch. 3	17 Sept. 1940
Campion, Leading Aircraftsman Michael, Royal Air Force	Ch. 9	5 July 1940
Chalmers, Petty Officer Robert Mills, Royal Navy		18 June 1926
Chant, Private Frederick, Dorset Regiment		2 June 1923
Charrington, Harold Francis	Ch. 9	8 March 1940
Child, Frederick William Henry Maurice		5 May 1939
Clark, Joseph		3 May 1927
Close, Pilot Officer Gerald Charles Neil, Royal Air Force		21 Dec. 1937
Cobham, Lieutenant - Commander Anthony John, Royal Navy		1 Jan. 1930
Crossley, Edwin		25 Feb. 1936
Deeds, Major Richard, King's Shropshire Light Infantry		8 May 1934
Din, Lance-Naik Mata, 19th Hyderabad Regiment		19 Nov. 1935

	Reference	Date of London Gazette
Name		
Douglas, Flying Officer Robert Ewing, Royal Air Force		27 March 1931
d'Souza, Shri Babtist Joseph		3 June 1931
Duffin, Charles Godfrey		1 Feb. 1937
Elston, Private Ernest Matthew, West Yorkshire Regiment		19 Nov. 1935
Farr, John Henry		26 July 1940
Fattah, Capt. Rashid Abdul, Transjordan Frontier Force		12 July 1938
Fleming, William George		30 June 1924
Frost, Aircraftsman Ernest Ralph Clyde, Royal Air Force	Ch. 9	5 July 1940
Golandez, Abus Samid Abdul Wahid		4 June 1934
Graveley, Flight Lieutenant Reginald Cubitt, Royal Air Force	Ch. 9	11 Nov. 1939
Gurung, Chitrabrabahadur		19 Nov. 1935
Hand, Sergeant William George MM, Dorset Regiment		2 June 1923
Harrison, Able Seaman George Willet, Royal Navy		1 Jan. 1931
Hemeida, Captain El Amim Effendi, Sudan Defence Force		23 June 1936
Henderson, Herbert Reuban		18 March 1927
Henshaw, Lance-Corporal George, Queen's Royal Regiment		19 Nov. 1935
Hodge, Captain Alexander Mitchell, VRD, Royal Naval Volunteer Reserve	Ch. 11	2 Aug. 1940
Humphries, Lieutenant Patrick Noel, Royal Navy		12 Nov. 1937
Idris, Sergeant Taha, Blue Nile Province Police		2 March 1934
Imam, El Yebia		1 Jan. 1932
Jamieson, William		23 June 1936
*Jolly, Commander Richard Frank, Royal Navy	Ch. 11	23 Dec. 1939
Kahn, Suedar-Major Pir, Indian Army		28 June 1940

Name	Reference	Date of London Gazette
Kelly, Cecil Francis		1 Feb. 1937
*Low, Lieutenant Niven Angus, Royal Navy	Ch. 11	16 Aug. 1940
Lungley, Battery Sergeant-Major Alfred, Royal Artillery		19 Nov. 1935
McAvoy, Private Thomas, Green Howards		25 July 1939
*McCabe, John	Ch. 10	31 May 1940
McClymond, Corporal John McIntosh, Auxiliary Air Force	Ch. 9	19 July 1940
McKechnie, Wing Commander William Neil, Royal Air Force		18 Oct. 1929
McTeague, Warrant Officer Thomas Patrick DCM, Royal Air Force		12 April 1929
Mahoney, Stoker Petty Officer Herbert John		23 Dec. 1927
Maltby, Staff Sergeant Reginald Harry, 11th Armoured Car Company		5 June 1926
March, Frederick Hamilton MBE		5 Dec. 1924
*Miller, Able Seaman Henry James, Royal Navy	Ch. 11	16 Aug. 1940
Miller, Private Thomas Frank, Dorset Regiment		2 June 1923
Mohammed, Mirghany Ahmed		2 Jan. 1933
Mohammed, Nafar Mohammed Abdulla		12 Dec. 1924
Mohi-ud-Din, Ghulum		3 June 1931
Morteshed, Francis Austin		3 June 1924
Mott, Private Joseph Edward, Essex Regiment		25 Feb. 1938
Naughton, Private Frank, Royal Tank Corps		1 Feb. 1937
Negib, Sol Ibrahim		12 Dec. 1924
Niven, Able Seaman George Paterson, Royal Navy		1 Jan. 1930
O'Hagen, Leo Francis	Ch. 10	6 Feb. 1940
Omara, Edwardo		9 Oct. 1934
Orr, Samuel		3 June 1924

Name	Reference	Date of London Gazette
O'Shea, The Rev. John Michael		30 June 1924
Parker, Flight Lieutenant Edward Donald, Royal Air Force Volunteer Reserve	Ch. 9	6 Aug. 1940
Pearson, Section Officer Joan Daphne Mary, Women's Auxiliary Air Force	Ch. 9	19 July, 1940
Pramar, His Excellency Bhupendra Singh, Rajah of Barwari		19 June 1934
Reynolds, Major Edward Womersley, Royal Engineers	Ch. 3	17 Sept. 1940
Rimmer, Sergeant Reginald, Bombay Police		3 June 1931
Rodriques, Assistant Surgeon, George David, Indian Medical Department		2 June 1923
Sewell, Stanley William	Ch. 10	6 Feb. 1940
Singh, Babu Ranjit		1 Jan. 1935
Singh, Baldev		1 Jan. 1932
Singh, Jemedar Barkat, 2nd Punjab Regiment		1 Jan. 1938
Stewart, Lieutenant-Colonel James Ernest, Royal Engineers		26 June 1928
Sylvester, William George	Ch. 10	6 Feb. 1940
Taha, El Jack Effendi, Khartoum Police Force		12 Dec. 1924
Talbot, 2nd Lieutenant Ellis Edward, Royal Engineers	Ch. 3	17 Sept. 1940
Tandy-Green, Lieutenant-Colonel Charles William, Bengal Public Works Department		19 June 1934
Taylor, Captain Sir Patrick Gordon MC, Late Royal Air Force		9 July 1937
Thapa, Havildar Nandlal, 8th Ghurka Rifles		19 Nov. 1935
Thomas, Dorothy Louise		2 March 1934
Tollemache, Squadron Leader Anthony Henry Hamilton, Auxiliary Air Force	Ch. 9	6 Aug. 1940

Name	Reference	Date of London Gazette
Townsend, Emma Jose		6 Sept. 1932
Troake, Private Frederick Henry, Dorset Regiment		2 June 1923
Turner, Radio Officer James Gordon Melville, Merchant Navy	Ch. 11	13 Oct. 1939
Tutton, Cyril James		18 March 1927
Waterfield, Albert		30 Dec. 1922
Wild, Robert		22 Oct. 1926
Wiltshire, Pilot Officer Sidney Noel, Royal Air Force		31 Jan. 1930
Winter, Gerald	Ch. 9	28 June 1940
Yar, Havildar-Major Ahmed, Royal Artillery		19 Nov. 1935

PART II

Men and women awarded the George Cross for acts of Gallantry performed since the institution of the award:

Name	Reference	Date of London Gazette
Alderson, Thomas Hopper	Ch. 2	30 Sept. 1940
*Ansari, Captain Matreen Ahmed, Rajput Rifles	Ch. 12	18 April 1946
Archer, Lieutenant-Colonel Bertram Stuart Trevelyan, Royal Engineers	Ch. 3	30 Sept. 1941
Armitage, Lieutenant Robert Selby GM, Royal Naval Volunteer Reserve	Ch. 8	27 Dec. 1940
*Axon, John	Ch. 14	17 May 1957
Babington, Lieutenant-Commander John Herbert OBE, Royal Naval Volunteer Reserve	Ch. 8	27 Dec. 1940
*Bailey, Sergeant Eric George, New South Wales Police Force	Ch. 13	29 Oct. 1946
Bamford, John	Ch. 14	16 Dec. 1952

Name	Reference	Date of London Gazette
*Banks, Sergeant Arthur, Royal Air Force Volunteer Reserve	Ch. 5	1 Nov. 1946
Barefoot, Major Herbert John Leslie ARIBA, Royal Engineers	Ch. 3	22 Jan. 1941
*Beckett, Sergeant John Archibald, Royal Air Force	Ch. 9	16 Dec. 1947
*Benner, 2nd Lieutenant Michael Paul, Royal Engineers	Ch. 14	17 June 1958
Biggs, Major Kenneth Alfred, Royal Army Ordnance Corps	Ch. 10	11 Oct. 1946
*Blaney, Captain Michael Floud BEng, Royal Engineers	Ch. 3	15 April 1941
Bridge, Lieutenant John GM, Royal Naval Volunteer Reserve	Ch. 8	20 June 1944
*Broadfoot, Radio Officer David, Merchant Navy	Ch. 11	6 Oct. 1953
Brooke-Smith, Sub-Lieutenant Francis Haffey, Royal Naval Reserve	Ch. 8	27 June 1941
Bywater, Richard Arthur Samuel GM	Ch. 10	26 Sept. 1944
*Campbell, 2nd Lieutenant Alexander Fraser, Royal Engineers	Ch. 3	22 Jan. 1941
Charlton, Squadron Leader Wilson Hodgson, Royal Air Force	Ch. 8	21 Jan. 1941
Churchill, Odette—See Hallowes.		
*Clarke, Donald Owen, Merchant Navy	Ch. 11	20 July 1943
Copperwheat, Lieutenant Dennis Arthur, Royal Navy	Ch. 7	17 Nov. 1942
*Craddock, Frederick John	Ch. 14	10 Sept. 1943
Dankwerts, Sub-Lieutenant Peter Victor, Royal Naval Volunteer Reserve	Ch. 8	20 Dec. 1940
*Davies, Frederick, National Fire Service	Ch. 14	5 Feb. 1946
Davies, Lieutenant Robert, Royal Engineers	Ch. 3	30 Sept. 1940
Dinwoodie, Squadron Leader Hubert OBE, MC, Royal Air Force Volunteer Reserve	Ch. 8	4 Feb. 1947

| | *Date of* |
Name	*Reference*	*London Gazette*
*Dolphin, Albert Ernest	Ch. 2	17 Jan. 1941
Dowland, Squadron Leader John Noel, Royal Air Force	Ch. 8	7 Jan. 1941
*Duncan, Private Charles Alfred, Army Air Corps	Ch. 10	9 Nov. 1943
Durrani, Lieutenant-Colonel Mahood Khan, 1st Bahawalpur Infantry, Indian State Forces	Ch. 12	23 May 1946
Eastman, Colonel William Marsden, Royal Army Ordnance Corps	Ch. 8	24 Dec. 1940
Easton, Sub-Lieutenant Jack Maynard Cholmondeley, Royal Naval Volunteer Reserve	Ch. 8	23 Jan. 1941
*Ellingworth, Chief Petty Officer Reginald Vincent, Royal Navy	Ch. 8	20 Dec. 1940
Errington, Harry, National Fire Service	Ch. 2	8 Aug. 1941
Fairfax, Sergeant William, Metropolitan Police Force	Ch. 13	6 Jan. 1953
*Fasson, Lieutenant Francis Anthony Blair, Royal Navy	Ch. 11	14 Sept. 1943
*Ford, Captain Douglas, Royal Scots	Ch. 12	18 April 1946
*Foster, Lieutenant William, Home Guard	Ch. 10	27 Nov. 1942
Fox, Leslie Owen	Ch. 2	20 Feb. 1945
*Fraser, John Alexander	Ch. 12	29 Oct. 1946
Gibson, Sergeant Michael, Royal Engineers	Ch. 3	22 Jan. 1941
Gidden, Lieutenant Ernest Oliver, Royal Naval Volunteer Reserve	Ch. 8	9 June 1942
*Gillett, Aircraftsman Ivor John, Royal Air Force	Ch. 9	3 Oct. 1950
Gimbert, Benjamin	Ch. 10	25 July 1944
Goldsworthy, Lieutenant-Commander Leon Verdi GM, DSC, Royal Australian Naval Volunteer Reserve	Ch. 8	19 Sept. 1944
Goodman, Lieutenant George Herbert MBE, Royal Naval Volunteer Reserve	Ch. 8	15 Sept. 1942

Name	Reference	Date of London Gazette
Gosse, Lieutenant-Commander George, Royal Australian Naval Volunteer Reserve	Ch. 8	30 April 1946
*Gravell, Leading Aircraftsman Karl Mander, Royal Canadian Air Force	Ch. 9	11 June 1942
*Gray, Flight Lieutenant Hector Bertram AFM, Royal Air Force	Ch. 12	19 April 1946
*Gray, Flying Officer Roderick Borden, Royal Canadian Air Force	Ch. 9	13 March 1945
*Grazier, Able Seaman Colin, Royal Navy	Ch. 11	14 Sept. 1943
Guerisse, Dr Albert Marie OBE (Late Royal Navy—Alias Patrick O'Leary)	Ch. 5	5 Nov. 1946
Hallowes, Odette Marie Celina MBE, First Aid Nursing Yeomanry	Ch. 4	20 Aug. 1946
Hardy, Private Benjamin Gower, 22nd Australian Garrison Battalion	Ch. 12	1 Sept. 1950
Harris, Lieutenant-Colonel Roy Thomas, Royal Engineers	Ch. 3	17 Dec. 1940
Harrison, Pilot Officer Leonard Henry, Royal Air Force	Ch. 8	3 Jan. 1941
Heming, Albert Edward	Ch. 2	17 July 1945
*Henderson, Sub-Officer George Campbell, Gibraltar Dockyard Fire Brigade	Ch. 10	20 Nov. 1951
*Hendry, Corporal James, Royal Canadian Engineers	Ch. 10	2 April 1943
Hiscock, Lieutenant-Commander William Ewart, Royal Navy	Ch. 8	16 June 1942
Hollowday, Corporal Vivian, Royal Air Force	Ch. 9	21 Jan. 1941
*Horsfield, Corporal Kenneth, Manchester Regiment	Ch. 10	23 March 1945
*Howard, Charles Henry George B.Sc., Earl of Suffolk and Berkshire	Ch. 3	18 July 1941
*Hughes, Driver Joseph, Royal Army Service Corps	Ch. 10	23 March 1946

Name	Reference	Date of London Gazette
*Inayat-Khan, Section Officer Nora, Women's Auxiliary Air Force	Ch. 4	1 April 1949
*Inwood, Section Commander George Walter, Home Guard	Ch. 2	27 May 1941
*Islam-ud-Din, Lance Naik, 6/9th Raj Regiment	Ch. 10	5 Oct. 1945
Jephson-Jones, Brigadier Robert Llewellyn, Royal Army Ordnance Corps	Ch. 8	24 Dec. 1940
*Jones, Private Ralph, 22nd Australian Garrison Battalion	Ch. 12	1 Sept. 1950
*Kelly, Able Seaman Raymond Thomas, Merchant Navy	Ch. 11	10 Feb. 1948
*Kempster, Major Andre Gilbert, Royal Armoured Corps	Ch. 10	9 Nov. 1943
Kinne, Fusilier Derek Godfrey, Royal Northumberland Fusiliers	Ch. 12	13 April 1954
*Latutin, Captain Simmon, Somerset Light Infantry, seconded to Somalia Gendarmerie	Ch. 10	10 Sept. 1946
Lewin, Sergeant Raymond Mayhew, Royal Air Force	Ch. 9	11 March 1941
*Madden, Private Horace William, Royal Australian Regiment	Ch. 12	30 Dec. 1955
MALTA, The Island of	Ch. 6 & 7	15 April 1942
Martin, Major Cyril Arthur Joseph MC, Royal Engineers	Ch. 3	11 March 1943
Mason, Captain Dudley William, Merchant Navy	Ch. 7	8 Sept. 1942
*Matthews, Captain Lionel Colvin MC, Australian Corps of Signals	Ch. 12	28 Nov. 1947
Merriman, Lieutenant-Colonel Arthur Douglas OBE, Royal Engineers	Ch. 3	3 Dec. 1940
*Miles, Leonard John	Ch. 2	17 Jan. 1941
Miller, Sub-Lieutenant John Bryan Peter, Royal Naval Volunteer Reserve	Ch. 8	14 Jan. 1941

Name	Reference	Date of London Gazette
Moore, Sub-Lieutenant Richard Valentine, Royal Naval Volunteer Reserve	Ch. 8	27 Dec. 1940
Mosedale, Station Officer William Radenhurst, National Fire Service	Ch. 2	28 March 1941
Moss, Special Constable Brandon, Coventry Police Force	Ch. 2	13 Dec. 1940
Mould, Lieutenant John Stewart GM, Royal Naval Volunteer Reserve	Ch. 8	3 Nov. 1942
*Moxey, Squadron Leader Eric Lawrence, Royal Air Force Volunteer Reserve	Ch. 8	13 Dec. 1940
Newgass, Lieutenant-Commander Harold Reginald, Royal Naval Volunteer Reserve	Ch. 8	4 March 1941
*Newnham, Colonel Lanceray Arthur MC, Middlesex Regiment	Ch. 12	18 April 1946
*Nicholls, Brigadier Arthur Frederick Crane, Coldstream Guards	Ch. 5	1 March 1946
*Nightall, James William	Ch. 10	25 July, 1944
O'Leary, Lieutenant-Commander Patrick Albert DSO, Royal Navy (See Guerisse)		
*Osborne, Leading Aircraftsman Albert Mathers, Royal Air Force	Ch. 10	10 July 1942
*Parish, Sergeant Graham Leslie, Royal Air Force Volunteer Reserve	Ch. 9	2 April 1943
Patton, Lieutenant John MacMillan Stevenson, Royal Canadian Engineers	Ch. 8	13 Dec. 1940
*Pugh, The Rev. Herbert Cecil MA, Royal Air Force	Ch. 11	1 April 1947
Quinton, Flight Lieutenant John Alan, Royal Air Force	Ch. 9	23 Oct. 1951
*Ram, Naik Kipra, 8th Battalion, Frontier Force Rifles	Ch. 10	15 March 1946
*Ram, Sowar Ditto, Central India Horse	Ch. 14	13 Dec. 1945
Rawing, Awang Anak	Ch. 14	20 Nov. 1951

Name	*Reference*	*Date of London Gazette*
*Reed, Gunner Henry Herbert, Merchant Navy	Ch. 11	23 Sept. 1941
Rehman, Havildar Abdul, 3/9th Jat Regiment	Ch. 14	10 Sept. 1946
Rennie, Sergeant John, Argyll and Sutherland Highlanders of Canada	Ch. 10	26 May 1944
Rogerson, Staff Sergeant Sidney George, Royal Army Ordnance Corps	Ch. 10	11 Oct. 1946
Ross, Air Commodore Arthur Dwight OBE, Royal Canadian Air Force	Ch. 9	27 Oct. 1944
Rowlands, Group Captain John Samuel OBE, Royal Air Force Volunteer Reserve	Ch. 8	10 Aug. 1943
Russell, Lance-Corporal David, 2nd New Zealand Expeditionary Force	Ch. 5	24 Dec. 1948
*Ryan, Lieutenant-Commander Richard John Hammersley, Royal Navy	Ch. 8	20 Dec. 1940
Sansom, Odette—See Hallowes		
Scully, Corporal James Patrick, Royal Pioneer Corps	Ch. 2	8 July 1941
*Seagrim, Major Hugh Paul DSO, MBE, 17th Hyderabad Regiment	Ch. 12	12 Sept. 1946
*Silk, Private Joseph Henry, Somerset Light Infantry	Ch. 10	13 June 1944
Sinclair, Air Vice Marshal Sir Lawrence Frank KCB, KBE, DSO, Royal Air Force	Ch. 9	17 Jan. 1941
Smith, Anthony	Ch. 2	30 May 1944
Smith, Sub-Lieutenant Francis Haffey Brooke—See Brooke-Smith		
*Smith, Signalman Kenneth, Royal Corps of Signals	Ch. 10	19 Oct. 1945
*Southwell, Able Seaman Bennett, Royal Navy	Ch. 8	23 Jan. 1941
*Spooner, Leading Aircraftsman Kenneth, Royal Canadian Air Force	Ch. 9	7 Jan. 1944

Name	Reference	Date of London Gazette
Stevens, Constable Henry William, Metropolitan Police	Ch. 13	21 Oct. 1958
Stronach, Chief Officer George Preston, Merchant Navy	Ch. 11	23 Nov. 1943
Subramanian, Subadar IDSM, Queen Victoria's Own Madras Sappers and Miners	Ch. 10	30 June 1944
Suffolk and Berkshire, Earl of (See Howard)		
Syme, Lieutenant Hugh Randall GM, Royal Naval Volunteer Reserve	Ch. 8	3 Aug. 1943
*Szabo, Violette, First Air Nursing Yeomanry	Ch. 4	7 Dec. 1946
Taylor, George Anthony	Ch. 14	22 April 1952
*Taylor, Robert George	Ch. 13	1 Aug. 1950
Taylor, Lieutenant-Commander William Horace, Royal Naval Volunteer Reserve	Ch. 8	14 Jan. 1941
*Thompson, Captain Jenkin Robert Oswald, Royal Army Medical Corps	Ch. 11	2 Feb. 1945
Tuckwell, Able Seaman Stephen John, Royal Navy	Ch. 8	14 Jan. 1941
Tunna, Norman	Ch. 10	24 Jan. 1941
Turner, Lieutenant Geoffrey Gledhill, Royal Naval Volunteer Reserve	Ch. 8	27 June 1941
*Waters, Lieutenant Terence Edward, West Yorkshire Regiment	Ch. 12	13 April 1954
*Woodbridge, Flight Sergeant Stanley James, Royal Air Force Volunteer Reserve	Ch. 12	28 Sept. 1948
Wylie, Corporal George Cameron, Royal Engineers	Ch. 3	30 Sept. 1940
Yeo-Thomas, Wing Commander Forest Frederick Edward MC, Royal Air Force Volunteer Reserve	Ch. 5	15 Feb. 1946
*Young, Lieutenant St John Graham, Royal Tank Regiment	Ch. 14	20 July 1945

*Posthumous award.

APPENDIX II

++

ROYAL WARRANT DEFINING THE
CONDITIONS OF THE GEORGE CROSS

(Note: This Royal Warrant, contained in the London Gazette of 31st January 1941, replaced the original Royal Warrant of 24th September 1940 which was never published in the London Gazette.)

THE GEORGE CROSS
Royal Warrant

GEORGE R.I.

GEORGE THE SIXTH, by the Grace of God, of Great Britain, Ireland and the British Dominions beyond the Seas King, Defender of the Faith, Emperor of India, to all to whom these Presents shall come, GREETING!

WHEREAS We have taken into Our Royal consideration the many acts of heroism performed both by male and by female persons, especially during the present war:

And whereas We are desirous of honouring those who perform such deeds:

We do by these presents for Us, Our Heirs and Successors institute and create a new Decoration which we desire should be highly prized and eagerly sought after.

First: It is ordained that the Decoration shall be designated and styled "The George Cross."

Secondly: It is ordained that the Decoration shall consist of a plain cross with four equal limbs, the cross having in the centre a circular medallion bearing a design showing St. George and the Dragon, that the inscription "For Gallantry" shall appear round this medallion, and in the angle of each limb of the cross the Royal cypher "G. VI" forming a circle concentric with the medallion, that the reverse of the Cross shall be plain and bear the name of the recipient and the date of the award, that the Cross shall be suspended by a ring from a bar adorned with laurel leaves, and that the whole shall be in silver.

Thirdly: It is ordained that the persons eligible for the Decoration of the Cross shall be

(1) Our faithful subjects and persons under Our protection in civil life, male and female, of Our United Kingdom of Great Britain and Northern Ireland, India, Burma, Our Colonies, and of Territories under Our Suzerainty, Protection or Jurisdiction,

(2) Persons of any rank in the Naval, Military or Air Forces of Our United Kingdom of Great Britain and Northern Ireland, of India, of Burma, of Our Colonies, and of Territories under Our Suzerainty, Protection or Jurisdiction, including the Home Guard and in India members of Frontier Corps and Military Police and members of Indian States' Forces and in Burma members of the Burma Frontier Force and Military Police, and including also the military Nursing Services and the Women's Auxiliary Services,

(3) Our faithful subjects and persons under Our protection in civil life, male and female, within, and members of the Naval, Military or Air Forces belonging to, any other part of Our Dominions, Our Government whereof has signified its desire that the Cross should be awarded under the provisions of this Our Warrant, and any Territory being administered by Us in such Government.

The Cross is intended primarily for civilians and award in Our military services is to be confined to actions for which purely military Honours are not normally granted.

Fourthly: It is ordained that awards shall be made only on a recommendation to Us, for civilians by Our Prime Minister and First Lord of the Treasury, and for Officers and members of Our Naval, Military or Air Forces, as described in the previous Clause of this Our Warrant, only on a recommendation by Our First Lord of the Admiralty, Our Secretary of State for War or Our Secretary of State for Air, as the case may be.

Fifthly: It is ordained that the Cross shall be awarded only for acts of the greatest heroism or of the most conspicuous courage in circumstances of extreme danger, and that the Cross may be awarded posthumously.

Sixthly: It is ordained that every recommendation for the award of the Cross shall be submitted with such description and conclusive proof as the circumstances of the case will allow, and attestation of the act as the Minister or Ministers concerned may think requisite.

Seventhly: It is ordained that the Cross shall be worn by recipients on the left breast suspended from a ribbon one and a quarter inches in width, of dark blue, that it shall be worn immediately after the Victoria Cross and in front of the Insignia of all British Orders of Chivalry, and that on those occasions when only the ribbon is worn, a replica in silver of the Cross in miniature shall be affixed to the centre of the ribbon.

Provided that when the Cross is worn by a woman, it may be worn on the left shoulder, suspended from a ribbon of the same width and colour, fashioned into a bow.

Eighthly: It is ordained that the award of the George Cross shall entitle the recipient on all occasions when the use of such letters is customary, to have placed after his or her names the letters "G.C."

Ninthly: It is ordained that an action which is worthy of recognition by the award of the Cross, but is performed by one upon whom the Decoration has been conferred, may be recorded by the award of a Bar to be attached to the ribbon by which the Cross is suspended, that for each such additional award an additional Bar shall be added, and that for each Bar awarded a replica in silver of the Cross in miniature, in addition to the emblem already worn, shall be added to the ribbon when worn alone.

Tenthly: It is ordained that the names of all those upon or on account of whom We may be pleased to confer or present the Cross, or a Bar to the Cross, shall be published in the London Gazette, and that a Register of such names shall be kept in the Central Chancery of the Orders of Knighthood.

Eleventhly: It is ordained that from the date of this Our Warrant, the grant of the Medal of the Order of the British Empire, for Gallantry, which was instituted and created by His late Majesty King George the Fifth, shall cease, and a recipient of that Medal, living at the date of this Our Warrant, shall return it to the Central Chancery of the Orders of Knighthood and become instead a holder of the George Cross: provided that there shall be a similar change in relation to any posthumous grant of the Medal of the Order of the British Empire, for Gallantry, made since the commencement of the present war.

Twelfthly: It is ordained that reproductions of the Cross, known as a Miniature Cross, which may be worn on certain occasions by those to whom the Decoration is awarded shall be half the size of the George Cross.

Thirteenthly: It is ordained that it shall be competent for Us, Our Heirs and Successors by an Order under Our Sign Manual and on a recommendation to that effect by or through Our Prime Minister and First Lord of the Treasury, Our First Lord of the Admiralty, Our Secretary of State for War, or Our Secretary of State for Air, as the case may be, to cancel and annul the award to any person of the George Cross and that thereupon the name of such person in the Register shall be erased: provided that it shall be competent for Us, Our Heirs and Successors to restore the Decoration so forfeited when such recommendation has been withdrawn.

Lastly: We reserve to Ourself, our Heirs and Successors, full power of annulling, altering, abrogating, augmenting, interpreting, or dispensing with these rules and ordinances, or any part thereof by a notification under Our Sign Manual.

> Given at Our Court at St. James's, the twenty-fourth of September, one thousand nine hundred and forty, in the fourth year of Our Reign.

By His Majesty's Command,

Winston S. Churchill.

PRINCIPAL
BRITISH GALLANTRY AWARDS

The Victoria Cross: (1856) For outstanding valour in the presence of the enemy. The ribbon is deep red and, when worn alone, it has a miniature replica of the cross fastened to it. Additional replicas are worn where the Cross has been won more than once by the same person. It may be awarded posthumously.

The Distinguished Conduct Medal: (1862) Awarded to warrant officers and non-commissioned ranks of the army for gallantry in action. The ribbon is dark blue with red edges.

The Albert Medal: (1866) Awarded for bravery in saving life. Since the institution of the George Cross and the George Medal it has only been given posthumously. The ribbon is blue for saving life at sea and red for saving life on land. There are four narrow white stripes on the ribbon of a gold Albert Medal and two on the ribbon of a bronze one.

The Conspicuous Gallantry Medal: (1874) Originally this medal was the naval equivalent of the Distinguished Conduct Medal and was awarded to non-commissioned ranks of the Royal Navy for bravery in action. In addition, it is now issued to non-commissioned ranks of all the fighting services for gallantry in the air. The ribbon has blue edges and a white centre if given for a naval action. The centre is light blue if given for an air action.

The Distinguished Service Order: (1886) Awarded to officers of the fighting services and the Merchant Navy for conspicuous service under fire. The ribbon is red with blue edges.

The Distinguished Service Cross: (1901) Awarded to junior officers and warrant officers of the fighting services for distinguished services at sea in the presence of the enemy. The ribbon is divided into three stripes of equal width; the outer ones being dark blue and the centre one white. It was originally called the Conspicuous Service Cross and had its title changed in 1914.

The Edward Medal: (1907) Awarded for bravery in industry. Today it is only given posthumously. The ribbon is dark blue and has yellow edges.

The Queen's Police Medal for Gallantry: (1909) Originally called the King's Police Medal, it was awarded to police and firemen for gallantry on duty. Today it is given only to police officers and only posthumously. The ribbon is dark blue with white stripes and has narrow red stripes in the centre of the white ones.

The Distinguished Service Medal: (1914) Awarded to petty officers and ratings of the Royal Navy for gallantry under fire that is not sufficiently outstanding to merit the award of the Conspicuous Gallantry Medal. The ribbon is dark blue with two narrow white stripes in the centre.

The Military Cross: (1914) Awarded to junior officers and warrant officers of the fighting services for conspicuous conduct in the presence of the enemy on land. The ribbon is divided into three stripes of equal width; the centre one being purple and the outer ones white.

The Military Medal: (1916) Awarded to non-commissioned ranks of the army for conspicuous service under fire. The ribbon is white with narrow blue edges and two narrow red stripes in the centre.

The Distinguished Flying Cross: (1918) Awarded to officers and warrant officers of the fighting services for bravery in air operations against the enemy. The ribbon has diagonal white and purple stripes.

The Distinguished Flying Medal: (1918) Awarded to non-commissioned ranks of the Royal Air Force for bravery in air operations against the enemy. The ribbon is similar to that of the Distinguished Flying Cross but the stripes are narrower.

The Air Force Cross: (1918) Awarded to officers and warrant officers of the fighting services for gallant conduct in flying operations not against the enemy. The ribbon has diagonal red and white stripes.

The Air Force Medal: (1918) Awarded to non-commissioned ranks of the Royal Air Force for gallant conduct in flying operations not against the enemy. The ribbon is similar to that of the Air Force Cross but the stripes are narrower.

The George Cross: (1940) For great heroism or conspicuous courage in circumstances of extreme danger. The ribbon is garter blue and, when worn alone, it carries one or more miniature replicas in the manner of the Victoria Cross. Like the V.C. it may be awarded posthumously.

The George Medal: (1940) Awarded in similar circumstances to the George Cross where the act of bravery has not been sufficiently outstanding to merit the latter award. The ribbon is red with five narrow blue stripes.

The Queen's Fire Service Medal for Gallantry: (1954) Awarded to firemen for acts of gallantry in fighting fires. The medal is unique in that, since its institution, it has only been awarded posthumously. The ribbon is scarlet with narrow yellow stripes.

Footnote.—The British Empire Medal has not been included in the above list although it has been awarded many times for what can only be regarded as acts of gallantry. According to the conditions governing its award, however, it is intended for 'meritorious service'.

COLLEGE OF HERALDS' WARRANT AUTHORISING THE USE OF THE GEORGE CROSS IN MALTA'S ARMS, SEALS, SHIELDS AND BANNER

GEORGE R.I.

GEORGE THE SIXTH by the Grace of God of Great Britain, Ireland and the British Dominions beyond the Seas King, Defender of the Faith, Emperor of India To our Right Trusty and Right Entirely Beloved Cousin and Counsellor Bernard Marmaduke, Duke of Norfolk, Knight of Our Most Noble Order of the Garter, Earl Marshal and Our Hereditary Marshal of England. Greeting!

WHEREAS We have been pleased to award to the island fortress of Malta the Decoration of the George Cross, to bear witness to the heroism and devotion of its brave people.

AND WHEREAS for the greater honour and distinction of Our Island of Malta and its Dependencies, we are desirous that the Armorial Bearings thereof should contain fit and proper allusion to this especial mark of Our Royal Favour.

KNOW Ye THEREFORE that we of Our Princely Grace and Special Favour do by these Presents ratify, confirm and assign the following Armorial Bearings, that is to say for Arms, Perpale Argent and Gules on a Canton Azure a representation of the George Cross proper, as depicted in the painting hereunto annexed, to be borne for Our Island of Malta and its Dependencies upon Seals, Shields, Banners or otherwise according to the Laws of Arms.

Our Will and Pleasure therefore is that you the said Bernard Marmaduke, Duke of Norfolk, to whom the cognizance of matters of this nature doth properly belong do require and command that this Our concession and Declaration be recorded in Our College of Arms in order that Our Officers of Arms and all other Public Functionaries whom it may concern may take full notice and have knowledge thereof in their several and respective Departments. And for so doing this shall be your Warrant.

> Given at Our Court at St. James's this twenty-eighth day of December 1943, in the Eighth year of Our Reign

By His Majesty's Command

Oliver Stanley

I hereby certify that the foregoing copy of the Royal Warrant assigning Armorial Ensigns to the Island of Malta and its Dependencies is faithfully extracted from the Records of the College of Arms, London. As witness my hand at the said College this twenty-fourth day of June 1946.

(sd.) Algar Howard

Garter King of Arms

APPENDIX V

++

ORDINANCE No. XVI of 1943

AN ORDINANCE to regulate the use of the emblem of the George Cross.

Be it enacted by the Governor with the advice and consent of the Council of Government as follows:—

Short title.

1. This Ordinance may be cited as the George Cross (Restriction of Use) Ordinance, 1943.

Prohibition of use of emblem of George Cross, etc.

2.—(*1*) As from the commencement of this Ordinance it shall not be lawful for any person to use or to continue to use for the purposes of his trade or business, or for any other purpose whatsoever, without the authority of the Governor, the emblem of the George Cross or any colourable imitation thereof or the words "George Cross" whether alone or in combination with any other word or words, and, if any person acts in contravention of this provision, he shall be guilty of an offence against this Ordinance, and shall be liable on conviction by the Court of Magistrates of Judicial Police to a fine (*multa*) of not less than fifty pounds nor more than two hundred pounds, and to forfeit any goods upon or in connection with which the emblem or words was or were used:

Provided that where such emblem or words is or are already being used on the date of assent and an application in writing is made to the Governor, within one month of the date of commencement of this Ordinance, for permission to continue to use the same, it shall be deemed that the person concerned has a provisional authority to use such emblem or words, as the case may be, until the Governor's decision on the application is made known to that person.

(2) The Governor may, at any time, in his absolute discretion, vary or revoke an authority previously given by him under subsection (*1*) of this section.

Where offence is committed by company or society.

3. Where a company or society is guilty of a contravention against section *1*, every director, manager, secretary and other officer of the company or society who is knowingly a party to the contravention shall be guilty of an offence against this Ordinance and liable to the like penalty.

Consent of Attorney General for prosecutions under this Ordinance.

4. Proceedings under this Ordinance shall not be instituted without the consent of the Attorney General.

Prohibition of registration of trade-marks containing emblem.

5. For the purposes of section 85 of the Law for the Protection of Industrial Property, the Comptroller shall not register any trade-mark containing the said emblem or words without the special authority of the Governor whose decision shall be final.

Passed by the Council of Government at Sitting No. 67 of the 22nd July, 1943.

P. P. DE CESARE,
Acting Clerk to the Council of Government.

APPENDIX VI

++

BIBLIOGRAPHY

The History of the Corps of Royal Engineers Vol. VIII by Major-General R. P. Pakenham-Walsh CB, MC (Published privately, 1958.)

Odette by Jerrard Tickell (Chapman & Hall, 1949)

Malta Besieged by R. Leslie Oliver (Hutchinson & Co Ltd, 1944)

Malta Magnificent by Francis Gerard (Cassell & Co Ltd, 1943)

The Unconquered Island by Ian Hay (Hodder & Stoughton Ltd, 1943)

For Gallantry by Kenneth Hare-Scott (Peter Garnett, 1951)

King George VI, His Life and Reign by Sir John W. Wheeler-Bennett (Macmillan & Co Ltd, 1958)

Unexploded Bomb by Major A. B. Hartley GM, MBE RE (Cassell & Co Ltd, 1958)

Gallantry by Sir Arnold Wilson MP and Captain J. H. F. McEwan MP (Oxford University Press, 1939)

Ribbons and Medals by Tapprell Dorling and F. Guille (George Phillip & Sons Ltd, 1956)

Gallant Deeds of the War by Stanley Rogers (Blackie & Son Ltd, 1941)

Specially Employed by Maurice J. Buckmaster (The Batchworth Press, 1952)

The Second World War by Sir Winston S. Churchill (Cassell & Co Ltd, 1948-54)

Special Operations Edited by Patrick Howarth (Routledge & Kegan Paul, 1955)

The Way Back by Vincent Brome (Cassell & Co Ltd, 1957)

Duel of Wits by Peter Churchill (Hodder & Stoughton, 1953)

The Undaunted by Ronald Seth (Fredrick Muller Ltd, 1956)

Open The Ports by J. Grosvenor and Lieut.-Comd. L. M. Bates (William Kimber, 1956)

The White Rabbit by Bruce Marshall (Evans Brothers Ltd, 1952)

The Blitz by Constantine FitzGibbon (Allan Wingate, 1957)

History of the Second World War, Civil Defence by T. H. O'Brian (H.M. Stationery Office & Longmans)